The Meaning of
American Democracy

D1709827

Edited by

ROBERT Y. SHAPIRO

THE ACADEMY OF POLITICAL SCIENCE
NEW YORK

Published by
The Academy of Political Science
475 Riverside Drive, Suite 1274
New York, NY 10115

This volume contains the following essays that have appeared in *Political Science Quarterly*:

Robert A. Dahl, "What Political Institutions Does Large-Scale Democracy Require?" 120 (Summer 2005): 187–197. Adapted from Robert A. Dahl, *On Democracy* (New Haven, CT: Yale University Press, 1998).

Michael Lind, "Prescriptions for a New National Democracy" 110 (Winter 1995–1996): 563–586.

Alexander Keyssar, "Shoring Up the Right to Vote for President: A Modest Proposal" 118 (Summer 2003): 181–203.

Paul T. McCartney, "American Nationalism and U.S. Foreign Policy from September 11 to the Iraq War" 119 (Fall 2004): 399–423.

Louis Fisher, "Deciding on War Against Iraq: Institutional Failures" 118 (Fall 2003): 389–410.

Steven Kull, Clay Ramsay, and Evan Lewis, "Misperceptions, the Media, and the Iraq War" 118 (Winter 2003–2004): 569–598.

Gary C. Jacobson, "Polarized Politics and the 2004 Congressional and Presidential Elections" 120 (Summer 2005): 199–218.

James E. Campbell, "Why Bush Won the Presidential Election of 2004: Incumbency, Ideology, Terrorism, and Turnout" 120 (Summer 2005): 219–241.

Excerpts have been taken from *Hamdi v. Rumsfeld*, 542 U.S. ____ (2004).

Cover design: Loren Morales Kando

Cover credits: White House photo

Library of Congress Cataloging-in-Publication Data

The meaning of American democracy/edited by Robert Y. Shapiro.
    p. cm.
  ISBN-13: 978-1-884853-05-0
  1. Democracy—United States. 2. Representative government and representation—United States. 3. Political participation—United States. 4. Elections—United States. 5. September 11 Terrorist Attacks, 2001. 6. Iraq War, 2003. 7. United States—Politics and government—2001-

JK1726.M42 2005
320.973'09'0511—dc22

                                   2005015483

Printed in the United States of America
p 5 4 3 2 1

Contents

Preface and Acknowledgements

This book is one of a series published by the Academy of Political Science on topics of particular importance in public and international affairs. At this point, no other issue is more topical or important than the viability of American democracy, which requires competitive elections, checks and balances by separate institutions sharing power, and living with the Constitution's limitations on what that democracy can do. In order to understand better the complicated nature of our democracy, we offer a series of articles published also in *Political Science Quarterly*, and an original introduction and concluding essay by the book's editor, Robert Y. Shapiro, and myself.

The Academy of Political Science is a nonpartisan, nonprofit organization founded in 1880 with a threefold mission: to contribute to the scholarly examination of political institutions, processes, and public policies; to enrich political discourse and channel the best social science research in an understandable way to political leaders for use in public policy making and the process of governing; and to educate members of the general public so that they become informed voters in the democratic process. The major vehicles for accomplishing these goals are its journal, *Political Science Quarterly*; Academy conferences; and the publication of books.

Published continuously since 1886, *PSQ* is the most widely read and accessible scholarly journal on government, politics, and policy, both international and domestic. Dedicated to objective analysis based on evidence, *PSQ* has no ideological or methodological slant and is edited for both specialists and general readers who have a serious interest in public and foreign affairs.

I thank the authors of the essays in this collection. I am especially grateful to Robert Shapiro, colleague and member of *PSQ's* editorial advisory board, not only for organizing this book, but also for having, over the years, provided much assistance and advice. Others who warrant my warm thanks are Kathleen Doherty, my research assistant and organizer; Marylena Mantas, *PSQ*'s managing editor; and Loren Morales Kando, who as business manager, production manager, and vice president for operations at the Academy of Political Science, does everything she can to make my life easier. Ms. Kando also designed the book's cover. We publish this book in hope that the American constitutional democracy will remain healthy even in this era of perpetual war on terrorism.

DEMETRIOS JAMES CARALEY
President, The Academy of Political Science
Editor, *Political Science Quarterly*

Part I:
INTRODUCTION

The Meaning of American Democracy

ROBERT Y. SHAPIRO

America in the twenty-first century continues to be faced with questions about how democratic government should work. These include recurrent debates about the excessive influence of "special interests" and the inequality of political power and influence, which have challenged the twentieth-century proponents of democratically oriented pluralist theory in the United States.[1] Recent events and circumstances have made questions about the meaning of democracy ever more pressing. The election of 2000, the terrorist attacks on 11 September 2001, the wars in Afghanistan and then Iraq, and the 2004 election have raised issues concerning the central normative requirements of democracy in America. By democracy, we mean, specifically, republican democracy or representative government, by which the wants of the American people are made part of and are respected by government. The normative requirements are: First, that there be institutions and procedures that facilitate control by the American people, which can be called "procedural" or "institutional" democracy; second, that there be recognizable representation of the people in what government does, which can be referred to as "substantive" democracy; and third, that there be vigorous protections of the individual rights and liberties of the people. This essay will take up each of these and provide a framework for understanding the chapters that follow. The chapters are articles reprinted from *Political Science Quarterly*, and this essay and the final one have been written for this volume.

---

[1] Cf. David B. Truman, *The Governmental Process: Political Interests and Public Opinion*, 2nd ed. (New York: Alfred A. Knopf, 1971); Robert A. Dahl, *Who Governs: Democracy and Power in an American City* (New Haven, CT: Yale University Press, 1961); and Mancur Olson, *The Logic of Collective Action: Public Goods and the Theory of Groups* (Cambridge, MA: Harvard University Press, 1965).

ROBERT Y. SHAPIRO is a professor of political science at Columbia University and a researcher at Columbia's Institute for Social and Economic Research and Policy. He is coauthor of *Politicians Don't Pander: Political Manipulation and the Loss of Democratic Responsiveness*, and *The Rational Public: Fifty Years of Trends in Americans' Policy Preferences*. He completed this volume while he was a visiting fellow at the Council on Foreign Relations.

Institutional Democracy

What republican democracy means to some theorists and others is the existence of rules, procedures, and entities that enable voters to hold political leaders accountable and that prevent abuses of power. The existence of these kinds of *effective* procedures and mechanisms, which can be subsumed by the term *institutions*, is sufficient for a system to be democratic. The public, as citizens, controls what government does through periodic elections that allow for the selection of new elites to lead the nation. Once in office, these elites are free to—indeed, are expected to—act independently of public opinion as "trustees" of the national interest (in contrast to "delegates" expected to follow directly the wishes of their constituents). It is sufficient for representative democracy that citizens judge and vote in or out these leaders at the time of the next election, when old leaders, if defeated, will give way to the new. This is what the Framers of the American Constitution established through direct and indirect elections of members of the legislative and executive branches, and it was sufficient for them to consider the constitutional system a republican democracy.[2] A number of essays in this volume address directly this aspect of American democracy.

Substantive Democracy

In contrast to institutional democracy, *substantive democracy* refers to how public opinion, to an identifiable extent, matters in policy making—that is, it has a place in shaping government policy. A challenge to this that V. O. Key, perhaps the most famous student of public opinion and political leadership, feared was the possibility "that democracy only amounts to a hoax, a ritual, whose performance serves to only delude the people and thereby convert them into willing subjects of the powers that be."[3] The original pluralists thought it was not a hoax because there was ultimately democratic competition among organized groups, and the "new pluralists," as Jacob Hacker and Paul Pierson have called them, emphasize the more general influence of public opinion and voters, which can be studied through comparisons of public opinion poll results with the policies government enacts.[4] The extent and nature of this influence is one standard against which democracy in the United States can be gauged.

---

[2] See Alexander Hamilton, James Madison, and John Jay, *The Federalist Papers* (New York: The New American Library, 1961 [1788]); Joseph A. Schumpeter, *Capitalism, Socialism, and Democracy* (New York: Harper, 1950); and John C. Wahlke, Heinz Eulau, William Buchanan, and Leroy C. Ferguson, *The Legislative System* (New York: Wiley, 1962).

[3] V. O. Key, *Public Opinion and American Democracy* (New York: Alfred A. Knopf, 1961), 7. Cf. Harrold D. Laswell, *Democracy Through Public Opinion* (Menasha, WI: Banta, 1941); and Benjamin Ginsberg, *The Captive Public: How Mass Opinion Promotes State Power* (New York: Basic Books, 1986).

[4] Jacob S. Hacker and Paul Pierson, "Abandoning the Middle: The Bush Tax Cuts and the Limits of Democratic Control," *Perspectives on Politics* 3 (March 2005): 33–53. Representative of the new pluralism are Robert S. Erikson, Michael B. MacKuen, and James A. Stimson, *The Macro Polity*

Some essays in this volume focus on the nature of this influence, though not the extent of this influence, which is a subject of substantial debate. The common wisdom is that politicians and policy makers today slavishly follow public opinion polls and do not take action without knowing from their pollsters that this is what the public wants. The critique is that polling is bad and that the solution, according to political pundits like Arianna Huffington, is for the public to refuse to talk to pollsters: Leaders should lead and not be swayed by poll results, which critics see happening perpetually. President Bill Clinton was the poster child for this. But is there evidence to support this? There was the case of Clinton's pollster influencing where Clinton went on vacation. More compelling, during the 1996 election, public opinion figured into Clinton's decision to sign welfare reform into law and also into the Republicans voting for an increase in the minimum wage. But what is wrong with political leaders responding to the threat of being held accountable by voters? Constitutionally, this is the one shot that voters get every two and four years. The Founders of the American Republic would permit no more than this, and they attempted to create a political system in which the nation's leaders were insulated from the "whims and passions" of the masses. In fact, to this day, it is politically incorrect for any political leader to go on record as saying that polling is useful for responding to public opinion.[5] George W. Bush has gone out of his way to criticize politicians paying attention to polling, but he and the Republicans, just like John Kerry and the Democrats, paid close attention to the polls during the campaign, and this has continued after the election.[6]

(New York: Cambridge University Press, 2002); Benjamin I. Page and Robert Y. Shapiro, *The Rational Public: Fifty Years of Trends in Americans' Policy Preferences* (Chicago, IL: University of Chicago Press, 1992); and Benjamin I. Page and Robert Y. Shapiro, "Effects of Public Opinion on Policy," *American Political Science Review* 77 (March 1983): 175–190. See also Jeff Manza, Fay Lomax Cook, and Benjamin I. Page, eds., *Navigating Public Opinion: Polls, Policy, and the Future of American Democracy* (New York: Oxford University Press, 2002); and Carroll J. Glynn, Susan Herbst, Garrett O'Keefe, Robert Y. Shapiro, and Mark Lindeman, *Public Opinion* (Boulder, CO: Westview Press, 2004), 355–404.

[5] See Lawrence R. Jacobs and Robert Y. Shapiro, *Politicians Don't Pander: Political Manipulation and the Loss of Democratic Responsiveness* (Chicago, IL: University of Chicago Press, 2000).

[6] See Richard W. Stevenson, "With Bush Safely Re-elected, Rove Turns Intensity to Policy," *The New York Times*, 28 March 2005; John F. Harris, "Policy and Politics by the Numbers," *Washington Post*, 31 December 2000; James Carney and John F. Dickerson, "Behind the Rhetoric: Polling for the Perfect Pitch," *Time*, 9 October 2000; Mimi Hall, "New White House, New 'War Room' for Strategizing," *USA Today*, 5 July 2001; and Joshua Green, "The Other War Room: President Bush Doesn't Believe in Polling—Just Ask His Pollsters," *The Washington Monthly*, April 2002. The history of presidential polling is described in Lawrence R. Jacobs and Robert Y. Shapiro, "The Rise of Presidential Polling: The Nixon White House in Historical Perspective," *Public Opinion Quarterly* 59 (Summer 1995): 163–165; Robert M. Eisinger, *The Evolution of Presidential Polling* (New York: Cambridge University Press, 2003); Diane J. Heith, *Polling to Govern: Public Opinion and Presidential Leadership* (Stanford, CA: Stanford University Press, 2003); John G. Geer, *From Tea Leaves to Opinion Polls: A Theory of Democratic Leadership* (New York: Columbia University Press, 1996); Jacobs and Shapiro, *Politicians Don't Pander*; and Shoon Kathleen Murray and Peter Howard, "Variation in White House Polling Operations: Carter to Clinton," *Public Opinion Quarterly* 66 (Winter 2002): 527–558.

After elections, however, the situation is very different. If policy makers were following the dictates of polls, research on the relationship between public opinion and specific policies would show historically a very strong correspondence, issue by issue, between short-term public opinion changes and subsequent government policies, and even a relationship that is becoming increasingly strong. What existing research shows, however, is that the opinion–policy relationship is very far from perfect. While we can debate many aspects of the data, there is no support for the extreme claims in one direction or the other: Policy makers do not purely respond to public opinion, nor do they purely attempt to lead it.[7] The fact that political parties and politicians do polls does not mean that they are doing them so that they will do things that are acceptable to the public. Why is that? The reason is that politicians and policy makers have policy and ideological goals that they attempt to pursue between elections. George W. Bush has shown this on a number of issues, especially the Iraq war, his efforts to reform Social Security, and his active support of maintaining Terri Schiavo on life support. Information about public opinion historically has been used in ways that are hardly characterized by responsiveness to national public opinion but rather, it has been used for other purposes. It is not possible to describe here the variety and complexity of this history in few minutes, but these uses have substantially been for purposes of *leading* or *manipulating* public opinion to attain policy goals or for other political purposes. There may be a fine line between leading and manipulating, which will be considered further below, but this hardly represents politicians slavishly doing what polls tell them. Rather, they have attempted to use information from opinion polls to move the public in the direction they want to go.[8] It is this need to gain public support that some of the essays that follow address.

But assessing American "democracy" requires more than seeing if government policies coincide with the wishes of the citizenry. What also matters is how this coincidence has come about and the nature and quality of that public opinion that supports government policies. Here, what matters is whether the public has received available information sufficient to make a judgment that is in its—and the nation's—best interest. It is therefore necessary to examine the process by which the public is informed about those policies that it comes to want, including, especially, those that the nation's leaders bring to its attention.

Democratic Rights and Liberties

Democracy requires more than effective institutions that hold leaders accountable and prevent them from abusing their powers, and more than evidence that the public often gets government to do what it wants. It is also essential that the rights

[7] See Erikson, MacKuen, and Stimson, *The Macro Polity*; Page and Shapiro, "Effects of Public Opinion on Policy"; Manza, Cook, and Page, eds., *Navigating Public Opinion*; Glynn, Herbst, O'Keefe, Shapiro, and Lindeman, *Public Opinion*, 355–404; and Jacobs and Shapiro, *Politicians Don't Pander*.
[8] Jacobs and Shapiro, *Politicians Don't Pander*.

and liberties of individuals be protected from possible abusive actions of government, its leaders, or majorities of the citizenry. These protections are provided for in the Constitution and its amendments, and American democracy requires that such rights and liberties be defended and upheld.

The chapters that follow are divided into four sections. The first offers appraisals of democracy, institutions, and rights; the second section takes up some of what transpired from 11 September 2001 through the subsequent war in Iraq; the third examines the 2004 elections; and the last section offers a historical and further normative perspective on current politics and challenges to American democracy.

DEMOCRACY, INSTITUTIONS, AND RIGHTS

In "What Political Institutions Does Large-Scale Democracy Require," Robert Dahl states that if a country is to be governed democratically, it requires certain political arrangements, institutions, or practices that go a long way toward meeting ideal democratic criteria. These consist of elected officials who represent the people and, in addition, free, fair, and frequent elections. This would presumably require a process that provides for something approximating one person, one vote, and also that all votes be correctly counted, and that elected officials thereby be held accountable. Further, there would be provisions for freedom of expression, associational autonomy, and inclusive citizenship, including the right to vote, which would be guaranteed as civil rights and liberties. Last, but not least, there would be alternative sources of information available to the country's citizens, which would subsume the press, the mass media more broadly, communications with other citizens, and information and guidance provided by a variety of leaders and other elites, including not only government leaders but also experts on any matter at hand. Guaranteeing associational autonomy clearly worked against the American Founders' desire to limit the expansion groups that would constitute divisive political factions, and this, along with the electoral system that was established, paved the way for political parties. However, the rest of the system that the Founders put together succeeded in preventing the dire consequences of factions that they feared. Inclusive citizenship was initially, to be sure, the least-well-advanced characteristic of American democracy (as when Alexis de Tocqueville visited). Dahl sees these institutions as crucial for democratic countries because these countries are "large."

The importance of the institutions lies in how they help fulfill the "democratic criteria" that Dahl sees as crucial: effective political participation, control of the agenda, equality of voting, and enlightened understanding. It is with the debate on full inclusion that rights and liberties get hammered out, and they are also related to voting equality, effective participation, and the free speech and free press aspects of enlightened understanding. Free expression means not only the right of individuals to be heard but also the right to be informed by others, leaving it to the individual to accept or reject such information. Citizens must also have access to alternative forms of information that are not under the control of the government or dominated by any other group or point of view.

Dahl does not address substantive democracy directly, but it would certainly come into play with equality of voting and frequent elections to hold government leaders/policy makers accountable. The last section of his essay emphasizes the importance of effective participation of independent associations as a source of "civic education and enlightenment," and how they provide opportunities for discussion, deliberation, and acquiring political skills. This discussion is all to the good and echoes some of the related concerns of Robert Putnam and others concerning the shortfalls of "social capital" in American civic life.[9] America's ills, for Dahl, however, are related to other aspects of democracy. Dahl raises the question of whether the United States, as a large established democracy, has institutions that have met the minimum standard for modern representative democracy or "polyarchal democracy." While the United States has in place the necessary institutions, have they been sufficient for achieving Dahl's democratic criteria? He concludes that against these criteria, American institutions reveal many shortcomings. The nation needs to determine how to improve its existing level of democracy before attempting to move beyond polyarchal democracy.

Michael Lind, too, wants to move American national democracy forward, and his essay, "Prescriptions for a New National Democracy," offers an expansive discussion and highly provocative recommendations regarding rights and inclusiveness. He emphasizes what he sees as three central elements of American democracy: individual rights, equal voting power, and the social market. Lind opposes what he sees as current nation-dividing racial preferences, plutocratic politics, and free-market capitalism. To start, he categorically rejects all racial labeling, as a prelude to ending all racial preferences, and, by extension, he also rejects racial gerrymandering designed to create and preserve "majority-minority" districts. He would depend on the courts to remain the battleground for determining violations of color-blind individual rights on a victim-specific basis, and the courts would cease to pursue group-based remedies. At the same time, Lind wants antidiscrimination laws to be expanded to include new categories of individuals, such as homosexuals. Where a new *national* democracy comes into play is in Lind's desire to nationalize, through federal laws governing rights, both "liberal" sexual privacy rights and also "conservative" property rights. Whether simply for practical reasons or for normative ones, personal and property rights, as Lind sees them, should not depend on the laws of the state or local jurisdiction within which one lives; such laws should be in conformity nationwide.

Equal voting, for Lind, is the one-person, one-vote standard that fully covers the equal empowerment of each individual—from the selection of candidates and the influence of money in campaigns, and the promotion of multi-

---

[9] Robert Putnam, *Bowling Along: The Collapse and Revival of American Community* (New York: Simon & Schuster, 2000).

party democracy, to abolishing the malapportioned United States Senate. Lind flags the 1976 *Buckley v. Valeo* decision as institutionalizing the electoral advantage for rich people by protecting the unlimited spending of their own money in running for office. Coming after Lind's writing, the most recent Bipartisan Campaign Finance Reform Act (BCRA) of 2002, while ending the unlimited "soft money" contributions to parties of the past (and thereby the power of soft-money contributors), also increased the limits on hard money (candidate- and campaign-specific) contributions to candidates and the parties. This changed campaign fund-raising strategies (encouraging efforts to obtain larger numbers of the now greater hard-money donations). Lind also cites the problems of special moneyed interests and paid advertising that BCRA's reforms also indirectly took on, but new organizations (the "527" organizations named after the new legal provision) have emerged that can spend funds during campaigns at least partly equivalent to past soft-money contributions.[10] Lind's best recommendation is to ban paid advertising and impose free ad time requirements on the media. It is curious here that he does not cite other reforms that have long been debated.

On party representation, Lind suggests that the Founders might have given proportional representation (PR) voting systems, had they been invented, some consideration in determining how members of the House of Representatives should be elected. In the spirit of a democracy, it would allow more votes to translate into representation of more individuals, in contrast to our plurality first-past-the-post system. In addition to other largely standard arguments for PR regarding electing women and minorities and providing for the representation of women's and minorities' interests,[11] it would do away with any need for partisan or racial gerrymandering. Doing away with the malapportioned Senate in favor of a national body preferably elected through PR fits in with Lind's aims. But here Lind misses out on further claims for how the states' allocations of senators distort elections themselves in the apportionment of presidential electors, which would lead logically to challenging the existence of the electoral college. Also, one of the smaller but more blatant cases of inequality is the lack of full House and Senate representation for residents of the District of Columbia, which has long been a gray if not black mark for American democracy.

Lind's final proposal is for a new social market contract to replace the New Deal system to ensure good jobs and benefits for the lower skilled. He would have government disconnect Social Security and health care benefits from specific employers, to be financed by progressive taxes. Further, he would have government encourage higher wages by restricting immigration by the unskilled, and pass

---

[10] Proponents of campaign finance reform did not fully foresee the unintended consequences of BCRA; see the analyses of the need for reform in Anthony Corrado, Thomas E. Mann, and Trevor Potter, eds., *Inside the Campaign Finance Battle: Court Testimony and the New Reforms* (Washington, DC: Brookings Institution Press, 2003).

[11] Douglas J. Amy, *Real Choice/New Voices: The Case for Proportional Representation Elections in the United States* (New York: Columbia University Press, 1993).

laws that would lessen reliance on temporary workers instead of full-time employees, discourage teens from working, and encourage caregivers to leave the job market or work outside only part time. The effects on the economy of immigration restrictions would be offset by encouraging automation, and government would impose what he calls a "social tariff" to deter relocation by employers to less-tight and otherwise cheaper labor markets. These policies would help preserve middle-class living standards. To deal further with oligarchy and inequality and to make social mobility easier, Lind would seriously consider controversial options, such as altering professional educational and licensing practices, to allow for intermediate professions in law and medicine, and also outlawing legacy preferences in higher education. He would have government work more actively through charitable and religious institutions to engage in more-direct tutelage of poor youth. While Lind does not state it explicitly, his approach to improving social welfare seems heavily class based, and it is nationalistic in a different sense from his other proposals, in that it attempts to minimize questions of inconclusive citizenship that have racial and ethnic dimensions.

Alexander Keyssar picks up further on the right of equal voting power in "Shoring Up the Right to Vote for President: A Modest Proposal." His essay is followed by a lively panel discussion of his proposal and the larger issues surrounding it. In the wake of the 2004 election, his assertions are as apt as they were after the election of 2000: It should be startling to the world that in the United States, there is no constitutionally guaranteed right to vote for the electors of the president, to say nothing of the fact that Americans do not directly elect the president. Keyssar's modest proposal is simply to amend the United States Constitution "to affirmatively guarantee the right of American citizens to vote for president and to have those votes determine each state's vote in the electoral college." The amendment would ratify current practices in the states, much as the passage of the Seventeenth Amendment to the Constitution institutionalized the then ongoing trend in state governments to get voters' input into the selection of senators, who were originally not directly elected by voters but selected by the state legislatures. Moreover, Keyssar's proposal would prevent the possibility of state legislatures claiming, as the Florida legislature threatened to do in 2000, the right to determine—late in the elections season—the means of choosing the electors. Not surprisingly, what Keyssar would prefer is that citizens be allowed to elect presidents directly, but he is settling for a much less controversial proposal as a means of establishing an important and widely assumed right.

Clearly, the right to vote and to have citizens' votes counted—and done so accurately—has been on the minds of many since the 2000 election, and the electoral college ought to once more be an issue for public debate. Since George W. Bush in 2004 won both the electoral vote and the popular vote, the nation's concern about the electoral college has subsided. The relevance of the electoral college, however, and the arguments made for keeping it—and what interests benefit from it—have become increasingly unclear. George Edwards has written a compelling book-length treatment of the subject, which shows how uncertain the arguments are concerning whether small or large states benefit from the electoral college and its winner-take-all system.[12] Because of the very close two-party competition that exists today (as the volume's two articles on the 2004 election show), the country seems likely to continue to have close presidential races. Moreover, because the last two presidential contests have boiled down to the outcomes of races in about a dozen closely contested states, it is not just small states that are in danger of being ignored, but all states in which one party tends to dominate the presidency. Indeed, in 2004, the small states of New Hampshire and, surprisingly, Hawaii received unexpected attention as Election Day approached and their elections seemed close, whereas the citizens in three of the largest states—New York, California, and Texas— received disproportionately little attention from the candidates after the Democratic primaries played themselves out. Thus, one strong argument against the electoral college is that it prevents citizens in the fullest number of states from being engaged by the candidates to compete for their votes. Ironically, it was only because of fund-raising efforts, potential inequalities and all, that the parties devoted any attention to loyal voters in the uncontested states as possible financial contributors within the parameters of the new campaign finance laws. It may, in the end, be the case that the clearest rationale for the electoral college at the founding and a century later was how it benefited whites in Southern states. Initially, when slaves, who could not vote, were counted as three-fifths in determining congressional representation, Southern slave states benefited from this in their number of electoral votes. Later, not long after the Civil War, and somewhat ironically, these same states benefited even further when their freed slaves and the slaves' descendants were prevented from voting through Jim Crow laws but were fully counted toward congressional representation and thereby also toward the clout of these states in the electoral college.[13]

Questions about the electoral college aside, the issues that remained more urgent have concerned the right to vote without barriers and delays and to have the votes accurately counted. Keyssar and the panelists also acknowledge the right of convicted felons to vote, depending on state laws and how these laws are implemented. There was not the major debate about this after the 2004 election that there was in 2000, but this is an aspect of the right to vote that is likely to surface again.[14] There were, however acrimonious debates about irregularities on Election Day related to long lines, defective equipment, and possible vote tampering and fraud. Related in part to the integrity of the vote count, there was a widely debated controversy concerning the quality of the exit polls

[12] George C. Edwards III, *Why the Electoral College Is Bad for America* (New Haven, CT: Yale University Press, 2004).

[13] Ibid.

[14] See Christopher Uggen and Jeff Manza, "Democratic Contraction? The Political Consequences of Felon Disenfranchisement in the United States," *American Sociological Review* 67 (December 2002): 777–803.

used in predicting and explaining the election results. There were calls for congressional investigations of voting procedure and equipment, as in 2000, and also of the problems with the exit polls. The latter controversy hearkened back to the pre-election polling fiasco of 1948, when there were investigations of the polling and prediction of the Gallup Poll organization. There was also a replay of the response to this by the social science community when the Social Science Research Council (SSRC) convened a committee to review and report on election and voting procedures and the quality of the exit polling, covering a wide range of possible problems, irregularities, and even fraud. The SSRC report was not, however, able to pinpoint irregularities that challenged the presidential election outcome, and it accepted the report about the exit polling operation from Edison Media Research/Mitofsky International, who conducted the exit polls for the National Election Pool of news media organizations. What the SSRC report did criticize was the lack of available data and transparency that would have enabled the report's authors to track fully all aspects of voting procedures, the kinds of voting equipment used, and what happened at the precincts where the exit polling occurred. The report was less a definitive statement on the 2004 election than a call for ways of more closely monitoring elections, voting, and polling in the future.[15]

FROM SEPTEMBER 11 TO IRAQ

The next section of the volume examines the ramifications of the new political realities and the challenges related to this for American democracy. There have been major transformations on the international front and in the United States's role in it. The Cold War has been replaced by the United States's struggle against international terrorism and its finding its way as the single military superpower capable of projecting its power around the world. This capability refers not just to the size of its military forces but also to its willingness to deploy them worldwide, on its own if necessary. American actions in Afghanistan and especially Iraq, and how the United States is proceeding more

[15] See Frederick Mosteller and others, *The Pre-Election Polls of 1948: Report to the Committee on Analysis of Pre-election Polls and Forecasts*, Bulletin 60 (New York: Social Science Research Council, 1949); Edison Media Research and Mitofsky International for the National Election Pool (NEP), "Evaluation of Edison/Mitofsky Election System 2004, 19 January 2005; Michael Traugott, Benjamin Highton, and Henry E. Brady, "A Review of Recent Controversies Concerning the 2004 Presidential Election Exit Polls," The National Research Commission on Elections and Voting, Social Science Research Council, 10 March 2005; Henry E. Brady, Guy-Uriel Charles, Benjamin Highton, Martha Kropf, Walter R. Mebane, Jr., and Michael Traugott, "Interim Report on Alleged Irregularities in the United States Presidential Election of 2 November 2004," The National Research Commission on Elections and Voting, Social Science Research Council, 22 December 2004; and R. Michael Alvarez and others, "Challenges Facing the American Electoral System: Research Priorities for the Social Sciences," The National Research Commission on Elections and Voting, Social Science Research Council, 1 March 2005.

broadly in international affairs, raise questions related to substantive democracy, political institutions, and the protections of the rights of individuals.

In addressing "American Nationalism and U.S. Foreign Policy from September 11 to the Iraq War," Paul McCartney raises questions about American political leadership that are relevant to making judgments about substantive democracy in the United States. McCartney's article, as part of his broader book project, is relevant to the meaning of American democracy today, because it lays out the content of the leadership strategy that firmed up and maintained the American public's support for Bush's foreign policy after September 11 and through the Iraq war and the nation building that is still in progress in Iraq (at the time of this writing in April 2005).

The leadership process was one in which the Bush administration was able to fill in an important gap left by the ending of the Cold War. With the end of the Cold War came the end of the usefulness of the framework that had enabled the American public to understand and evaluate American foreign policy. This framework (or "schema," as political psychologists might put it) both facilitated presidential leadership in foreign policy during the Cold War and constrained it, in the sense that it very likely prevented political leaders from persuading the public to support initiatives that did not advance, and might even have threatened, the Cold War objective of containing and constraining the Soviet Union and communism worldwide. Without this framework to inform and guide the public, the public was more dependent than ever on its political leaders and the press to explain and justify the country's actions abroad and, ideally, to provide a new framework for simplifying how to understand international politics in the post-Cold War world. In this sense, presidential leadership became easier, although some analysts thought that the end of the Cold War would give the press more influence, in that it could provide new frames for understanding American foreign policy.[16]

Leadership of public opinion did indeed become easier with the attacks of September 11, when, as McCartney argues, Bush offered an "official" and persuasive interpretation of what was then occurring. Bush provided a context in which Americans could understand and accept broader policy goals than any simple and direct response to the particular attacks would have indicated. He offered a new national focus and purpose, replacing the objectives of the Cold War, and called for a war against the "evil" perpetrators. This laid the groundwork in the public's mind for militaristic objectives against Saddam Hussein's Iraq,

---

[16] Cf. Robert Y. Shapiro and Lawrence R. Jacobs, "Who Leads and Who Follows? U.S. Presidents, Public Opinion and Foreign Policy" in Brigitte L. Nacos, Robert Y. Shapiro, and Pierangelo Isernia, eds., *Decisionmaking in a Glass House: Mass Media, Public Opinion, and American and European Foreign Policy in the 21st Century* (Boston, MA: Rowman and Littlefield Publishers, 2000), 223–245; Robert M. Entman, *Projections of Power: Framing News, Public Opinion, and U.S. Foreign Policy* (Chicago, IL: University of Chicago Press, 2004); and Robert Y. Shapiro and Lawrence R. Jacobs, "Public Opinion, Foreign Policy, and Democracy: How Presidents Use Public Opinion" in Manza, Cook, and Page, eds., *Navigating Public Opinion*, 184–218.

which were central to the administration's new vision for the United States's role in the world as described formally in the administration's National Security Strategy statement.

McCartney's analysis shows how the foreign policy that emerged can be interpreted, in one sense, as democratic and, in another sense, as undemocratic. It is democratic in the sense that Bush obtained public support through the use of rhetoric and symbols reflecting an American nationalism that was consistent with an established tradition in the United States—one for which there was underlying public support or for which public support could be evoked. McCartney describes the nature and origin of the missionary dimension of American national identity relevant to American foreign policy, and he maintains that the American style of foreign policy is a manifestation of an ideological and cultural interpretation of the United States and its role in the world as an "archetype of virtue and the locomotive of human progress." To the extent that the public's support for the new American foreign policy reflected such perceptions and beliefs, the end result could be called democratic, and, as McCartney concludes, any blame for American foreign policy rests not only with Bush but with all Americans.

On the other hand, that this is democratic assumes that Americans have an adequately informed understanding of the realities that have led them to see the national interest in a particular way. Was this the case in the decision to invade Iraq in March 2003? Arguably, this was not so.

Louis Fisher's analysis in "Deciding on War Against Iraq: Institutional Failures" suggests that U.S. foreign policy in the case of this war was undemocratic in both substantive and institutional terms. This occurred, significantly, for one reason: The Bush administration misinformed the public in a way that led the public to misperceive the national interest in going to war. The public saw the war in terms of preventing an allegedly near-term threat by Iraq to use chemical, biological, or nuclear "weapons of mass destruction" (WMDs) against the United States in some fashion, and of battling Iraq as part of the constellation of terrorist threats against the United States since September 11. In its confusion over what reasons to emphasize in its decision to invade Iraq, the administration, in the end, emphasized the WMDs, for which it had little unequivocal evidence, which meant that the public support for the war that the administration gained existed under a false pretense. The public believed a national interest that was unproven and that in the end turned out to be false. This would hardly make the decision to go to war against Iraq something we would want to call "democratic." Moreover, it is difficult to ignore here the comparison to the Gulf of Tonkin debate leading into the Vietnam War, having to do with the now well-documented confusion over attacks on U.S. patrol ships (the crucial second attack was never proven to have occurred and there were suspicious circumstances related to the first one) that led the United States into full-scale war.[17]

---

[17] See Edwin E. Moise, *Tonkin Gulf and the Escalation of the Vietnam War* (Chapel Hill: University of North Carolina Press, 1996).

Aside from the fact that Congress was also misinformed about the degree of threat from WMDs when it voted on giving the administration the green light to invade Iraq, the decision to go to war was undemocratic on other grounds—institutional ones.

First, Congress abandoned its responsibility to make the final decision to go to war. According to Fisher, the House International Relations Committee approved a resolution, thinking that providing the President with the authority he needed to use force would be the best way to avoid the actual use of force. Thus, Congress left the final decision to go to war, a decision that the Constitution gives to Congress alone, up to the President. Instead of representing public opinion in our republican form of government, Congress gave the President unchecked power in deciding to go to war. Fisher emphasizes especially that Congress was under political pressure before the 2002 midterm election, and this pressure on members of Bush's own party and on the Democrats benefited the President. Had the information on the Iraqi threat and the position of the United Nations been more ironclad, such pressure might have been construed differently and in a way more consistent with democratic norms. But it was not.

It is easy to understand how the public accepted the administration's justification for war in terms of the protection of an American national interest, once the confrontation over WMDs and weapons inspection had escalated and the Bush administration had offered a barrage of explanations as to why Saddam Hussein's regime should be deposed. The public, along with the world, waited to see how and when WMDs might be discovered, and what evidence might be found for a direct connection between Saddam Hussein and al Qaeda-supported terrorists. It is deeply troubling to many that no evidence, to this date, has been found that Iraq had WMDs at or near the ready, or that there was any direct connection between Saddam Hussein's regime and representatives of al Qaeda. These were the reasons that led to the war and that helped maintain public support for the war once the invasion was launched, and they have proven false.

Perhaps equally if not more troubling is what Steven Kull, Clay Ramsay, and Evan Lewis describe in "Misperceptions, the Media, and the Iraq War." They found that months into the war, when no evidence was found for either WMDs or an al Qaeda connection, a sizeable percentage of the public reported that such evidence had been found. The undemocratic nature of the administration's public statements and actions continued, in that the public continued to hold false beliefs that affected their support for the war and perceptions of what national interests were being protected by the Iraq invasion. The Bush administration ultimately admitted that no relevant evidence at issue was found, but it did not do so visibly enough to correct fully the misperceptions that persisted fully two years after the Iraq war began.[18] Nor have the news

[18] Gary Langer, "Two Years After War's Start, Deeper Doubts About its Cost," ABC News/Washington Post Poll: The War in Iraq, March 13, released 15 March 2005.

reports gotten the word out fully enough to reach all segments of the public, especially Republican partisans and Bush supporters, to correct these misperceptions. Kull, Ramsay, and Lewis's most provocative and controversial conclusion is that some evidently more-partisan television news outlets did worse than others in informing their audiences of actual developments with regard to WMDs and other factual claims in contention. Of course, now any questions about an al Qaeda connection are almost moot, since al Qaeda-affiliated insurgents are battling American and Iraqi government forces alongside Sunni and former Hussein supporters.

If Kull and his colleagues are correct, American democracy has been short-changed by both its leaders and the press. There is other evidence that drives this point home even further. The Bush administration apparently continued to attempt to manipulate, if not mislead, public opinion. It has admitted to engaging in a public relations campaign that included government-supported news reports for broadcast on local television stations.[19] The administration's veracity has also been questioned in its presentations of facts and analysis on other issues—most notably Social Security. It has described the Social Security system as going "bankrupt"—exaggerating the actual status of the flow of funds that will be available to pay benefits, as well as how any delay in enacting and implementing reforms enormously increases the deficit in funds for the program that is occurring.[20] In contrast to the issues that led to the Iraq war, however, Social Security is a policy area for which the executive does not have significant advantages in information and expertise compared to Congress and others, which has enabled the administration's opponents in Congress as well as other critics to make accurate counter-claims about the economic viability of Social Security and to offer concrete and workable alternatives for Social Security reform beyond the administration's preferred proposal for government-initiated "private" or "personal" retirement accounts.[21] These alternatives, moreover, are likely to be understandable to the public. In contrast, the administration has had better success at persuading—or manipulating—the public by the way that it has framed its support for fully repealing the estate tax (or "death tax" as the Republicans have called it) and for its tax cutting more generally, without drawing attention to the government spending trade-offs that will eventually have to come into play.[22]

September 11 and the Iraq war have not only produced problems for substantive and institutional aspects of democracy, they have also raised questions about threats to existing protections of rights and liberties in American life. This volume has reprinted excerpts from the Supreme Court case, *Yaser Esam Hamdi v. Don-*

[19] Anne E. Kornblut and David Barstow, "Debate Rekindles Over Government-Produced 'News,'" *The New York Times*, 15 April 2005.

[20] Paul Krugman, "The $600 Billion Man," *The New York Times*, 15 March 2005.

[21] For example, Robert M. Ball, Former Commissioner of Social Security, "Social Security Plus," December 2004, and personal communication, February 2005.

[22] See Hacker and Pierson, "Abandoning the Middle."

ald H. Rumsfeld, which is examined further by Demetrios Caraley in his concluding essay. This case is troubling, in that Hamdi, who was a U.S. citizen and a wartime detainee on U.S. soil, is requesting the simplest right to hear and respond
to charges against him. A majority of the Court grants this, although readers
may find it difficult to extract this from the different opinions offered by different subsets of justice. This murkiness may well epitomize the status of constitutionally based rights and protections. In passing the Patriot Act after September 11, Congress felt obligated to beef up the surveillance of individuals who
might pose a terrorist or other threat to the nation through such monitoring actions
as "secret searches," demands for library, medical, and other records, making it
illegal for the record holder to reveal that the government had requested the information, and the wide sharing of information among government units.[23]

Voting, Elections, and Partisanship

The 2004 election was the first presidential election after the period bracketed
by September 11 and the Iraq war and the challenges they have posed for
American democracy. Moreover, this has been a time in which the political parties have become increasingly competitive in their battle for control not only
over the White House but also over the House of Representatives and the Senate. In 1994, the Republicans ended the Democrats' long-standing control of
the House since the Harry Truman presidency, and this has given the Republicans the opportunity—which they have capitalized on—for unified control of
the executive and legislative branches after years during which Democratic
control of at least one branch of Congress has been the norm. Along with these
trends has been a period, since the mid-1970s, of increasing ideological polarization in Congress. Indeed, the 2004 election confirmed directly what political
scientists have tracked over the last thirty years: Politics in the United States has
become increasingly polarized at the elite level. Contrary to complaints that there
is no difference between the two major parties, the party leaders today are more
ideologically unified than they were in the 1970s—Republicans more coherently
conservative and Democrats more consistently liberal.[24] The moderating forces
within each party have disappeared: Gone from the Democratic Party are most
of the conservative Southerners; they have been replaced by—or become—
Republicans. Hence, we get Democrat Zell Miller's performance at the Republican convention, where he attacks his (presumably now former) party's presi-

[23] See Eric Lichtblau, "Justice Department Defends Patriot Act Before Senate Hearings: Critics
Say the Growing Use of Secret Search Warrants Raises the Risk of Abuse of Power," *The New York
Times*, 5 April 2005; Eric Lichtblau, "Antiterrorism Law Defended as Hearings Start: Opponents of
a Bill Make Their Case; Small Concessions Follow," *The New York Times*, 6 April 2005; and "Revising
the Patriot Act," *The New York Times*, 10 April 2005.

[24] See Nolan McCarty, Keith Poole, and Howard Rosenthall, *Income Redistribution and the Realignment of American Politics* (Washington, DC: American Enterprise Institute, 1997); and Jacobs and
Shapiro, *Politicians Don't Pander.*

dential candidate. Moderate Republicans—the Jacob Javitses and Everett Dirksens of old—are hard to find; and we are not surprised to hear criticism of Senator Arlen Specter's lack of fervor on the Senate Judiciary Committee toward appointing conservative judges.

The state of the political parties and their leaders has led to strident party conflict in the House and Senate that is magnified by the news media, which have incentives to emphasize conflict wherever it exists as important news, which it usually (but not necessarily always) is, and to attract audiences and maintain their status as viable, if not prosperous businesses.[25] The elite level—congressional—polarization story began with the two major parties realigning on the issue of civil rights in the 1960s, which then helped clarify the distinctions between the two parties. The parties also took different positions on the new social values issues that came to the fore, defining further the differences in the ideological liberalism/conservatism of the parties' leaders.[26]

What did the 2004 elections indicate? They mainly confirmed that the major parties are now evenly matched. The unified Republican control of Congress and the presidency led to the perception that the President, while not having clear claim to a "mandate," could muster enough support for his domestic agenda.[27] It is not clear at this writing, however, that he can get the public support that he needs. As Morris Fiorina persuasively shows in his recent book, *Culture Wars*, the polarization in politics does not extend to public opinion on economic and social issues. The public's opinions on issues do divide in the same way as they do on their parties' candidates, but differences in opinions within the public have not shown increasing partisan polarization on specific issues. Voters do not cast unequivocally ideological votes that correspond to issue differences between the parties, so that the 2004 election, as considered further below, was not a vote for the kinds of changes that Bush and conservative Republicans in Congress had in mind (the same would have held regarding liberal changes had the Democrats won by a comparably close margin).[28]

The next set of articles in the volume, James Campbell's "Why Bush Won the Presidential Election of 2004: Incumbency, Ideology, Terrorism, and Turnout," and Gary Jacobson's "Polarized Politics and the 2004 Congressional and Presidential Elections," show how partisan polarization has rubbed off on the electorate. The authors report some particularly striking findings: The differ-

[25] See Morris P. Fiorina, with Samuel J. Abrams and Jeremy Pope, *Culture War? The Myth of Polarized America* (New York: Pearson/Longman, 2005); and Jacobs and Shapiro, *Politicians Don't Pander*. For a discussion related to more recent politics, see Robert Y. Shapiro, "Bush's Harder Sell: The President May Dominate in Foreign Affairs, but He's Out of Step at Home," *Newsday*, 13 March 2005.

[26] See James A. Stimson, *Tides of Consent: How Public Opinion Shapes American Politics* (New York: Cambridge University Press, 2004).

[27] On presidents claiming "mandates," see Patricia Heidotting Conley, *Presidential Mandates: How Elections Shape the National Agenda* (Chicago, IL: University of Chicago Press, 2001).

[28] See Fiorina, *Culture Wars*; on past long-term trends that show little evidence for the public becoming more polarized on specific issues, see Page and Shapiro, *The Rational Public*, 285–320.

ences in Bush's approval ratings between Republican versus Democrat voters reached their highest levels of the last fifty years; the proportion of self-identified Democrats and Republicans who voted for their party's presidential candidate in 2004 was 90 percent; and the numbers of "strong" partisans in both parties increased to sizes last found during the 1950s, as reported originally in *The American Voter*.[29] What is remarkable about the partisan differences in Bush's approval rating is that the decline that occurred as the United States got bogged down in Iraq was driven exclusively by opinion changes among Democrats and Independents, with the President's approval rating among Republicans holding solidly at or above the 90 percent level.[30]

Where does this leave elected government in 2005? On the one hand, it is possible to argue that the United States has or is approaching a presidential system of government with "responsible political parties," which critics of American democracy have long desired, as exemplified by the 1950 American Political Science Association report.[31] The two major parties differ visibly on major issues and approaches to government, so that the party in power (controlling most or all of the executive and the legislature) can be held accountable by voters when compared to the choice by the opposition party out of power. On the other hand, the degree of conflict between the parties may have become too extreme, having unintended consequences for governance. This conflict is drawn out most visibly and acrimoniously when allegations of political scandals occur, such as those that led to Bill Clinton's impeachment and, at this writing, allegations against House majority leader Tom Delay; or when religious or otherwise emotion-laden moral values issues rise above other national problems—cases in point have been the issue of gay marriage and the widely publicized debate about euthanasia and terminating life support for Terri Schiavo.

Short of the parties voluntarily turning down the heat and volume, one way this conflict might be diminished, if not resolved, is through the ascendancy of one of the parties, where the Republicans would be the leading choice. Campbell sees this as a possibility if the Democratic Party continues to put forth liberal Northern candidates for the presidency. Beyond that, while Bush and the Republicans had the edge on what Campbell calls the three campaign fundamentals—public support for the in-party, the state of the pre-campaign economy, and incumbency—the Republicans can claim no lock on these, and they will lose the "second party term incumbency advantage" in the 2008 election. Jacobson sees, on net, close contests for control of Congress, with some structural advantage to the Republicans in terms of the numbers of states in the

---

[29] Angus Campbell, Philip E. Converse, Warren E. Miller, and Donald E. Stokes, *The American Voter* (New York: Wiley, 1960; Chicago, IL: University of Chicago Press, 1976).

[30] This deviates sharply from the normal expected pattern of more parallel changes in opinion among all subgroups; see Page and Shapiro, *The Rational Public*, 285–320.

[31] American Political Science Association, "Toward a More Responsible Government: A Report on the Committee on Political Parties," *American Political Science Review Supplement* 44 (September 1950): 1–96.

South that have shifted into the Republican camp since the 1960s. The Republican gains in the House were, however, due mainly to gerrymandering in Texas, so that the Democrats have maintained their competitiveness, and there are enough Republican seats vulnerable to unfavorable national forces—economic performance, Bush's approval rating, unpopular Republican action on Social Security or the budget, and disappointment in the situation in Iraq—that the Democrats could conceivably re-take the House of Representatives.[32]

CONCLUSIONS

What can we conclude about the status of American democracy and the questions that the essays in this volume have considered? In the volume's final section, Demetrios Caraley concludes that for American democracy to continue, elections are not enough. The first part of his essay reviews the historical establishment of American national elections, what elections do and what their limitations are with regard to government policy making, and, again, how it is still the case that there is no constitutional right for citizens to vote for presidential electors. Caraley agrees firmly with Keyssar and acknowledges that the states can choose to step in and impose limitations on the importance of statewide voting for electors, which became an issue during the 2000 presidential election and the *Bush v. Gore* court case. Such limitations clearly contradict the spirit, if not the essence, of Dahl's criteria for democracy.

Caraley explains how the Framers of the Constitution knew that the election or selection of the president, whether by citizen voters, presidential electors, or state legislatures, was not enough, in the normative sense, for representative democracy to thrive in the United States. The Founders required that powers be shared with vigor through the separation-of-powers system that the Constitution established. This has been particularly relevant to contemporary politics, given the frequency with which the same party has not controlled the presidency and the House of Representatives and the Senate. Further, the government's response to the terrorist attacks of September 11 and its initiation of war in Iraq have drawn renewed attention to the separation of Congress's power to *declare* war from the president's power to *conduct* wars as commander in chief. The Framers expected a lopsided balance of power here in Congress's favor, since the president could not make war without congressional authorization and resources.

In addition to this concern about potential elective tyranny in the executive branch, Caraley is also concerned about such tyranny in the legislature. He emphasizes how both electoral accountability, consistent with Dahl, and the separation of powers protect the people against oppression and tyranny by

---

[32] For another analysis of the limited likelihood of a further Republican surge, see Paul R. Abramson, John H. Aldrich, and David W. Rohde, "The 2004 Presidential Election: The Emergence of a Permanent Majority?" *Political Science Quarterly* 120 (Spring 2005): 33–57.

one or more branches of government. If such oppression were initiated by Congress or the president, both of whom could, in fact, be following a voting majority of citizens, the Constitution and its amendments, as ratified by the states, would provide protections from violations of fundamental rights and liberties. And if these protections were not abided, the judiciary could be brought into play. The key objective was that there would be ways for losers to particular majorities to survive as "outs," who would remain able to compete and win on another day. This protection was facilitated in general by the existence of multiple veto points.

Caraley is most concerned about the threat during the last two decades to other tenets of American democracy. First, with regard to voting in presidential elections and democratic legitimacy, the 2004 election struck a central nerve of the nation. In 2004, Bush almost lost the electoral vote and the election, even with a three million vote lead, and this once more raised questions about the electoral college's legitimacy, especially the way in which the votes of individuals do not count equally and the possible, in effect, disenfranchisement of minority party voters in the states. Second, Caraley criticizes further a campaign system that allows the buying of presidential and congressional elections.

Drawing further on the later work of Kull and his colleagues, Caraley is also highly critical of the way that the incomplete, if not inaccurate, media coverage of the facts related to the nation's most important issues limits the possibilities for fully enlightened political engagement by the public. This compounds further the problem for American democracy that comes with congressional abdication of its war powers, as the executive branch is allowed to monopolize information and go unchallenged in its justifications for its actions. His review of the separate opinions offered in *Hamdi v. Rumsfeld* confirms the seriousness of threats to the most basic constitutional guarantees of due process that have occurred since 11 September 2001. Caraley ends his essay with an impassioned assessment of what he sees as two serious—and not unrelated—threats to American democracy: the mean-spiritedness that has come with partisan conflict, and the religious intrusion into contemporary politics. This decline in "comity,"[33] to put it mildly, is reflected both in the behavior of mild-mannered Republican Speaker Dennis Hastert in setting the rules for partisan engagement of legislative proposals in the House, and in majority leader Tom DeLay's response to the investigations of his own behavior and to attacks by Democrats, as well as the zeal with which he wants Congress to alter the way the courts act as institutions, thereby threatening to undermine the role of the judiciary in the separation-of-powers system. This kind of behavior, in tandem with the religious fervor seen in the efforts to keep Terri Schiavo on life support—at odds with medical experts and public opinion[34]—has been an incendiary combination.

[33] On this general topic, see Eric M. Uslaner, *The Decline of Comity in Congress* (Ann Arbor: University of Michigan Press, 1993).

[34] Dalia Sussman and Gary Langer, "Two-Thirds Back Spouse in Right to Die Cases," ABC News/Washington Post Poll: Terri Schiavo, March 13, released 15 March 2005.

What, then, is the status of American democracy in 2005? The answer is complicated and, based on the essays in this volume, disconcerting. It is complicated because there are three aspects of American democracy to consider—institutional processes, substantive representation, and protections of rights and liberties. It is disconcerting because of the specific answers that rise to the top at this time. The country's institutions have fallen short in ways that need to be widely debated and resolved. This volume has raised serious questions about the right to vote and the nature of majority rule in the United States. The separation of powers that has served the nation well is facing challenges in contemporary politics because of events since September 11 and increases in partisan polarization. This polarization may have affected the extent to which government is substantively responsive to public opinion. The fact that polarized parties, by definition, have different agendas and preferred policies indicates that the parties are acting as "responsible parties" that offer voters clear choices, and they can be held responsible for these choices at election time. That the major parties and their candidates have ideological incentives to attempt to lead the public, and electoral incentives to be responsive, would seem to befit the term "American democracy."

Where there is a clear problem for substantive democracy is in the extent to which political leaders have resorted to using deceptive or outright false information and questionable efforts at public relations to manipulate public opinion. The nation's press has fallen short here—it has not been able to protect the public from such manipulation. This problem was clear in the decision to go to war with Iraq. In contrast, debate about Social Security reform has played in a way more consistent with democratic norms. The separation of powers, open debate, and the availability of information and the analyses of experts have made the politics of Social Security reform more democratic than the case of Iraq, and an engaged public on this issue has been taken into account in the political process.[35]

Last, regarding the protection of rights and liberties, debates about civil rights and political inclusiveness for racial and ethnic minorities have continued, along with concerns about how to deal with the increasing economic inequality. But what are currently taking their toll on American democracy are government actions that have encroached on individual rights and liberties in response to a perceived external threat to the nation. The courts do not always reassert the guarantees of these rights quickly and clearly. Historically, the challenges to individual rights and liberties have subsided in such cases when the threat has diminished.[36]

It is, in a sense, ironic that these challenges to American democracy have emerged during a period in which the United States should have been basking

---

[35] Gary Langer, "Bush's Social Security Plan Plays to a Tough Audience," ABC News/Washington Post Poll: Bush/Social Security, March 13, released 14 March 2005.

[36] See Page and Shapiro, *The Rational Public*, 81–89.

in its success. With the end of the Cold War, it was indisputably the world's leading military as well as economic power, and its biggest fears of the past and threats to security had diminished. Then came September 11. Perhaps more ironically, these challenges to democracy have occurred at a time when the goal of American foreign policy, as stated by the Bush administration, is to spread democracy and freedom worldwide. It may be the case that in this new century, what American democracy means may be affected, more so than ever before, not only by domestic politics but also by the what the United States does on the world stage.*

* The responsibility for all analysis and interpretation is the author's. He thanks Demetrios Caraley, Kathleen Doherty, Loren Morales Kando, and Marylena Mantas for their guidance, comments, and assistance, and Gary Langer for his timely survey reports and helpful discussions.

Part II:
DEMOCRACY, INSTITUTIONS, AND RIGHTS

What Political Institutions Does Large-Scale Democracy Require?

ROBERT A. DAHL

What does it mean to say that a country is governed democratically? Here, we will focus on the political institutions of *democracy on a large scale*, that is, the political institutions necessary for a *democratic country*. We are not concerned here, then, with what democracy in a very small group might require, as in a committee. We also need to keep in mind that every actual democracy has always fallen short of democratic criteria. Finally, we should be aware that in ordinary language, we use the word *democracy* to refer both to a goal or ideal and to an actuality that is only a partial attainment of the goal. For the time being, therefore, I'll count on the reader to make the necessary distinctions when I use the words *democracy, democratically, democratic government, democratic country*, and so on.[1]

How Can We Know?

How can we reasonably determine what political institutions are necessary for large-scale democracy? We might examine the history of countries that have changed their political institutions in response, at least in part, to demands for broader popular inclusion and effective participation in government and politi-

---

[1] Political *arrangements* sound as if they might be rather provisional, which they could well be in a country that has just moved away from nondemocratic rule. We tend to think of *practices* as more habitual and therefore more durable. We usually think of *institutions* as having settled in for the long haul, passed on from one generation to the next. As a country moves from a nondemocratic to a democratic government, the early democratic *arrangements* gradually become *practices*, which in due time turn into settled *institutions*. Helpful though these distinction may be, however, for our purposes it will be more convenient if we put them aside and settle for *institutions*.

ROBERT A. DAHL is Sterling Professor Emeritus of Political Science, Yale University. He has published many books on democratic theory and practice, including *A Preface to Democratic Theory* (1956) and *Democracy and Its Critics* (1989). This article was adapted from his recent book, *On Democracy*, Yale University Press.

FIGURE 1
What Political Institutions Does Large-Scale Democracy Require?

Large-scale democracy requires:
1. Elected officials
2. Free, fair, and frequent elections
3. Freedom of expression
4. Alternative sources of information
5. Associational autonomy
6. Inclusive citizenship

cal life. Although in earlier times those who sought to gain inclusion and participation were not necessarily inspired by democratic ideas, from about the eighteenth century onward they tended to justify their demands by appealing to
democratic and republican ideas. What political institutions did they seek, and
what were actually adopted in these countries?

Alternatively, we could examine countries where the government is generally referred to as democratic by most of the people in that country, by many
persons in other countries, and by scholars, journalists, and the like. In other
words, in ordinary speech and scholarly discussion the country is called a democracy.

Third, we could reflect on a specific country or group of countries, or perhaps even a hypothetical country, in order to imagine, as realistically as possible, what political institutions would be required in order to achieve democratic
goals to a substantial degree. We would undertake a mental experiment, so to
speak, in which we would reflect carefully on human experiences, tendencies,
possibilities, and limitations and design a set of political institutions that would
be necessary for large-scale democracy to exist and yet feasible and attainable
within the limits of human capacities.

Fortunately, all three methods converge on the same set of democratic
political institutions. These, then, are minimal requirements for a democratic
country (Figure 1).

THE POLITICAL INSTITUTIONS OF MODERN
REPRESENTATIVE DEMOCRACY

Briefly, the political institutions of modern representative democratic government are

- *Elected officials.* Control over government decisions about policy is constitutionally vested in officials elected by citizens. Thus modern, large-scale
  democratic governments are *representative.*
- *Free, fair and frequent elections.* Elected officials are chosen in frequent and
  fairly conducted elections in which coercion is comparatively uncommon.

- *Freedom of expression.* Citizens have a right to express themselves without danger of severe punishment on political matters broadly defined, including criticism of officials, the government, the regime, the socioeconomic order, and the prevailing ideology.
- *Access to alternative sources of information.* Citizens have a right to seek out alternative and independent sources of information from other citizens, experts, newspapers, magazines, books, telecommunications, and the like. Moreover, alternative sources of information actually exist that are not under the control of the government or any other single political group attempting to influence public political beliefs and attitudes, and these alternative sources are effectively protected by law.
- *Associational autonomy.* To achieve their various rights, including those required for the effective operation of democratic political institutions, citizens also have a right to form relatively independent associations or organizations, including independent political parties and interest groups.
- *Inclusive citizenship.* No adult permanently residing in the country and subject to its laws can be denied the rights that are available to others and are necessary to the five political institutions just listed. These include the right to vote in the election of officials in free and fair elections; to run for elective office; to free expression; to form and participate in independent political organizations; to have access to independent sources of information; and rights to other liberties and opportunities that may be necessary to the effective operation of the political institutions of large-scale democracy.

THE POLITICAL INSTITUTIONS IN PERSPECTIVE

Ordinarily these institutions do not arrive in a country all at once; the last two are distinctly latecomers. Until the twentieth century, universal suffrage was denied in both the theory and practice of democratic and republican government. More than any other single feature, universal suffrage distinguishes modern representative democracy from earlier forms of democracy.

The time of arrival and the sequence in which the institutions have been introduced have varied tremendously. In countries where the full set of democratic institutions arrived earliest and have endured to the present day, the "older" democracies, elements of a common pattern emerge. Elections to a legislature arrived early on—in Britain as early as the thirteenth century, in the United States during its colonial period in the seventeenth and eighteenth centuries. The practice of electing higher lawmaking officials was followed by a gradual expansion of the rights of citizens to express themselves on political matters and to seek out and exchange information. The right to form associations with explicit political goals tended to follow still later. Political "factions" and partisan organization were generally viewed as dangerous, divisive, subversive of political order and stability, and injurious to the public good. Yet because political associations could not be suppressed without a degree of coercion that an increasingly large and influential number of citizens regarded as intolerable, they were often able to exist as more or less clandestine associations until they emerged from the shadows into the full light of day. In the legislative bodies, what once were "factions" became political parties. The "ins" who served in the government of the day were opposed by the "outs," or what in Britain came to be officially styled His (or Her) Majesty's Loyal Opposition. In eighteenth-century Britain, the faction supporting the monarch and the opposing faction supported by much of the gentry in the "country" were gradually transformed into Tories and Whigs. During that same century in Sweden, partisan adversaries in Parliament somewhat facetiously called themselves the Hats and the Caps.[2]

During the final years of the eighteenth century in the newly formed republic of the United States, Thomas Jefferson, the vice president, and James Madison, leader of the House of Representatives, organized their followers in Congress to oppose the policies of the Federalist president, John Adams, and his secretary of the treasury, Alexander Hamilton. To succeed in their opposition, they soon realized that they would have to do more than oppose the Federalists in the Congress and the cabinet: they would need to remove their opponents from office. To do that, they had to win national elections, and to win national elections they had to organize their followers throughout the country. In less than a decade, Jefferson, Madison, and others sympathetic with their views created a political party that was organized all the way down to the smallest voting precincts, districts, and municipalities, an organization that would reinforce the loyalty of their followers between and during election campaigns and make sure they came to the polls. Their Republican Party (soon renamed Democratic Republican and, a generation later, Democratic) became the first popularly based *electoral* party in the world. As a result, one of the most fundamental and distinctive political institutions of modern democracy, the political party, had burst beyond its confines in parliaments and legislatures in order to organize the citizens themselves and mobilize party supporters in national elections.

By the time the young French aristocrat Alexis de Tocqueville visited the United States in the 1830s, the first five democratic political institutions described above had already arrived in America. The institutions seemed to him so deeply planted and pervasive that he had no hesitation in referring to the United States as a democracy. In that country, he said, the people were sovereign, "society governs itself for itself," and the power of the majority was unlimited.[3] He was astounded by the multiplicity of associations into which Americans organized themselves, for every purpose, it seemed. And towering among these associations were the two major political parties. In the United States, it appeared to Tocqueville, democracy was about as complete as one could imagine it ever becoming.

[2] "The Hats assumed their name for being like the dashing fellows in the tricorne of the day. . . . The Caps were nicknamed because of the charge that they were like timid old ladies in nightcaps." Franklin D. Scott, *Sweden: The Nation's History* (Minneapolis: University of Minnesota Press, 1977), 243.

[3] Alexis de Tocqueville, *Democracy in America*, vol. 1 (New York: Schocken Books, 1961), 51.

During the century that followed, all five of the basic democratic institutions Tocqueville observed during his visit to America were consolidated in more than a dozen other countries. Many observers in Europe and the United States concluded that any country that aspired to be civilized and progressive would necessarily have to adopt a democratic form of government.

Yet everywhere, the sixth fundamental institution—inclusive citizenship—was missing. Although Tocqueville affirmed that "the state of Maryland, which had been founded by men of rank, was the first to proclaim universal suffrage," like almost all other men (and many women) of his time he tacitly assumed that "universal" did not include women.[4] Nor, indeed, some men. Maryland's "universal suffrage," it so happened, also excluded most African Americans. Elsewhere, in countries that were otherwise more or less democratic, as in America, a full half of all adults were completely excluded from national political life simply because they were women; in addition, large numbers of men were denied suffrage because they could not meet literacy or property requirements, an exclusion supported by many people who considered themselves advocates of democratic or republican government. Although New Zealand extended suffrage to women in national elections in 1893 and Australia in 1902, in countries otherwise democratic, women did not gain suffrage in national elections until about 1920; in Belgium, France, and Switzerland, countries that most people would have called highly democratic, women could not vote until after World War II.

Because it is difficult for many today to grasp what "democracy" meant to our predecessors, let me reemphasize the difference: in all democracies and republics throughout twenty-five centuries, the rights to engage fully in political life were restricted to a minority of adults. "Democratic" government was government by males only—and not all of them. It was not until the twentieth century that in both theory and practice democracy came to require that the rights to engage fully in political life must be extended, with very few if any exceptions, to the entire population of adults permanently residing in a country.

Taken in their entirety, then, these six political institutions constitute not only a new type of political system but a new kind of popular government, a type of "democracy" that had never existed throughout the twenty-five centuries of experience since the inauguration of "democracy" in Athens and a "republic" in Rome. Because the institutions of modern representative democratic government, taken in their entirety, are historically unique, it is convenient to give them their own name. This modern type of large-scale democratic government is sometimes called *polyarchal* democracy.

Although other factors were often at work, the six political institutions of polyarchal democracy came about, in part at least, in response to demands for inclusion and participation in political life. In countries that are widely referred to as democracies today, all six exist. Yet you might well ask: Are some of these institutions no more than past products of historical struggles? Are they no

---

[4] Tocqueville, *Democracy in America*, 50.

longer necessary for democratic government? And if they are still necessary today, why?[5]

THE FACTOR OF SIZE

Before answering these questions, I need to call attention to an important qualification. We are considering institutions necessary for the government of a democratic *country*. Why "country"? *Because all the institutions necessary for a democratic country would not always be required for a unit much smaller than a country.*

Consider a democratically governed committee, or a club, or a very small town. Although equality in voting would seem to be necessary, small units like these might manage without many elected officials: perhaps a moderator to preside over meetings, a secretary-treasurer to keep minutes and accounts. The participants themselves could decide just about everything directly during their meetings, leaving details to the secretary-treasurer. Governments of small organizations would not have to be full-fledged *representative* governments in which citizens elect representatives charged with enacting laws and policies. Yet these governments could be democratic, perhaps highly democratic. So, too, even though they lacked political parties or other independent political associations, they might be highly democratic. In fact, we might concur with the classical democratic and republican view that in small associations, organized "factions" are not only unnecessary but downright harmful. Instead of conflicts exacerbated by factionalism, caucuses, political parties, and so on, we might prefer unity, consensus, agreement achieved by discussion and mutual respect.

The political institutions strictly required for democratic government depend, then, on the size of the unit. The six institutions listed above developed because they are necessary for governing *countries*, not smaller units. Polyarchal democracy is democratic government on the large scale of the nation-state or country.

To return to our questions: Are the political institutions of polyarchal democracy actually necessary for democracy on the large scale of a country? If so, why? To answer these twin questions, let us recall what a democratic process requires (Figure 2).

[5] Polyarchy is derived from Greek words meaning "many" and "rule," thus "rule by the many," as distinguished from rule by the one, or monarchy, and rule by the few, oligarchy or aristocracy. Although the term had been rarely used, a colleague and I introduced it in 1953 as a handy way of referring to a modern representative democracy with universal suffrage. Hereafter I shall use it in that sense. More precisely, a polyarchal democracy is a political system with the six democratic institutions listed above. Polyarchal democracy, then, is different from representative democracy with restricted suffrage, as in the nineteenth century. It is also different from older democracies and republics that not only had a restricted suffrage but lacked many of the other crucial characteristics of polyarchal democracy, such as political parties, rights to form political organizations to influence or oppose the existing government, organized interest groups, and so on. It is different, too, from the democratic practices in units so small that members can assemble directly and make (or recommend) policies or laws.

FIGURE 2
Why the Institutions Are Necessary

In a unit as large as a country, these political institutions of polyarchal democracy ...	are necessary to satisfy the following democratic criteria:
1. Elected representatives...	Effective participation
	Control of the agenda
2. Free, fair and frequent elections...	Voting equality
	Control of the agenda
3. Freedom of expression...	Effective participation
	Enlightened understanding
	Control of the agenda
4. Alternative information...	Effective participation
	Enlightened understanding
	Control of the agenda
5. Associational autonomy...	Effective participation
	Enlightened understanding
	Control of the agenda
6. Inclusive citizenship...	Full inclusion

WHY (AND WHEN) DOES DEMOCRACY REQUIRE ELECTED REPRESENTATIVES?

As the focus of democratic government shifted to large-scale units like nations or countries, the question arose: How can citizens *participate effectively* when the number of citizens becomes too numerous or too widely dispersed geographically (or both, as in the case of a country) for them to participate conveniently in making laws by assembling in one place? And how can they make sure that matters with which they are most concerned are adequately considered by officials—that is, how can citizens *control the agenda of* government decisions?

How best to meet these democratic requirements in a political unit as large as a country is, of course, enormously difficult, indeed to some extent unachievable. Yet just as with the other highly demanding democratic criteria, this, too, can serve as a standard for evaluating alternative possibilities and solutions. Clearly the requirements could not be met if the top officials of the government could set the agenda and adopt policies independently of the wishes of citizens. The only feasible solution, though it is highly imperfect, is for citizens to elect their top officials and hold them more or less accountable through elections by dismissing them, so to speak, in subsequent elections.

To us that solution seems obvious. But what may appear self-evident to us was not at all obvious to our predecessors.

Until fairly recently the possibility that citizens could, by means of elections, choose and reject representatives with the authority to make laws remained largely foreign to both the theory and practice of democracy. The election of representatives mainly developed during the Middle Ages, when monarchs realized that in order to impose taxes, raise armies, and make laws, they needed to win the consent of the nobility, the higher clergy, and a few not-so-common commoners in the larger towns and cities.

Until the eighteenth century, then, the standard view was that democratic or republican government meant rule by the people, and if the people were to rule, they had to assemble in one place and vote on decrees, laws, or policies. Democracy would have to be town meeting democracy; representative democracy was a contradiction in terms. By implication, whether explicit or implicit, a republic or a democracy could actually exist only in a small unit, like a town or city. Writers who held this view, such as Montesquieu and Jean-Jacques Rousseau, were perfectly aware of the disadvantages of a small state, particularly when it confronted the military superiority of a much larger state, and were therefore extremely pessimistic about the future prospects for genuine democracy.

Yet the standard view was swiftly overpowered and swept aside by the onrushing force of the national state. Rousseau himself clearly understood that for a government of a country as large as Poland (for which he proposed a constitution), representation would be necessary. And shortly thereafter, the standard view was driven off the stage of history by the arrival of democracy in America.

As late as 1787, when the Constitutional Convention met in Philadelphia to design a constitution appropriate for a large country with an ever-increasing population, the delegates were acutely aware of the historical tradition. Could a republic possibly exist on the huge scale the United States had already attained, not to mention the even grander scale the delegates foresaw?[6] Yet no one questioned that if a republic were to exist in America, it would have to take the form of a *representative* republic. Because of the lengthy experience with representation in colonial and state legislatures and in the Continental Congress, the feasibility of representative government was practically beyond debate.

By the middle of the nineteenth century, the traditional view was ignored, forgotten, or, if remembered at all, treated as irrelevant. "It is evident," John Stuart Mill wrote in 1861

> that the only government which can fully satisfy all the exigencies of the social state is one in which the whole people participate; that any participation, even in the smallest public function, is useful; that the participation should everywhere be as great as the general degree of improvement of the community will allow; and that nothing less can be ultimately desirable than the admission of all to share in the sov-

[6] A few delegates daringly forecast that the United States might ultimately have as many as one hundred million inhabitants. This number was reached in 1915.

ereign power of the state. But since all cannot, in a community exceeding a single small town, participate personally in any but some very minor portions of the public business, it follows that the ideal type of a perfect government must be representative.[7]

WHY DOES DEMOCRACY REQUIRE FREE, FAIR, AND FREQUENT ELECTIONS?

As we have seen, if we accept the desirability of political equality, then every citizen must have an *equal and effective opportunity to vote, and all votes must be counted as equal.* If equality in voting is to be implemented, then clearly, elections must be free and fair. To be free means that citizens can go to the polls without fear of reprisal; and if they are to be fair, then all votes must be counted as equal. Yet free and fair elections are not enough. Imagine electing representatives for a term of, say, twenty years! If citizens are to retain *final control over the agenda*, then elections must also be frequent.

How best to implement free and fair elections is not obvious. In the late nineteenth century, the secret ballot began to replace a public show of hands. Although open voting still has a few defenders, secrecy has become the general standard; a country in which it is widely violated would be judged as lacking free and fair elections. But debate continues as to the kind of voting system that best meets standards of fairness. Is a system of proportional representation (PR), like that employed in most democratic countries, fairer than the first-past-the-post system used in Great Britain and the United States? Reasonable arguments can be made for both. In discussions about different voting systems, however, the need for a fair system is assumed; how best to achieve fairness and other reasonable objectives is simply a technical question.

How frequent should elections be? Judging from twentieth-century practices in democratic countries, a rough answer might be that annual elections for legislative representatives would be a bit too frequent and anything more than five years would be too long. Obviously, however, democrats can reasonably disagree about the specific interval and how it might vary with different offices and different traditional practices. The point is that without frequent elections, citizens would lose a substantial degree of control over their elected officials.

WHY DOES DEMOCRACY REQUIRE FREE EXPRESSION?

To begin with, freedom of expression is required in order for citizens to *participate* effectively in political life. How can citizens make their views known and persuade their fellow citizens and representatives to adopt them unless they can express themselves freely about all matters bearing on the conduct of the government? And if they are to take the views of others into account, they must

[7] John Stuart Mill, *Considerations on Representative Government* [1861] (New York: Liberal Arts Press, 1958), 55.

be able to hear what others have to say. Free expression means not just that you have a right to be heard. It also means that you have a right to hear what others have to say.

To acquire an *enlightened understanding* of possible government actions and policies also requires freedom of expression. To acquire civic competence, citizens need opportunities to express their own views; learn from one another; engage in discussion and deliberation; read, hear, and question experts, political candidates, and persons whose judgments they trust; and learn in other ways that depend on freedom of expression.

Finally, without freedom of expression, citizens would soon lose their capacity to influence *the agenda* of government decisions. Silent citizens may be perfect subjects for an authoritarian ruler; they would be a disaster for a democracy.

WHY DOES DEMOCRACY REQUIRE THE AVAILABILITY OF ALTERNATIVE AND INDEPENDENT SOURCES OF INFORMATION?

Like freedom of expression, the availability of alternative and relatively independent sources of information is required by several of the basic democratic criteria. Consider the need for *enlightened understanding.* How can citizens acquire the information they need in order to understand the issue if the government controls all the important sources of information? Or, for that matter, if any single group enjoys a monopoly in providing information? Citizens must have access, then, to alternative sources of information that are not under the control of the government or dominated by any other group or point of view.

Or think about *effective participation* and influencing the *public agenda.* How could citizens participate effectively in political life if all the information they could acquire were provided by a single source, say the government, or, for that matter, a single party, faction, or interest?

WHY DOES DEMOCRACY REQUIRE INDEPENDENT ASSOCIATIONS?

It took a radical turnabout in ways of thinking to accept the need for political associations—interest groups, lobbying organizations, political parties. Yet if a large republic requires that representatives be elected, then how are elections to be contested? Forming an organization, such as a political party, gives a group an obvious electoral advantage. And if one group seeks to gain that advantage, will not others who disagree with their policies? And why should political activity cease between elections? Legislators can be influenced; causes can be advanced, policies promoted, appointments sought. So, unlike a small city or town, the large scale of democracy in a country makes political associations both necessary and desirable. In any case, how can they be prevented without impairing the fundamental right of citizens to participate effectively in governing? In a large republic, then, they are not only necessary and desirable but inevitable.

Independent associations are also a source of *civic education and enlighten-ment.* They provide citizens not only with information but also with opportunities for discussion, deliberation, and the acquisition of political skills.

WHY DOES DEMOCRACY REQUIRE INCLUSIVE CITIZENSHIP?

We can view the political institutions summarized in Figure 1 in several ways. For a country that lacks one or more of the institutions, and is to that extent not yet sufficiently democratized, knowledge of the basic political institutions can help us to design a strategy for making a full *transition* to modern representative democracy. For a country that has only recently made the transition, that knowledge can help inform us about the crucial institutions that need to be *strengthened, deepened, and consolidated.* Because they are all necessary for modern representative democracy (polyarchal democracy), we can also view them as establishing a *minimum level for democratization.*

Those of us who live in the older democracies, where the transition to democracy occurred some generations ago and the political institutions listed in Figure 1 are by now solidly established, face a different and equally difficult challenge. For even if the institutions are necessary to democratization, they are definitely not *sufficient* for achieving fully the democratic criteria listed in Figure 1. Are we not then at liberty, and indeed obligated, to appraise our democratic institutions against these criteria? It seems obvious to me, as to many others, that judged against democratic criteria, our existing political institutions display many shortcomings.

Consequently, just as we need strategies for bringing about a transition to democracy in nondemocratic countries and for consolidating democratic institutions in newly democratized countries, so in the older democratic countries, we need to consider whether and how to move beyond our existing level of democracy.

Let me put it this way. In many countries, the task is to achieve democratization up to the level of polyarchal democracy. But the challenge to citizens in the older democracies is to discover how they might achieve a level of democratization *beyond* polyarchal democracy.

Prescriptions for a New National Democracy

MICHAEL LIND

Americans tend to think of their history as one of unbroken continuity. The United States has been governed under the same federal constitution since the eighteenth century, and its borders have remained unchanged since the nineteenth century (with the exception of the admission to statehood of Alaska and Hawaii). This superficial continuity disguises the discontinuities between three successive American regimes or republics, each separated from its predecessor by a violent upheaval, each marked by a distinctive set of rules governing citizenship, race, and immigration. The First Republic of the United States, Anglo-America, lasted from the adoption of the U.S. Constitution in 1787–1789 until the Civil War. Its successor, Euro-America, coalesced in the aftermath of the Civil War and lasted until the Civil Rights Revolution of the 1950s and 1960s. The present American regime, Multicultural America, was assembled in the late 1960s and early 1970s.

Each republic of the United States to date has had its own political creed. The political creed of Anglo-America was federal republicanism; even before the Civil War inaugurated the Euro-American republic, this was giving way to federal democracy, as class-based restrictions on suffrage (at least among white men) were abolished. In Multicultural America, federal centralization has been combined with a cooptive system of racial preferences; in effect, territorial federalism has been overlaid by racial federalism. The idea of racial federalism is democracy *within* races, not democracy *across* races; its symbol is the racially gerrymandered majority-minority district.

The philosophy of liberal nationalism offers an alternative to the multicultural conception of American society. Liberal nationalists reject the multicultural idea of the United States as a federation of half a dozen biologically defined ethnocultural groups in favor of a conception of the American community as a concrete historic nation engendered by cultural fusion and ethnic and racial amalgam-

MICHAEL LIND, the author of a number of books on American politics and history, is the Whitehead Senior Fellow at the New America Foundation in Washington, DC. This article is adapted from his book, *The Next American Nation: The New Nationalism and the Fourth American Revolution* (The Free Press, 1995).

ation. If American nationality is defined by the use of American English and participation in a common vernacular culture, then most Americans of all races, with the exception of recent immigrants, are members of the transracial national majority.

What I call "national democracy" would be the political creed of a Fourth Republic of the United States based on the liberal-nationalist idea of American identity. National democracy has three elements: individual rights, equal voting power, and the social market. Realizing the ideal of national democracy in the United States would require a return to the original project of liberal integrationists of completely eliminating race as a legitimate category in American law and politics. It would require, as well, a genuine democratization of our money-dominated political system and a commitment to the kind of social democratic reforms that the color-blind integrationists of the 1960s envisioned as the next logical step after the eradication of formal white supremacy. In the Fourth American Republic, the nation-dividing mixture of racial preference, plutocratic politics, and free-market capitalism that defines the politics of Multicultural America would be replaced by a nation-uniting synthesis of color-blind individualism in civil rights, equal voting power, and social market capitalism.

INDIVIDUAL RIGHTS

Every American republic to date has embodied its conception of the American nation (or nations) in civil rights law. In Anglo-America and Euro-America, to be a "real" American one had to be white, and the laws requiring or permitting racial segregation reflected this idea. Today's racial preference laws are based on two quite different notions; first, that America is a federation of five racial nations and second, that it is just and reasonable to discriminate against members of the "non-Hispanic white" category in the interests of the other four.

The liberal nationalist conception of American identity is completely at odds with this idea. Liberal nationalists reject not merely racial preferences, but the very definitions of the races themselves. The lines of culture and the lines of race do not coincide in the United States; and nationality, properly understood, is a matter of culture, not race. The division of humanity into three, or five, or sixteen "races" is an inherently arbitrary activity; in the United States, the arbitrary is joined by the absurd when dubious categories are linked to real government-enforced benefits and disabilities.

Racial labeling by the government must be ended, as soon as possible. The U.S. government should no longer give any official sanction to arbitrary color-coded identities—white, black, brown, yellow, red—that do not correspond to the way that Americans actually think about themselves. According to a recent study sponsored by the Ford Foundation, most "Hispanics" prefer to be identified by their country of origin—Mexico, Cuba, or Puerto Rico—rather than as "Hispanics" or "Latinos." The same survey revealed that English is the primary language for most U.S.-born Hispanics, and that Mexicans, Puerto Ricans, and

Cubans think better of "Anglos" than of other Hispanic national-origin groups. Most, furthermore, are indifferent to Latin America and oppose increased immigration.[1] The federal government should not make a bad situation worse by adding new official races (like the "multiracial" category that is promoted by some mixed-race Americans). Even less should the government substitute a linguistic-cultural criterion, distinguishing Trans-Americans of all races from culturally different but genetically related groups (though such a system would approximate reality better than our present official categories).

The time for racial classification schemes like the five-race pattern promulgated in 1977 by the Office of Management and Budget (OMB) in Statistical Directive 15 is past. The color-blind liberals were right, in the early 1960s, to favor the complete elimination of government racial labels. The U.S. government should no more classify native-born American citizens as whites, blacks, Hispanics, or Asians, or for that matter as mixed-race, than it classified white Americans as Swedish- or Irish-Americans. There should no longer be an ominous-sounding Division of Racial Statistics at the Census Bureau. If people are to be labeled for record-keeping purposes, it should be solely on the basis of country of *personal* (not ancestral) national origin. For government record-keeping, there should be only two categories of U.S. citizens—native-born citizens, and naturalized immigrants (the two groups, or course, would have absolutely identical rights). Only naturalized Mexican-born immigrants to the United States would be described as Mexican-Americans. As far as the U.S. government is concerned, their children, born and raised in the United States, would be Americans.

The government should not be hostile to subcultural identities within the Trans-American nation, but it should exhibit a principled indifference toward them. If self-described Asian-Americans wish to perpetuate themselves as a distinct population by limiting marriage among themselves to Americans of Chinese, Indian, Filipino, Korean, and Malaysian descent, and by teaching their children a fabricated Sino-Indo-Filipino-Korean-Malaysian tradition, similar to the fake African-American and pan-Hispanic traditions, they are welcome to do so—but this should be a purely private matter, like the perpetuation of Polish- or Italian-American identities (and mythologies). Complete obliviousness to race is not necessary for national integration, merely the decline of powerful racial identities in "symbolic ethnicities," so that Americans eventually think of themselves as black or white or Asian in the same way that white Americans now think of themselves as Irish or Anglo or Polish. Conventionally defined race would be one of the facts people note about each other, like height and build, but it would have lost its social connotations and emotional valence. If this seems utopian, recall that only a few generations ago even thinkers on the left like Horace Kallen thought that the white "races" of America—the Germans, the Italians, the Irish—were immutable groups that would forever define the identities of individual Americans.

---

[1] "Latinos: Speaking in Their Own Voices," *News from the Ford Foundation*, 15 December 1992.

It might be objected nonetheless that for many generations to come the public would continue thinking in terms of traditional racial distinctions, even if the government ceased labeling citizens by race. The argument from popular prejudice to government policy is unconvincing. Suppose that a majority of Americans were misguided enough to believe that Jews are a race. Should the pseudoracial category of Hispanics be joined by a pseudoracial category of Hebraics? In the nineteenth century, many thought that the Irish formed a distinctive Celtic race. Does the need to overcome the legacies of anti-Irish prejudice justify labeling Irish-Americans as Celts and putting Anglo-, German-, and Scandinavian-Americans together in the category of Teutons?

Four centuries of racial labeling are enough. Let the U.S. Census of 2000 A.D. be the first in American history that does not ask citizens to identify themselves by quasi-fictive categories of race.

The end of racial labeling should be accompanied by the abolition of all racial preference policies, whether carried out by the government or private-sector institutions. Subnational racial group entitlements should be replaced by individual rights and entitlements that are the same for all members of the American citizenry, no matter what their ancestries. The civil rights laws of the Fourth Republic of the United States should be founded on a principle rejected by the drafters of the first three American republics: absolutely color-blind law.

In his dissent in *Plessy v. Ferguson* (1896), the case that legitimated Jim Crow segregation, Supreme Court Justice John Marshall Harlan summarized the color-blind ideal of individual rights:

> There is no caste here. Our Constitution is color-blind and neither knows nor tolerates classes among citizens. In respect of civil rights all citizens are created equal before the law. The law regards man as man and takes no account of his surroundings or of his color when his civil rights as guaranteed by the supreme law of the land are involved.

Three quarters of a century later, another justice, William O. Douglas (one of the most influential liberals ever to sit on the Court, it should be noted) denounced the emerging system of racial preferences in his dissent in *Defunis v. Odegaard* (1974) as passionately as Harlan had denounced the emerging system of Jim Crow in his day:

> The Equal Protection Clause commands the elimination of racial barriers, not their creation in order to satisfy some theory of how society ought to be organized. The purpose of [the university] cannot be to produce Black lawyers for Blacks, Polish lawyers for Poles, Jewish lawyers for Jews, and Irish lawyers for the Irish. . . . A segregated admissions process creates suggestions of stigma and caste no less than a segregated classroom, and in the end it may produce that result despite contrary intentions.

The color-blind ideal was repudiated by the governing class in both Euro-America and Multicultural America. Let Trans-America be the first republic of the United States in which a citizen's race has no legal consequences whatsoever.

All racial preference programs should be consigned to the junkyard of history. Racial gerrymandering to produce "majority-minority" districts by carving up electorates that happen to be the wrong color should be outlawed. All minority set-asides should be eliminated. Busing in order to achieve racial balance should be forbidden by law. Giving preference to individuals on the basis of their race in hiring, promotion, or college admissions, for whatever purpose, should be banned by federal law. Colleges and universities should be forced to end scholarships limited to members of one race, on pain of losing their federal tax-exempt status and federal funding and being subject to antidiscrimination suits. The present amendments to the Voting Rights Act of 1965 that force the racial gerrymandering of districts are scheduled to expire, unless renewed, in 2007. That year should be set as the date by which all race-conscious provisions of American law and public policy are repealed or allowed to lapse. Whether racial preference is eliminated by federal law or by a constitutional amendment is a matter of expedience. However it goes, it must go.

Without racial quotas, some ask, how will poor black and Hispanic Americans ever move out of poverty? And how will upwardly mobile middle-class and upper-middle-class nonwhites be able to overcome the almost invisible but strong and resilient webs of nepotism and inherited advantage that link members of the white overclass?

The social mobility of many blacks and Hispanic Americans is impeded by three quite different kinds of obstacles—active racism, barriers to entry in the economy and politics, and acquired disabilities. No single strategy is appropriate for all three obstacles. Active racism against individuals must be neutralized by rigorous enforcement of antidiscrimination law. Barriers to entry in the economy and politics have to be dismantled by sweeping legislative reforms of how business is done and how elections are carried out in the United States. Acquired disabilities—by which I mean the very real culture of poverty that equips many children of the ghetto and barrio with attitudes making them unfit for the mainstream, workaday community—are the most difficult, because the most subtle, of all obstacles. To the solution of all these problems, racial preference is irrelevant.

A serious attempt to integrate American society would consist of coordinate efforts in different spheres—the judicial (antidiscrimination law), the political (legislative reform of education, the professions, electoral methods, and government structures) and the economic (targeted programs to liberate the hereditary poor, as well as broader programs like universal health care and public education benefiting all wage-earning Americans).

Under a new, color-blind legal regime of individual rights, there would continue to be redress in the courts for individuals who suffer as individuals from actual discrimination. The abolition of government racial labeling need not affect antidiscrimination law at all; it is already against the law for employers to discriminate against people on the basis of religion, even though employers are not required to keep records of the religious status of their employees. However, in all cases where racial discrimination has been proven redress should be victim-specific, not collective. If an employer discriminates against a black American in promotion, then only the victim of the discrimination should be entitled to redress. The employer should not be required to go beyond ceasing to discriminate against blacks to promising to promote other blacks in some arbitrary quota fixed by a judge, just as an employer who discriminates against one Catholic should not be compelled to hire other Catholics according to some mathematical formula. Such collective justice is dehumanizing. It assumes that all members of a particular group of the population are interchangeable, identical units.

The abolition of racial preference, then, need not affect antidiscrimination law at all. Indeed, even as group preferences are being abolished, the scope of individualistic antidiscrimination law should be expanded to protect (not favor) new categories of individuals. To name one example, the federal government should strike down all remaining sodomy laws and prohibit public or private discrimination against homosexuals in all areas outside of family law (a complex area where even the rights of heterosexual citizens are far from absolute or simple). It should be against the law to refuse to hire, or to fire, or to refuse to rent to any American citizen on the basis of sexual orientation.

Not only "liberal" sexual privacy rights, but "conservative" property rights should be extended by federal legislation, too—when it comes to important matters, property owners and businesses should not be at the mercy of local governments and state legislatures. As the United States has increasingly become a single continental society, rather than a confederation of regional subsocieties, the argument in favor of permitting extreme variation in basic individual rights from state to state is weaker then ever. Why should restrictions on abortion vary between New York and Nevada? Why should a company have to deal with entirely different rules for tax assessment in Florida and Maine? Why should a homosexual employee of IBM be considered a law-abiding citizen in Massachusetts and a felon in Alabama, to which he is transferred by the corporation he works for? What is the point of national citizenship at all, if one's most basic personal rights—not just those touching on sex and marriage and parenthood, but also property rights—depends on the territorial jurisdiction in which one happens, perhaps temporarily, to live?

The argument that state legislatures are closer to the people begs the question—*which* people? When it comes to one's individual rights as a citizen, the only relevant population is the American nation as a whole. Perhaps the conclusion would be different if the states corresponded to actual social units, like the German-, French-, Italian- and Romansch-speaking cantons in Switzerland. Most state lines, however, are purely arbitrary, cutting across more natural geographic, cultural, and economic regions. State populations are not genuine moral communities. There is no "Louisiana" morality, no "Massachusetts" morality. A social conservative in Louisiana has more in common with a social conservative in Massachusetts than with a libertarian who happens to be a fellow citizen of Louisiana.

No one, in proposing a constitution for new democracies today—say, in Eastern Europe—would be demented enough to propose that the basic sexual and property rights of citizens should depend on the accident of their residence in a particular state or province. Some forms of federalism are justifiable, but civil rights federalism is an evil anachronism. The more basic the right, the more important that it be protected by the national government from bigoted or misguided local majorities that are national minorities. The twentieth century has seen a gradual nationalization of civil rights in the United States. In the twenty-first century, the process should be completed. Congress, with the help of the federal judiciary, should preempt and codify state legislation in many areas, imposing uniform basic rights laws in place of fifty separate state legal codes, in matters of racial equality, sexual privacy, family law, and the rights of property and business. The basic individual rights of all American citizens should be exactly the same, everywhere on American soil.

Defenders of group preferences often point out that these have always existed in the United States; for generations, civil and political rights were limited to white men. The evolution of notions of citizenship, however, was in the direction of universal individual rights, before the tragic perversion of the color-blind Civil Rights Revolution into a racial and gender preference revolution. Insofar as there is not a single consequence of white-supremacist racial preference that cannot be best addressed by color-blind socioeconomic reforms of the kind I describe later, we are justified in trying to make Justice Harlan's dissent the new consensus: *There is no caste here.*

EQUAL VOTING POWER

After color-blind individual rights, the ideal of equal voting power is the second element of the liberal nationalist creed of national democracy. Equal voting power means more than formal equality in voting for candidates who have been preselected by a small group of wealthy donors. It means the substantive realization of the one-person, one-vote ideal. In the United States, realizing this ideal requires success in three major reforms: the separation of check and state, the promotion of multiparty democracy, and the transformation of the malapportioned federal Senate into a new, national Senate.

Separation of Check and State

Today's U.S. government is democratic in form but plutocratic in substance. The American campaign finance system could not work better if it had been deliberately designed to ensure government of the rich, by the rich, and for the rich. In a misguided 1976 decision, *Buckley v. Valeo*, the Supreme Court held that Congress could not limit spending by rich Americans promoting their own candidacies. This decision was to the equalization of voting power what *Dred Scott* was to abolitionism. In *The Yale Law Review*, Jamin Raskin and

John Boniface have argued that political candidates in the United States must win a "wealth primary." Candidates without enormous amounts of money, either from their own fortunes or from rich individuals and special interest groups, cannot hope to win party primaries—much less general elections. Indeed, the *Buckley* decision is one reason why more than half of the members of the Senate today are millionaires.[2] The bias toward the rich embodied in American campaign finance practices makes a mockery of America's democratic ideals. Genuine democracy requires not only juridical equality among races when it comes to individual rights, but also political equality among the different socioeconomic classes of citizens.

It is time to build a wall of separation between check and state. Curing the disease of plutocratic politics requires a correct diagnosis of its cause: the costs of political advertising. The basic problem is that special interests buy access and favors by donating the money needed for expensive political advertising in the media. Elaborate schemes governing the flow of money do nothing to address the central problem: paid political advertising. Instead of devising unworkable limits on campaign financing that leave the basic system intact, we should cut the Gordian knot of campaign corruption by simply outlawing paid political advertising on behalf of any candidate for public office. The replacement of political advertising by free informational public service notices in the electronic and print media would level the playing field of politics and kill off an entire parasitic industry of media consultants and spin doctors.

An outright ban on paid political advertising and the imposition of free time requirements on the media are radical measures, but nothing less is necessary if we are to prevent our government from continuing to be sold to the highest bidders. The argument against strict public regulation of money in politics is based on a false analogy between free spending and free speech protected under the First Amendment. The analogy is false, because limits on campaign finance do not address the *content* of speech—only its volume, as it were. It is not an infringement on free speech to say that, in a large public auditorium, Douglas will not be allowed to use a microphone unless Lincoln can as well.

Indeed, the separation of check and state might permit us to re-create, in modern conditions, something like the American democracy of a century ago. When Illinois voters had to choose between Abraham Lincoln and Stephen A. Douglas, they were not treated to different thirty-second spots—an "image" commercial for Lincoln showing a slave in chains and then cutting to a blurry, idealized log cabin, an "attack" commercial by Douglas showing quotes from Lincoln opposing the Civil War, taken out of context to make him look like a traitor. Instead, nineteenth-century Illinois voters could see Lincoln and Douglas debate for several hours. Today, television technology permits such debates without requiring candidates to travel from town to town. Our televised public debates, sponsored by nonpartisan bodies like the League of Women Voters,

[2] E. J. Dionne, Jr., "Democracy or Plutocracy," *Washington Post*, 15 February 1994.

represent the best part of our campaign system; the paid political advertisements are the worst. The advertisements should go, the debates remain.

Campaign finance reform is not properly described as a free speech issue at all; it is, first and foremost, a civil rights issue. The progressive exclusion of monetary advantage from the civic sphere, and its confinement to the marketplace, is one of the clearest signs of political progress. When the ideal of popular democracy has triumphed over plutocratic democracy, future generations will look back on the practice of buying access and votes from politicians by means of campaign contributions with the same amazement, horror, and disgust with which we regard the poll tax, the selling of exemptions from the draft to the sons of wealthy families during the height of the Civil War, or the college-student exemption to the Vietnam draft. Today progress means, in the words of E. J. Dionne, making sure "that the votes of majorities matter more than the dollars of minorities."[3]

Multiparty Democracy

The United States is one of the few democracies in the world that retains the archaic plurality system for electing legislators. Under the plurality system—sometimes known as "first past the post" or "winner take all"—a representative is elected by a plurality of voters in a single district. The drawbacks of this system are obvious. A candidate who gets 40 percent of the vote, as long as he gets more votes than any other candidate, can be elected—even though 60 percent of the voters voted against him. In what sense is that 60 percent majority represented by the candidate thus elected? Even worse, the plurality system encourages a two-party monopoly, because votes for third parties are wasted. Finally, plurality systems reward the gerrymandering of single-member districts to give parties (or, in the United States, particular racial groups) built-in advantages.

Proportional representation (PR) is free from these defects. In the most common form of PR, the party-list system, a country, or subunit like a state, county, or city, is divided into multimember districts. Several parties present lists of candidates within each multimember district. The voters vote for the parties, rather than the candidates. Seats are allocated among the parties, on the basis of the proportion they receive of the total vote.

The kinds of distortions that take place routinely in plurality systems are impossible in PR systems. Under a PR system, a party that wins 40 percent of the vote in a multimember district will win only 40 percent of the seats. PR encourages multiparty democracy, because it permits even small parties to elect representatives (in order to discourage tiny, extremist parties, most democracies with PR now require that parties pass a minimum threshold of the total vote; in Germany, extremist parties have been checked by a 5 percent threshold). PR also reduces the incentives to engage in partisan or racial gerrymandering. Under

---

[3] Ibid.

PR, in multimember districts every significant party or voting bloc will be represented more or less in proportion to its strength in the entire electorate, regardless of how the district lines are drawn. Only in "winner-take-all" plurality systems, in which the voters in an area of several blocks may make the difference between losing everything and winning everything by a few percentage points, is there an incentive to gerrymander.

In the United States, proportional representation would permit us to do away with both partisan and racial gerrymandering, while, at the same time, increasing the political options (as new parties formed) and making it easier for members of minority groups—not only racial, but religious and cultural—to elect at least one member of multimember delegations. PR achieves the goal of the Voting Rights Act—greater voting power for black and Hispanic Americans—but by color-blind, nonintrusive means that benefit members of numerical minorities in general. Under PR, black and Hispanic voters would find it much easier to elect black and Hispanic candidates, if they chose. They would not, however, be maneuvered into such a choice by being electorally ghettoized in safe minority-majority districts. They would not have to live in minority neighborhoods in order to enjoy a greater range of options, and to wield greater individual power at the polls.

PR could be easily adopted for city councils, county commissions, and state legislatures simply by changes in state law. Furthermore, although many people believe mistakenly that winner-take-all plurality elections and their inevitable result, the two-party monopoly, are enshrined in the U.S. Constitution, nothing more than an act of Congress would be required to establish the election of members of the House of Representatives by PR.[4]

Our archaic first-pass-the-post plurality electoral system preserves a two-party monopoly rejected by a growing number of alienated American voters, forces many Americans to waste their votes, and effectively disfranchises substantial numerical minorities. There are practically no arguments in its favor, other than the fact that it is more than two hundred years old. The Founding Fathers, however, did not so much choose the plurality method as take it for granted. They were not able to consider the merits of proportional representation as an electoral method, because it had not been invented yet. Noting that "the highly cultivated members of the community" find it difficult to be elected under a winner-take-all plurality system, John Stuart Mill wrote, "Had a plan like Mr. Hare's [for proportional representation] by good fortune suggested itself to the enlightened and patriotic founders of the American Republic, the

---

[4] Article I, Section 4 of the Constitution provides: "The Times, Places and Manner of holding Elections for Senators and Representatives shall be prescribed in each State by the Legislature thereof; *but the Congress may at any time by Law make or alter such Regulations*, except as to the Places of chusing Senators" (emphasis added). Congress, then, has the power to preempt all state electoral laws governing the election of members of the House and to mandate a system of multimember districts and PR. For a more detailed discussion of how PR elections to the U.S. Congress might work, see Michael Lind, "A Radical Plan to Change American Politics," *The Atlantic*, August 1992, 73–83.

Federal and State Assemblies would have contained many of these distinguished men, and democracy would have been spared its greatest reproach and one of its most formidable evils." The Founding Fathers did not know of alternatives to the inherited electoral system. We do not have that excuse.

The National Senate

It would be relatively easy to begin electing representatives by PR from new multimember districts in the fifty states. PR would not work for elections to the U.S. Senate, as it is now designed. All the more reason, then, to redesign the U.S. Senate.

The Senate has been the most defective branch of American government. In the Anglo-American republic, the Southern planter class, thanks to the informal compromise embodied in the sectional balance between slave states and free states, was able to exaggerate its political power. Had there been no Senate, or had the Senate been elected on the basis of population, slavery probably would have been abolished in the United States by the northern majority much sooner. In late-nineteenth-century Euro-America, the Senate became the favorite branch of government of the new industrial plutocracy. The only major structural change in the Constitution in more than two centuries was that effected by the Seventeenth Amendment, which provided for the direct election of senators, who had formerly been elected by state legislatures whose members auctioned off senatorial seats to corporations and trusts. The Seventeenth Amendment did not alter the malapportionment built into the Senate; it merely gave small-state populations, instead of small-state legislatures, an unfair weighted vote in federal policy making.

That weighted vote grows heavier with every passing year. Today, thanks to Senate malapportionment, 16 percent of the nation can elect half the Senate—and thwart the senators representing the 84 percent of the public who live in the twenty-five most populous states.[5] Since most population growth, as a result of replacement and immigration, is taking place in a few populous states, the disparity can only grow over time. Will 10 percent of the public elect half the Senate in 2010? 5 percent in 2020? 2 percent in 2050? If the Constitution is not amended, by the middle of the twenty-first century a tiny, almost exclusively white minority of the U.S. population, living in the largely empty states of the continental interior, may control a majority of the seats in the Senate. As it happens, small-state whites tend to be political allies of reactionary members of the white overclass in the large states. A few generations from now, conservative small-state whites may use their weighted vote to consistently block every program beneficial to the mixed-race or nonwhite majority, most of whose members will live in a few populous coastal states like California, Texas, and New York. This trend is already ominously apparent, in the way that public-spending programs that would benefit nonwhites and whites alike in the populous states are routinely killed by small-state senators

[5] Tom Geoghegan, "The Infernal Senate," *The New Republic*, 21 November 1994, 17–23.

in the Senate, after having been passed by the more responsive and representative House.

How are black and Hispanic Americans—to say nothing of big-state whites—going to react, when it becomes evident that the policies they favor are being consistently thwarted by senators representing a tiny number of mountain and prairie state whites? If the U.S. Congress is perceived to be held in a choke hold by a shrinking sliver of a white population that is itself shrinking, pressures will grow for the presidency or the courts to circumvent a deadlocked Congress altogether and take urgent policy-making tasks into their own hands. That way lies presidential dictatorship or government by judiciary.

Sooner or later, in some manner, Senate malapportionment must be eliminated. The best approach would be to sever the Senate from the states altogether. That senators represent the interests of state constituencies is already a fiction, inasmuch as most senators today depend more on out-of-state campaign contributions than on money raised at home. Our corrupt campaign finance system has already, in effect, nationalized the Senate. Let us formally nationalize it, clean it up, and, while we are at it, democratize it. Let senators be elected by proportional representation, in national elections, and serve four years, concurrent with the president. Members of the House, elected from small multimember districts by PR, would adequately represent local interests; senators, with their national constituencies, would tend to be more concerned with the nation as a whole.

These reforms may sound radical. In fact, they are conservative. Their purpose is to conserve the essence of our constitutional system, by eliminating the factors—campaign finance abuses, unfair electoral methods, and malapportionment—that are alienating an every-growing number of Americans from the political process. In the words of Tennyson, "That man's the true conservative/Who lops the moulder'd branch away." The legitimacy of the United States Congress is at an all-time low. If it is not restored by timely reforms that restore the confidence of the American people in the institution, people will turn away from Congress and look for leadership elsewhere—in a quasi-dictatorial presidency; even, if they despair enough, in a military strongman. If the historic succession of Republics of the United States is not to be replaced by a succession of pseudo-democratic executive regimes—Protectorates, Directories, Consulates, Empires—we must, sooner rather than later, realize the ideal of equal voting power: not one dollar/one vote, nor one acre/one vote, but one citizen/one vote.

The Social Market Contract

Social mobility in twenty-first century America will require good jobs for unskilled and low-skilled Americans at good wages with good benefits. All of this, in turn, requires a new social contract—the social market contract—between the national government, employers, and workers, to replace the New Deal system, which has been breaking down since the 1960s. A post-New Deal social market contract must promote high wages for American workers without bankrupting either employers or the government, or imposing excessive rigidity in the labor market.

A new social market contract might have the following features. Benefits which are now linked to employment and paid out of payroll taxes, like Social Security and most health care, should be completely severed from any connection with a particular job (though a requirement of work of some kind should be enforced to prevent the development of a class of idle parasites). Employer mandates would be replaced by direct government-to-citizen transactions, financed out of progressive income taxes and consumption taxes (from which staples would be excluded). Higher wages could be encouraged, by ending the influx of unskilled immigrant labor, by passing laws against reliance on temporary workers instead of full-time employees, by discouraging teens from working (they should be studying), and by encouraging caregivers, male or female, to leave the job market or enter it only part-time in order to care for children or aged relatives.

The most promising way to quickly raise wages at the bottom of the income ladder in the United States is to restrict immigration. In the furor over California's Proposition 187, much of the overclass press has attempted to smear all proponents of immigration restriction as immigrant-bashing nativists. No doubt prejudice against the new immigrants—against Hispanic immigrants, in particular—accounts for opposition to immigration on the part of some Americans. Concern about high levels of immigration, however, cannot in itself be dismissed as racism. A sober look at the numbers might be enough to make a restrictionist of the most humanitarian liberal.

Thanks to ever-growing legal immigration, the U.S. Census Bureau has revised its estimate of annual immigration upward *by 50 percent* to 880,000 per year, and now predicts growth from 252 million in 1991 to 383 million in 2050. Largely as a result of the post-1965 immigration wave, the population in 2050 is projected to be 82 million greater than it would have been if immigration had ended in 1991. The U.S. rate of 1.1 percent per year, though it sounds low, is enough to double the U.S. population in sixty four years.[6]

In addition to enlarging the U.S. population much more rapidly than may be desirable, mass immigration, by increasing the availability of low-wage labor, may have retarded the progress of automation in the United States by making it cheaper for corporations to hire immigrant workers rather than invest in labor-saving technology. Even worse, the continual enlargement of the low-wage labor pool in the United States by immigration since the 1960s is probably one of the reasons that wages have stagnated or declined at the bottom of the American class system. Cutting off the competition of native-born or naturalized Americans with new immigrants for jobs could have salutary effects for the bottom half of the American population. Although the ethnic basis of early-twentieth-century U.S. immigration restrictions was objec-

[6] Virginia D. Abernethy, *Population Politics* (New York: Plenum Press, 1993), 259–261.

tionable, the overall effects of the restriction of immigration in the 1920s were positive. Immigration restriction helped black Americans by opening up good entry-level jobs that would otherwise have gone to newly arrived Europeans. The postwar American economic boom could hardly have occurred if immigration levels had continued at their turn-of-the-century levels, with impoverished and illiterate Europeans crowding into the big cities, and employers using immigrants in sweat-shops to evade labor laws and break American unions. If immigration restriction had these beneficial effects once, why not once again?

The restriction of legal immigration should not be limited to low-wage workers who compete with the native-born poor and working poor for a limited number of unskilled jobs. The United States has benefited, and one hopes will always benefit, from a moderate influx of foreign scientists, scholars, journalists, and other educated immigrants. Furthermore, no immigration policy that turns away people in danger of genocide would be acceptable. Even so, there must be some limit to the number of skilled immigrants who are admitted, if educated Americans, along with low-skilled Americans, are not to see their incomes dragged down. Today many college-educated Americans are being forced to settle for noncollege jobs. Since 1970, the proportion of college graduates taking jobs that do not require college degrees has doubled to 20 percent.[7] From 1990 to 2005 the growth of job openings for college graduates will diminish while the number of bachelor's degrees awarded grows.[8] When growing numbers of college-educated Americans cannot find work worthy of their training, why should they have to compete with skilled immigrants for a diminishing number of places in good universities and desirable jobs? If we must import well-educated foreigners to be scientists and engineers, clearly we are failing to equip native white, Hispanic, black, and Asian-Americans with the necessary skills or necessary attitudes. The East Asian countries managed to create first-rate science and engineering professionals by educating their own people, rather than by bringing in great numbers of Americans and Western Europeans; why can't we, too, raise up the bottom half of the population?

One can debate how much immigration should be reduced, in order to create a tight labor market, boost American wages, and increase opportunities for upward mobility. The best policy might be one of "zero net immigration"— limiting the number of legal immigrants to the number of people who voluntarily emigrate from the United States each year, around 200,000 (down from 7–800,000 today), and reducing the number of illegal immigrants to as near zero as possible.

One result of immigration restriction might be to encourage the flight of U.S. manufacturing abroad. If immigration restriction denied U.S. business access to an ever-growing pool of cheap, nonunionized labor within U.S. borders, more businesses might follow the precedent of transferring production abroad to countries where wages and benefits are kept low by inherited poverty,

---

[7] "Training Up America," *The Economist*, 15 January 1994.

[8] John Judis, "Why Your Wages Keep Falling," *The New Republic*, 14 February 1994, 29.

overpopulation, or tyrannical governments that suppress workers. Immigration restriction therefore should be accompanied by checks upon the expatriation of American industry. A social tariff, in the amount of the difference between American and foreign wage rates, might deter American employers in some industries from responding to rising wages in a tight American labor market by transferring production abroad. Any price advantage that, say, Motorola gained by manufacturing in Malaysia rather than in California would be eliminated by the imposition of a social tariff on imports from Motorola's Malaysian factories. Since the same social tariffs would be imposed on all imports, American businesses would not be penalized in competing with foreign manufacturers seeking to sell to the American market.

Social tariffs imposed to deter the relocation of production by employers seeking to evade generous wage and labor laws need not wreck the world economy, if they are adopted by most or all of the advanced industrial democracies. For example, the United States, Canada, and the EC might create a common high-wage trading bloc—a common social market—with a common social tariff. American or German corporations transferring production to low-wage countries would be penalized, if they tried to export to the common social market. Within the common social market, however, trade barriers might be progressively eliminated, so that trade flows increased, say, between the United States and Germany. Unlike free trade between a First World and a Third World country, free trade between First World countries tends to be an unalloyed good, inasmuch as companies derive their advantages from superior quality, organization, or technology, rather than from a particular country's low wages or low regulatory standards. As a general rule, then, free trade should be encouraged between high-wage countries but trade between high-wage and low-wage countries should be regulated in order to prevent mobile transnational corporations from using the poverty of available workers in the latter to drive down wage and benefit levels in the former.

The most compelling argument for the adoption of a common social tariff by the high-wage industrial countries is the preservation of middle-class living standards in the First World. The goal of U.S. economic policy is to raise the living standards of ordinary Americans; whether the pursuit of high incomes for Americans happens to promote global welfare is a matter of secondary importance. A common social tariff, protecting a common social market, might, however, have an incidentally beneficial effect, insofar as it encouraged Third World countries to develop by creating well-paid workforces and large domestic markets, instead of by treating the poverty of their people as a resource in a never-ending competition to host offshore production facilities owned by American, European, and Japanese corporations. The common social tariff would not affect investment from the developed countries, as long as that investment was limited to transplant factories making goods for local consumption. While American investors would be discouraged from making computers in, say, India for the American market, they would be free to grow rich by investing in Indian factories producing for the local Indian market. The United States, Japan, and Germany developed on the basis of production for protected domestic markets, with the help of foreign investment. The claim of free-market globalists that the successful development by protectionism of the three leading capitalist countries of our day can never be repeated, and that Third World countries can only hope to develop by specializing in low-wage piecework for foreign-owned companies and foreign markets, finds no support in history.

The point is not to promote protectionism in the abstract against free trade in the abstract, but to promote pragmatism in trade and investment policy. We do not assume that a single tax policy is best, for all countries, at all levels of development, in all phases of world history; why should we assume that a single trade policy should be the *only* trade policy? Trade-building is like road-building; the dogma that we always need more roads, and it does not matter where they are or where they go, would be a poor guide to rational decisions about building a national infrastructure. We must be pragmatic and experimental in our national and multinational economic strategy, not guided by abstract rules that purport to be the best for all times and all places. *Realpolitik* in military and diplomatic strategy needs to be joined by a pragmatic policy of economic realism promoting the interests of the salaried majority in the United States and similar high-wage countries: *Realekonomik*.

The combination of immigration restriction with a social tariff, by dramatically reducing the effective labor pool for corporations selling goods and services in the United States, would tend to drive up the average American wage. Employers would have a choice between paying higher wages—thereby arresting the economic decline of the least fortunate Americans—or moving toward automation, something that, however disruptive in the short term, would promote the long-term evolution of the U.S. economy as a capital-intensive and technology-intensive rather than labor-intensive economy. The low-wage, low-investment strategy that American business has followed since the 1960s, a strategy made possible by a constantly renewed supply of cheap immigrant labor and low-wage overseas production sites, would be replaced by a high-wage, technology-intensive strategy. Robots in American factories, yes; immigrant workers in America and workers in American-owned or funded sweatshops abroad, no.

This would not be a Luddite strategy, because it would welcome, even encourage, the replacement of workers by machines. Automation is already destroying not only traditional blue-collar industrial jobs but "pink-collar" secretarial and clerical jobs. The high-wage strategy would accelerate this new version of what the economist Joseph Schumpeter called creative destruction. Within a few generations, thanks to automation, the number of Americans engaged in factory work and routine office work may be as small as the number engaged in agriculture. If handled properly, this transition from a labor-intensive industrial economy to an automated industrial economy could usher in a new age of widespread affluence.

The potential for disaster, however, is high. America's ghettos are full of the children and grandchildren of rural Southern agricultural workers displaced by technology in the early twentieth century. The public housing estates of Europe and the shantytowns of Latin America, like the *favelas* of Brazil, are crowded by the white and mestizo urban underclasses similarly created by the dispossession of peasantries by mechanized agriculture. Prudent action by government will be required to prevent the decline of technologically obsolete blue-collar and pink-collar workforces into new hereditary urban or suburban underclasses composed of the alienated, the ignorant, and the unemployable.

Governmental redistribution of the gains from automation might take the form of increased spending on public services and amenities or subsidies to enable more people to obtain basic services and amenities in the private sector. The very distinction between the "public" and "private" sectors might become blurred, in a system of "voucher capitalism," in which citizens were given consumption vouchers not only for basic necessities like housing and transportation but for amenities like recreation and entertainment. Thanks to such consumption subsidies, the most important market for the services of middle-class workers would be other middle-class workers, not the wealthy few.

What would those middle-class service careers be? Many would be familiar in-person service jobs: teaching, nursing, cleaning, police and fire protection, janitorial work. Today these are poorly paying and low-status occupations. In a high-wage, high-tech economy, however, they might be transformed into respectable middle-class vocations, that not only command higher wages but demand higher skills. Tomorrow's nurses, police officers, and janitors may not be menial laborers; they may oversee complex robots and computers, which will perform many of the routine or degrading or dangerous tasks done by people today. Already, as "smart" or computer-controlled buildings become more common, the blue-collar "super" is giving way to a new breed of building superintendent or "resident manager" skilled in computer electronics as well as business and personal diplomacy.[9]

THE WAR ON OLIGARCHY

Will janitors be members of the solid, educated middle class in 2050? The idea seems strange today, but for the past few centuries formerly despised vocations have consistently moved upward in social status. Few people in 1850 could have imagined that despised mechanics like unionized auto workers would be the very model of middle American affluence in 1950, just as few in 1750 could have dreamed that merchants and lawyers—at that time the insecure, ridiculed members of the middle rung of an aristocratic social order—would be at the top of the status hierarchy in countries like the United States in 1850. Since

---

[9] Mervyn Rothstein, "Meet the New Super Super of the High-End Residence," *New York Times*, 25 September 1994.

the industrial revolution, as if they were on an escalator, the lower rungs of society have consistently moved up, in affluence and status, with one era's lower class becoming the next era's middle class.

The corollary trend has been the disappearance, or at least the marginalization, of a series of upper classes. In the Euro-American world, the landowning elite gave way to a proprietary industrial bourgeoisie, which then gave way, in the late nineteenth and early twentieth centuries, to the dominant professional classes of managers, lawyers, and financiers. As James Burnham and others were realizing as early as the 1930s, modern industrial organization, with its separation of ownership and control, has created a class or managers of large economic enterprises who tend to fuse with accredited professionals in a managerial-professional elite. The term "new class" originally referred to this elite, before it was distorted by conservative polemicists. The contemporary credentialed managerial-professional elite will not be automatically or painlessly transformed or replaced by the mere operation of economic processes. That will take the equivalent, for the upper class, or the war on poverty—a war on oligarchy.

The war on oligarchy would be the class-war strategy on a post-Marxist egalitarianism. Post-Marxist egalitarians would recognize that in a managerial society the ownership of the means of production may take many forms: concentration in the hands of a few families or trusts; decentralized private ownership by vast numbers of small shareholders (say, through pension funds); even government ownershop (where enterprises are allowed to pursue profits in a more or less rational way). All of these different patterns of ownership are compatible with the same monopolization of the best positions in the managerial-professional elite by a hereditary or quasi-hereditary social class. If the United States government nationalized all of the banks tomorrow, *and that were the only reform*, the class backgrounds of bank officials would be utterly unchanged. CEOs and professionals would, at least nominally, be civil servants, but in this new socialist United States the children of the white overclass would still predominate in the higher reaches of the economic bureaucracy, and black and brown Americans would be concentrated disproportionately in the lower tiers.

Real radicalism is not compensating the losers of a crooked game, but rewriting the rules of the game itself, so that more people can play and so that there are more opportunities to score. The rules of the class game in America revolve primarily around professional licensing and education. In a country where control of the means of production is more important than ownership of them, and where access to that control depends on credentials, the *real* class war must take the form of struggles over credentialing.

James Fallows, among others, has proposed that the professions be disaggregated into small subfields, each of which would have lower (and less expensive) barriers to entry. Medicine need not be monopolized by M.D.s, if nurse-practitioners were permitted to write some simple prescriptions; the J.D., who now must have four years of undergraduate education and three years of law school in addition in most states, could be replaced by a variety of legal-services specialists—say, conveyancers, who could make valid wills and trusts on the basis of an eight-month study course. A Ph.D., that nineteenth-century Germanic credential, would no longer be required for college teaching (much of which, anyway, is now done by underpaid graduate student teaching assistants). Brain surgeons, corporate lawyers, and distinguished academics would continue to meet high standards and command high fees, but much of what is now done by doctors and lawyers would be done by New Professionals, to the benefit of middle-class and working-class Americans (who would move into these newly multiplied trades) and of consumers of all classes (who would pay lower fees).

This is merely carrying the logic of capitalist rationalization of efficiency through the division of labor through to its conclusion. The professional generalist would continue to give way to the professional specialist. The legal profession would become the legal services industry, divided into dozens of specialized functions. Professional management would become management services. The professoriate would be replaced by the higher education services industry. The medical profession would give way to the medical services industry. In every case, subdivision would open up new jobs with lower entry requirements—that is, new opportunities for working-class and middle-class Americans.

A national debate over professional educational and licensing practices is long overdue. The federal government has no business trying to determine fair compensation for CEOs, lawyers, or doctors. It can, however, assume the task of professional regulation from the fifty state governments, and investigate and proscribe attempts by the great guilds of management, law, and medicine to artificially drive up salaries and fees by prevailing on state legislatures to write monopolistic guild regulations into law. What is more, the federal government has the right and the responsibility to determine not only what the requirements for entry into the professions should be, but how the professions are defined in the first place. A reform like dividing the Great Guilds of law, medicine, management, and the professoriate into dozens of modest vocations is the sort of thing that democratic legislatures are supposed to do. The professions, after all, are artificial creatures of statute; new professions can be formed from old ones and existing professions broken down with the stroke of a pen.

The final redoubt of oligarchy in the managerial-capitalist United States, after the great professions like law, management, medicine and the professoriate, is our caste-like educational system. Without diluting standards of intellectual excellence, the rules of the educational game, as well as the rules of professional accreditation, need to be rewritten to make social mobility easier in America—to the benefit not only of black, Hispanic, and Asian-Americans but of a majority of white Americans as well.

For generations, Americans have perceived the link between universal public education and social mobility. That link needs to be restored, by efforts that revitalize the public school system—for example, by equalizing funding for all public schools (a reform underway in a number of states) and imposing statewide and national standards to measure how much students actually learn.

Experiments with vouchers and student choice might be worthwhile, as long as their purpose is to reinvigorate public education, not destroy it.

We should also give some thought to turning higher education from a largely private luxury into a universal entitlement and a regulated public utility. The rationing of access to higher education by parental income and wealth—the chief means by which inherited money is converted into managerial-professional credentials—should be brought to an end. One way to achieve this goal might be the adoption, from some health care schemes, or a universal, single-payer system for higher education. Here is how it might work. Colleges and universities would be banned from accepting any payments from students or their parents except for government higher education vouchers, on pain of losing their federal tax-exempt status. All young adults in America would be entitled to a voucher, though the amounts would vary based on academic achievement, measured by achievement tests (which are less biased than IQ and aptitude tests) and other race-neutral and gender-neutral measures. Most Americans might receive two- or four-year vouchers; the top 10 or 20 percent, in terms of academic achievement, would get six- or eight-year vouchers. The vouchers would not be loans. They would be free of any obligation, except the obligation to adequately finish a course of study.

In order to prevent the costs of this new middle-class entitlement from spiraling out of control, the federal government would have to impose tuition caps on all colleges and universities, private or state, that accept the vouchers (and the tax-exempt status that comes with it). The tuition at Yale and Harvard would be exactly the same as the tuition at, say, the University of Nebraska—a few thousand a year. Would this tend to erase the difference between the expensive Ivy League schools and other colleges and universities? Naturally—and about time, too. The abolition of private financing of higher education, along with the outlawing of alumni preference, would force the Ivy League to abandon its historic role as a credentialing institution for a social oligarchy. The prestige of a college in the new system would depend on its attracting the brightest students, of all backgrounds, not on coaxing funds from rich alumni parents in return for warehousing their mediocre children for four years.

These suggestions seem radical now. But tuition cost inflation (driven by our inequitable system of loans, rather than grants, to middle-class students) is rapidly pushing American higher education toward bankruptcy. At some point in the twenty-first century, this design defect of our present system of financing higher education will have to be dealt with, if the college experience is not, as in the nineteenth century, to be limited to the children of the rich. Wealthy Americans have many advantages over middle-class Americans; the ability to buy a first-rate education for their children should no longer be one.

Even in the absence of sweeping reforms like these, equalizing access to higher education requires the outlawing by the federal government of one of the pillars of social oligarchy in America; legacy preference in college admissions. In an industrial, bureaucratic society in which access to wealth and power depend on educational credentials, alumni preference in university admissions is the managerial-professional equivalent of primogeniture. Legacy preference is affirmative action for the Haves.

The arguments in favor of legacy preference are so obviously specious that they need only be mentioned to be refuted. There is, for example, the argument that, in return for lower admissions standards for their offspring, wealthy alumni contribute money that goes to scholarship students. By this logic, it might save time and trouble simply to sell diplomas for their children to rich alumni parents through the mail.

The argument that outlawing legacy preferences would be a sort of sinister socialistic interference with private institutions is just not convincing. Private colleges and universities are chartered by government, the agent of the democratic citizenry, and they are bound to follow any regulations that the citizenry sees fit to impose—the ban on racial discrimination today, a ban on the class discrimination represented by alumni preference tomorrow. Eliminating legacy preference in college admissions would open up as much as a fifth of the spaces at elite schools for talented Americans of all races who are now passed over in favor of less qualified students with family connections.

Democratizing the professions, making higher education a universal civic entitlement rationed by demonstrated ability rather than by parental income, and outlawing the oligarchic institution of legacy preference—all of these can be seen as the latest in a series of historic reforms intended to realize the American ideal of a society in which individuals compete, sometimes fiercely, on the basis of their talents, not their family wealth or connections. The abolition of titles of nobility and primogeniture and entail, during the American Revolution; the elimination of property restrictions on citizenships in the Jacksonian period; the elimination of the ability to buy exemption from military service in wartime; the extension of civil rights to non-Christians, nonwhites, and women—all of these have pushed America a little closer to the goal of a meritocratic social order. The products of affluent and educated families will always derive indirect and informal benefits from their origins; they should not derive any direct and formal benefits. Family advantage may put one ahead at the starting line, but one should still be required to clear the hurdles all by oneself, at every point along the track, before reaching the finish line.

The social market contract would create a floor for wage earners; the war on oligarchy would create a new and more accessible ladder, or staircase. Neither can be taken advantage of by members of the American underclasses, as long as they are, metaphorically, in another room.

There are several hereditary underclasses in the United States. There is a rural white underclass, concentrated in the Appalachians and the Ozarks, and the makings of Hispanic underclasses in the barrios. As important as it is not to neglect these groups, it is even more important to rehabilitate, employ, and integrate the black ghetto underclass of the major metropolitan areas. The goal must not be to reupholster the ghetto, but to eliminate it completely, through the assimilation of its inhabitants to mainstream American norms, and their gradual dispersal throughout metropolitan suburbs.

It is difficult to image a successful program for dispersing the ghetto poor that would not have an intermediate stage of education and acculturation and, if necessary, rehabilitation. That stage would have to involve a period of separation from the ghetto environment and incentives for learning standard English, mainstream manners, and useful skills. The government, perhaps working through charitable or religious institutions, would have little choice but to assume moral as well as material tutelage of its poorest wards, in the hope of making them productive members of the national community. The model might be something like the settlement houses for European immigrants of Jane Addams and other turn-of-the-century social reformers. A government effort along these lines would combine idealism with a freedom from romantic illusions, like the fantasies of white overclass liberals about ghetto gangsters as romantic countercultural revolutionaries, or the equally romantic fantasies of laissez-faire conservatives about ghetto entrepreneurs. It would be paternalistic, in the best sense of the term. Instead of "maximum feasible participation," the ideal of the romantic countercultural liberals of the 1960s, the ideal would be "maximum feasible paternalism."

The reforms I have suggested here are intended as examples, not as an exhaustive enumeration of all possible liberal nationalist proposals. In discussing reforms, it is important not to lose sight of the basic perception of color-blind liberal nationalism—namely, that the answer to the problem of racial separation by class is not tokenism that chiefly benefits affluent nonwhite Americans but the weakening of class barriers and increasing mobility between classes, to the benefit of the transracial American majority. Greater movement from the lower ranks naturally corresponds to an accelerated eviction rate at the top; those moving up should be given a hand, and the skids should be greased for those going down. The goal is not to eliminate the abstract categories of rich and poor—there will be high- and low-income people in any capitalist society (and, in practice, in any noncapitalist society). The goal, rather, is to minimize the correspondence between income categories and *social classes*—to ensure that the rich do not tend to share a common upper-class accent and habits, and that the poor do not tend to have a similar complexion. To put it another way, the goal is a society in which the middle class, as a distinct social class, not merely an economic group, is overwhelmingly dominant. The rich would rise out of the middle class, but their offspring would quickly fall back into it; the ranks of the poor would be made up, for the most part, by unfortunates who had dropped out of the middle class temporarily, rather than by hereditary underclasses whose members are cut off more with each generation from middle-class customs and norms.

Neither of the two national parties today is hospitable to liberal nationalism, as I define it. The Democrats—under FDR, Truman, and LBJ, the great champions of the national state and national integration—since McGovern have been identified with the multicultural conception of America as a coalition of groups. The alienation of Democrats from the national sentiments of the American majority accounts, in large part, for the Democratic party's loss of both houses of Congress to the Republican party in the mid-term elections of 1994. Post-1960s Republicans, while they have almost monopolized the language and imagery of American patriotism, have lost contact with the older Republican tradition of strong national government and civil rights (Goldwater, the father of the modern Republican party, voted against the Civil Rights Act of 1964). Jacob Javits, in *Order of Battle* (1964), his defense of the Hamiltonian tradition in the GOP against Goldwaterite conservatives of the South and West, got it right: "This is the spirit which has represented the most dominant strain in Republican history. Hamilton-Clay-Lincoln and Theodore Roosevelt: they represent the line of evolution embodying this tradition."[10] No one of any influence in today's GOP thinks this way. The Democrats, it might be said, believe in the State but not the Nation, while the Republicans believe in the Nation but not the State. Neither party unites the two halves of Hamiltonian nationalism into a theory of the strong and integrated American nation-state.

The particular party or parties used as a vehicle for a liberal nationalist movement—populist Democrats, centrist Republicans, or a new reform party—is of secondary importance. What is important above all is the mobilization of an electoral majority around the liberal nationalist agenda, to arrest the slow decay of the United States into a pseudo-multicultural oligarchy and renovate it as a meritocratic, melting-pot nation-state under a government no longer dominated by the rich and their agents. Liberal nationalism, if successful, would redefine the consensus as to what constitutes American identity. Liberal nationalist concepts would define the terms of debate for *all* parties in the twenty-first century, in the same way that Appomattox and the Civil Rights Act of 1964 altered the meanings of conservatism and liberalism for generations afterward. The Trans-American "left" and "right" would debate the extent of civil rights for individuals, but both sides would agree that group preferences are illegitimate. Trans-American liberals and conservatives would disagree over the details of a new social market contract, not over the everlasting need for a third way between laissez-faire capitalism and unworkable socialism. If liberal nationalism were to succeed, talk of America as a multicultural society will sound as archaic and grotesque to the ears of twenty-first century Americans as talk of "the Anglo-Saxon mission" and Social Darwinism does to us today.

The difficulties confronting proponents of national renewal should not be underestimated. Machiavelli warns in *The Prince*: "It must be considered that there is nothing more difficult to carry out, nor more doubtful of success, nor more dangerous to handle, than to initiate a new order of things. For the reformer has enemies in all those who profit by the old order, and only lukewarm defenders in all those who would profit by the new."[11]

---

[10] Jacob K. Javits, *Order of Battle: A Republican's Call to Reason* (New York: Pocket Books, 1966), 63.

[11] Niccolo Machiavelli, *The Prince*, George Bull, trans. (London: Penguin Books, 1961), 51.

Cynics may argue that plans to radically improve American society and government are utopian projects that are doomed to fail. History suggests another conclusion. American society has been transformed dramatically for the better every few generations since 1776. When one considers the differences between the United States of 1800 and 1900 and 2000 A.D., then dramatic change seems much more thinkable. Less than a century ago, Americans reformed the Constitution to provide for direct election of senators and an income tax; only sixty years ago, the New Deal assured all Americans of basic economic security; and it was only thirty years ago that the three-century-old white-supremacist caste system was torn down. Again and again in our history, Americans have recreated their state and their society, to reflect new ideals, or to embody old ideals in a better way. Progressives at the end of the nineteenth century faced problems remarkably similar to those that we face at the end of the twentieth—the decline of the dominance of a superpower that had policed the world and promoted international free trade (Britain in their case, America in ours); the emergence of a new, multipolar world order based on regional military and economic blocs; massive immigration overburdening the institutions of assimilation; corrupt urban political machines and patronage systems; an unrepresentative Senate; the manipulation of politics by free-spending corporate interests and rich individuals; the coexistence of dreadful squalor with plutocratic opulence. Now, as then, renewing the American republic will require a new generation of bold leaders, no longer fighting the battles of the 1960s and 1970s, a generation of men and women sharing the vision and confidence of Secretary of State John Hay in his eulogy for the murdered President William McKinley almost a century ago:

> The past gives no clue to the future. The fathers, where are they? and the prophets, do they live forever? We are ourselves the fathers! We are ourselves the prophets![12]"

---

[12] *Congressional Record*, vol. 35, pts. 3–5, 57th Cong., 1st sess., (27 February 1902), 2202, quoted in Martin J. Sklar, *The Corporate Reconstruction of American Capitalism, 1890–1916* (Cambridge, England: Cambridge University Press, 1988), 440.

Shoring Up the Right to Vote for President: A Modest Proposal*

ALEXANDER KEYSSAR

One of the more remarkable features of election 2000 was its bringing to the surface of political life the peculiar fact that Americans do not possess a constitutionally-guaranteed right to vote for president of the United States. Even for those of us who study politics professionally, it was a bit as though a half-forgotten corpse had suddenly been jarred loose from the river bottom and floated upward into view.

This happened in two ways, both of which jolted political junkies without penetrating public consciousness very broadly. The first, of course, was when the Republican majority in Florida's legislature announced that the legislature itself would select the state's delegates to the electoral college if the outcome of the popular election remained legally unsettled on 12 December, the date by which electors were to be chosen. The legal basis of such an action, they claimed, was located in Article II, Section 1 of the Constitution, which specifies that "each state shall appoint in such manner as the legislature thereof may

* On 27 September 2002, there took place in the Iphigene Sulzberger Tower Suite at Barnard College, a symposium on various aspects of the question: "Should Americans Have the Constitutional Right to Vote for Presidential Electors?" The symposium was sponsored by the Academy of Political Science and the Barnard College Department of Political Science and was funded by the Carnegie Corporation of New York. The question addressed was provoked by the part of the Supreme Court decision in *Bush v Gore* which asserted that there is no constitutional right to vote for president, so voting directly for presidential electors can be given and taken away by state legislatures even after a popular vote. In this issue, we are publishing the paper prepared for the first panel of the symposium and the discussion that followed.

ALEXANDER KEYSSAR is the Matthew W. Stirling Jr. Professor of History and Social Policy at the Kennedy School of Government, Harvard University. He is the author of *The Right to Vote: The Contested History of Democracy in the United States* and coauthor of *Inventing America: A History of the United States*.

direct, a number of electors" who will meet and cast ballots for president. Happily for the future reputation of the sunshine state's legislature, the Supreme Court's rapid decision in *Bush v Gore* rendered this legislative hijacking of the election unnecessary. Yet there can be little doubt that a majority of Florida's legislators were prepared to take that step—and to assert their primacy over the state's citizenry—to guarantee the election of George W. Bush; had they done so, a political firestorm would almost certainly have ensued.

The second sighting of the floating corpse was provided by the Supreme Court itself. Justice Antonin Scalia cheerfully pointed to it on 1 December 2000 during oral arguments in *Bush v Palm Beach County Canvassing Board*, the first of the two cases to be heard by the high tribunal. While interrogating Al Gore's attorney, Laurence Tribe, Scalia noted that "in fact, there is no right of suffrage under Article II." Ten days later, in *Bush v Gore*, the majority opinion drove the point home, emphasizing that "the individual citizen has no federal constitutional right to vote for electors for the President of the United States unless and until the state legislature chooses a statewide election as the means to implement its power to appoint members of the electoral college." Citing the 1892 case of *McPherson v Blacker*, the Court even went a step further, pointing out that the state, "after granting the franchise in the special context of Article II, can take back the power to appoint electors." Thus had Florida's legislators acted on their own, the Supreme Court would have backed them up.[1]

The Court's flat assertion that American citizens have no constitutional right to vote for president attracted little public attention: few people ever read the convoluted opinion, and the press was understandably focused on the fact that George W. Bush had just become president-elect. As a matter of constitutional interpretation, moreover, the Court's assertion was not far-fetched and not nearly as much of a stretch as other ingredients in *Bush v Gore*. The federal Constitution never has contained any affirmative guarantee of a citizen's right to vote in federal elections. Article II, Section 1 does clearly seem to leave key decisions to state legislatures. All of the amendments to the constitution dealing with the right to vote (and they are numerous) are phrased negatively rather than positively: they prevent the states from denying people the franchise on particular grounds, but they do not directly confer the right to vote on anyone.

Yet as a statement about contemporary American political institutions, the Supreme Court's pronouncement, which is now the law of the land whether or not it was before December 2000, is extraordinary. The citizens of the nation that prides itself as the standard bearer of democracy on the world stage do not possess an unambiguous right to vote for the country's most powerful political office. The constitutions of more than a hundred nations around the world positively affirm the right of citizens to vote, but the Constitution of the United States does not. What if someone told the Taliban or China's ruling elite? What

[1] *Bush v Gore*, 121 S.Ct. 526, 529 (2000); *George W. Bush v Palm Beach County Canvassing Board*, oral arguments, 1 December 2000, 55.

if someone told Nebraska's farmers or New York's firemen or my Uncle Pat, all of whom think they have a right to vote?

At one level, of course, the issue is a technical one: in practice (and thanks to their state legislators), the vast majority of American citizens do possess a right to vote for their state's delegates to the electoral college; and that right is (at least obliquely) sheltered by a substantial array of constitutional amendments, statutes, and court decisions. Nonetheless, the events surrounding election 2000 inescapably bring the question of reform to the foreground. Should the federal Constitution be amended in order to affirmatively guarantee the right of American citizens to vote for president and to have those votes determine each state's vote in the electoral college?[2] My own answer to that is an unequivocal "yes." Such a step seems long overdue, and this is as good a time as any to make the move.

Making the Constitution Match Our Values

I should say at the outset that I personally would favor an even stronger measure: abolishing the electoral college altogether, and electing the president and vice-president by means of a national popular vote. The electoral college is a flawed and archaic institution that has wrought mischief in roughly 10 percent of our national elections. It functions at all only because it has long ceased to serve the deliberative function for which it was designed; and its granting of disproportionate weight to voters who live in the small states looms as an overt contradiction of the principle of "one person, one vote" that is at the heart of modern conceptions of democracy. That said, the chances of abolishing the electoral college (thanks in good part to the opposition of those small states) seem to be roughly on a par with the chances of Fidel Castro becoming governor of Florida.

The proposition discussed here, therefore, is more modest but more pragmatic: it might have some possibility of becoming law. As framed, the proposal would leave the small-state advantage intact while presumably permitting each state to decide how to allocate its electors—that is, by district or in one bloc. The proposal would nonetheless achieve two critical goals. It would prevent state legislatures from ever acting to select members of the electoral college on their own or in any way other than through popular election. More abstractly—but perhaps more critically—it would embed the value of a right to vote for the nation's highest office in the federal Constitution.

[2] There are, of course, a number of different types of amendments that could be proposed, some of which would affect all federal elections or all elections and others of which would abolish the electoral college outright. Here I discuss what might be regarded as a minimal constitutional intervention: an amendment that would guarantee to all American citizens the right to vote in presidential elections and to have those popular votes be decisive in selecting members of the electoral college. This would leave the electoral college untouched and presumably leave to states or state legislatures decisions about how to apportion electoral votes.

The most fundamental reason for amending the Constitution in this way is to bring a late eighteenth-century Constitution into harmony with late twentieth- or twenty-first-century ideals and values. The phrase "the right to vote" did not appear in our original Constitution, an omission that was only partially a consequence of the Founding Fathers' decision to leave most suffrage matters to the states. The phrase was absent, both from the first Constitution and, notably, from the Bill of Rights, because there was substantial uncertainty and disagreement among the Framers about whether voting was in fact a right. The more conservative among them (probably a majority) believed it to be a privilege; and even those who did call it a right were generally quick to point out that it was not by any means a universal right. As is well known, voters in nearly all states of the early republic were adult (usually white) male property owners or tax payers.

A great deal changed over the next century and three-quarters. Property and taxpaying requirements were stripped away during the first half of the nineteenth century, although they made some surreptitious returns thereafter. The Fourteenth and Fifteenth Amendments added the phrase "the right to vote" to the language of the Constitution, while giving formal (if contested and then flagrantly ignored) protection to the political rights of African Americans. The exclusion of women was prohibited in the first decades of the twentieth century. And the 1960s witnessed a stunning expansion of voting rights at the hands of both Congress and the Supreme Court, effectively ending discrimination based on race, literacy, poverty, and residential mobility. As I have recounted in detail elsewhere, these changes took a great deal of time; they were always contested; they were often rolled back in partial and incomplete ways. But the legal, political, and cultural environment did change profoundly.[3] Few Americans today would openly advocate disenfranchising blacks, Natives Americans, women, or poor people.[4]

The intellectual or ideological history of suffrage in the United States can be viewed as a prolonged process through which Americans came to view voting as a right rather than a privilege and also as a right similar to other rights, adhering to all citizens or at least all adult citizens. The two prongs of this issue infused debates about the franchise for many decades, leading, among other things, to distinctive contortions of language, argument, and rhetoric. As early as the revolutionary period, advocates of franchise expansion (to include those without property, for example) defended their position on the grounds that vot-

[3] See Alexander Keyssar, *The Right to Vote: The Contested History of Democracy in the United States* (New York: Basic Books, 2000).

[4] I use the word "openly" deliberately. I do not think that the embrace of genuinely democratic values is universal by any means; and I suspect that many Americans view universal suffrage as E. L. Godkin did in 1894: "it has, in spite of its imperfections and oddities, something of the majesty of doom." Quoted in Keyssar, *Right to Vote*, 126. Among other signs of something less than a full-scale embrace were the hundreds of thousands of Massachusetts and Rhode Island voters who opposed constitutional changes sanctioning the enfranchisement of paupers in the early 1970s.

ing was a right or even a natural right. Conservatives commonly sought to rebut such claims by pointing out that if voting were a right, then all men, even African Americans, should have it—and women and children too, as John Adams famously noted. On the other hand, if suffrage could reasonably be denied to any category of persons (and few were willing to argue the contrary), then it must not be a right but a privilege. As a privilege, it could reasonably and legitimately be restricted to those who would wield it "responsibly." Such arguments led throughout the nineteenth century to often murky claims that suffrage was an "earned" right or a "conferred" right, or one that could only be exercised by people with particular capacities or qualities. A delegate to the Indiana constitutional convention of 1850 announced that he believed in "the right of universal suffrage," which he asserted belonged only to "all free white male citizens over the age of twenty-one."[5] So much for universal.

It was during the cauldron of Reconstruction that prominent political leaders first began to openly embrace the full logic of the claim that suffrage was a right: as Senator Henry Wilson put it in words eerily predictive of public debates that would occur a century later, "Let us give all citizens equal rights, and then protect everybody in the United States in the exercise of those rights." His colleague, Oliver Morton, maintained that the same ideals that led him to favor enfranchising African Americans obliged him to oppose suffrage restrictions based on property, literacy, or nativity. In the 1870s and 1880s, numerous male delegates to state constitutional conventions applied that logic to women as well. "Women's right to the ballot seems so clear," noted an Ohioan in 1874, "that it is like some of the mathematical axioms." "Whatever rights are given to one citizen ought to be given . . . to every other citizen," claimed a California delegate four years later.[6]

These were not the views of most Americans in the 1860s and 1870s. Nor did they quickly become predominant: the latter decades of the nineteenth century witnessed a stunning backlash against franchise expansion in the North as well as the South. But the spectrum of public opinion had shifted enormously since the 1780s or even the 1830s, and the view that every adult citizen ought to be enfranchised had made its way into the ideological mainstream. There it has remained, gaining ground in fits and starts, until it was eventually catapulted into a majority ideal thanks to the combustible mix of World War II, the cold war, and the transformation of southern agriculture. The notion that suffrage was a right that belonged to all adults (with the noted exception of convicted felons) undergirded the passage of the Voting Rights Act and the Twenty-fourth Amendment, as well as the Supreme Court's repeated invocation of the equal protection clause to loosen numerous restrictions on the franchise. "It is wrong—deadly wrong—to deny any of your fellow Americans the right to vote," a president from Texas told Congress in 1965.[7]

[5] Keyssar, *Right to Vote*, 1, 44, 53, 172.
[6] Ibid., 98–99, 188.
[7] Ibid., 256–281.

It would be pollyannish to presume that everyone in the United States whole-heartedly believes that voting is a right belonging to all adult citizens. During election 2000 I found myself called a "democracy pimp" on a radio show in Dallas, and just months ago at a polling place a neighbor adamantly promoted the resuscitation of property requirements. But our nation's political, legal, and cultural embrace of democracy is unquestioned, and democracy has come to mean that all adult citizens participate in the selection of government leaders. In the words of Chief Justice Earl Warren, "the right to vote freely for the candidate of one's choice is of the essence of a democratic society." Amending our Constitution to bring it in line with our values, thus, hardly seems controversial. It would also follow a strong current of American history. In the 1860s, Charles Sumner acknowledged that racial bars to the franchise may have been "'republican' according to the imperfect notions of an earlier period," but that they were no longer appropriate in a changed world. His Republican colleagues in Congress argued for a broadened franchise with the lovely phrase (now gone from the language) that the Constitution should be amended according to "the lights we have before us," or "all the lights of our modern civilization."[8] In the year 2003, the lights we have before us make clear that all American citizens ought to possess a constitutionally guaranteed right to vote for president.

STATES' RIGHTS AND DEMOCRACY

One likely objection to an amendment of the type proposed here is that it would represent yet another incursion of the national government into an arena traditionally controlled by the states. State legislatures would relinquish the ability to select the manner in which delegates to the electoral college are chosen; all states would be compelled to hold popular elections.

One response to such an objection might, of course, be to point out that all states hold popular elections for president now and thus relatively little would change. But the historical record suggests a more powerful answer. Put simply, the cry of "states' rights," with respect to the breadth of the franchise, has almost invariably been a rhetorical and legal shield deployed to protect discriminatory behavior and a narrowing of the franchise. For most of our history, to be sure, the loosening of suffrage requirements came at the hands of state legislatures and constitutional conventions. In one notable instance—the alien declarant voting laws of the nineteenth century—the states were out ahead of the national government. (So far ahead that they eventually crept back into line.) But whenever the states and the federal government have been in overt conflict, it has been because Washington insisted on more democratic processes.

---

[8] Xi Wang, *The Trial of Democracy* (Athens: University of Georgia Press, 1997), 32; Keyssar, *Right to Vote*, 96–97, 284.

This dynamic was visible early on, as political leaders first grappled with the confusing structure that the Founding Fathers had erected for choosing a president. The Twelfth Amendment, ratified in 1804, was the work of Congress. Congress, moreover, played a key role in pressing the states to hold popular elections for president despite the latitude offered state legislatures by the Constitution. During the first decades of the nineteenth century, methods of selecting members of the electoral college varied greatly from state to state and even from election to election. Some state legislatures chose electors by themselves; six did so as late as 1824. In other states, electors were chosen in districts by popular vote; in still others, all electoral votes went to the winner of the popular vote. Practices tended to change for short-term and partisan reasons, thereby potentially undermining the legitimacy of the elections themselves. The North Carolina legislature's decision to choose electors by itself in 1812, although altogether legal, was the occasion of a "great excitement" in the state, and the last-minute decision of New Jersey's legislators to do the same for purely partisan reasons was treated as something of a scandal, even in a state which from birth seems to have been allergic to the nonpartisan enforcement of election laws. Similarly unpopular, at least in some quarters, was the congressional decision to deny Andrew Jackson the presidency in 1824 despite his having received the largest number of popular votes.[9]

This chaotic method of choosing a chief executive prompted members of Congress during the first quarter of the nineteenth century to introduce dozens of amendments calling for revamped and standardized methods of voting for president. Some called for the abolition of the electoral college, others for district voting; nearly all demanded that the people, not state legislatures, have the power to choose the president or at least presidential electors. Even after things had settled down in the early 1830s, Senator Thomas H. Benton of Missouri, with the support of his friend Andrew Jackson, continued to present to each Congress a proposed amendment mandating a national popular vote for president along district lines.[10]

Benton's rationale for such a proposal reflected both a growing faith in popular elections and a deepening distrust of intermediary institutions that could frustrate the popular will. On the floor of Congress, Benton insisted that his goal was "to keep the election wholly in the hands of the people, and to do this by giving them a direct vote for the man of their choice." Its underlying "principle"—not irrelevant to our own time—was "that liberty would be ruined by

---

[9] *Annual Report of the American Historical Association [AHA] for the Year 1896*, vol. II (entitled *Proposed Amendments to the Constitution, 1789 to 1889*, a prize essay by Herman V. Ames), *House Document No. 353, part 2*, 54th Congress, 2nd sess. (Washington, DC: 1897), 80–85; see also Jack N. Rakove, "The E-College in the E-Age" in Rakove, ed., *The Unfinished Election of 2000* (New York: Basic Books, 2001), 201–234; Edward Stanwood, *A History of Presidential Elections*, 4th ed. (Boston: Houghton-Mifflin, 1896), 60–61; Charles A. O'Neil, *The American Electoral System* (New York: G. P. Putnam's Sons, 1889), 106.

[10] AHA, *Annual Report*, 80–91.

providing any kind of substitute for popular election." President Jackson him-self in 1835 declared that "the experience of our country, from the formation of the government to the present day, demonstrates that the people cannot too soon adopt some stronger safeguard for their right to elect the highest officers known to the Constitution." Implicit in such claims was the notion that popular voting was a national value. Opposition to the amendments was grounded, rhe-torically at least, in a rejection of their assertion of national power over states' rights. Benton's proposal, according to John Tyler, "obliterated all state bound-aries and dictated a course of action as if we were a nation and not a compact of states."[11]

None of these amendments passed, although several garnered a great deal of support. Yet it was in the face of action in Washington that the states moved toward a uniform method of choosing presidential electors through popular election and with the winner-take-all system that has become so grimly familiar. By 1832, only South Carolina clung to the practice of having its legislature choose electors; and only Maryland continued to use the district system.[12]

The Reconstruction amendments also, of course, constituted a federal in-tervention in the name of democratic values, as did the Nineteenth Amend-ment ratified in 1920, which gave women the right to vote. Most importantly, the transformation of voting rights law that was centered in the 1960s—but which actually unfolded a bit more gradually from the 1940s through the early 1970s—represented the self-conscious assertion of the federal government as the guarantor of democratic rights. Recognizing that the southern states, by themselves, would not undertake democratizing reforms (to enforce the Fif-teenth Amendment, which had been on the books for nearly a century), Con-gress, the president, and the Supreme Court acted to enforce the national value of democracy. They were in effect asserting that no state or region of the United States could remain outside of a national consensus; in so doing, they acted precisely "as if we were a nation"—which, in fact, we are.

CONFRONTING THE DISENFRANCHISEMENT OF FELONS

Tinkering with suffrage laws has throughout American history meant prying the lid open on a Pandora's box. Replacing property with taxpaying require-ments meant calling into question why there should be any pecuniary qualifica-tions for voting at all. Advocates of black suffrage after the Civil War found themselves in sharp, sometimes bitter conflict with supporters of women's suf-frage. Southern suffragists in the early twentieth century encountered resis-tance from those who feared that any effort to change franchise requirements could break down the barriers against black voting.

---

[11] Ibid., 91; *Congressional Globe*, 24th Congress, 1st sess. (Washington, DC: 1836), 11; 28th Congress, 1st sess. (Washington, DC: 1844), 686.

[12] AHA, *Annual Report*, 85. See also Arthur M. Schlesinger, Jr., ed., *History of American Presiden-tial Elections: 1789–1968* (New York: McGraw-Hill, 1985).

In a far more limited way, the Pandora's box is present here as well. Any constitutional amendment that affirmatively guarantees the right of American citizens to vote in presidential elections will bump up against at least one knotty issue—the voting rights of felons and exfelons. This is so because any clearly and simply stated guarantee ("All American citizens shall have the right to vote for presidential electors in the state in which they reside") would appear to override state restrictions on voting by those convicted of crimes.[13] Circumventing this problem, on the other hand, would require wording ("All citizens not convicted of crimes" or "All citizens eligible to vote under state laws") that would thicken the barriers against the enfranchisement of felons and exfelons.

Either position will be controversial and have detractors; it is particularly easy to imagine opponents of a simply worded amendment latching onto and making much of the fact that it would enfranchise several million people who have committed crimes. (Willy Horton goes to the ballot box.) In states like Florida, Alabama, and Texas, with large numbers of excluded felons, this issue could jeopardize ratification of an amendment. On the other hand, language that sanctioned the disenfranchisement of felons would be unpopular within the black community and among many progressives who would generally be inclined to support an amendment guaranteeing the right to vote. None of which, to my mind, is a reason to back away from the issue: a national debate about the merits and demerits of felon exclusions may be well worth provoking. The same could also be said of another issue that might rear its head—the voting rights of American citizens residing in Puerto Rico. Public debates that challenge the American people to test their stated ideals against tricky concrete issues ought perhaps to be welcomed rather than avoided.

IT JUST MIGHT MATTER

Just as generals sometimes fall prey to the impulse to fight the last war, political reformers frequently attempt to keep the last crisis from happening again. Much of the election reform legislation now pending before Congress seems to be of this type: it is designed to keep the spectacle of hanging chads, butterfly ballots, Katherine Harris, and confused news analysts from dominating the national television screen for a month after some future election. Such a spectacle would be unlikely to recur in any event, but numerous legislative proposals seem to spring from an understandable impulse to at least do something—or to avoid the charge of having done nothing after the train wreck of election 2000. That said, there is nothing particularly harmful and much that is constructive about the package of bills awaiting action in Congress. That they remain

[13] If felons and exfelons were enfranchised in presidential elections, it would put immense pressure on the states to enfranchise them for local elections also. Unless the states did so, they would have to maintain different voting rolls and possibly voting machines for presidential and for state elections. The situation would be analogous to what loomed on the horizon with the eighteen-year-old vote before passage of the 26th Amendment.

pending over two years after election 2000 has less to do with the quality or significance of the reforms proposed (the package is bland at best) than with the simple fact that all election reforms have potential partisan implications and no party wants to surrender any procedural advantage.

The constitutional amendment discussed here is somewhat different and penetrates more deeply into our political structures. It is not a response to what happened or what was publicly debated or what filled the airwaves, but to what was revealed and to what almost happened. Election 2000 and *Bush v Gore* made clear that a partisan state legislature could legally hijack a presidential election. Is this likely to occur? Certainly not. But the events of November 2000 and September 2001 remind us in ways that we should not ignore that the unlikely can happen. Moreover, a legislative hijacking of an election is unlikely precisely because it would provoke a deep crisis of legitimacy in a nation whose citizens believe in popular elections. Stated somewhat differently, the largest barrier to abuse of the current legal configuration is the fact that the vast majority of the American people are unaware that this configuration exists and would regard it as incompatible with the nation's core political values. Making the Constitution congruent with those values would thus seem to be a worthy goal in and of itself. In addition, placing the right of citizens to vote for president firmly and squarely in the Constitution could well carry weight in future legal conflicts, the contours of which we cannot quite imagine at present.

The new and somewhat unfamiliar tones of uncertainty and unpredictability that mark public life in the United States in the wake of September 11, 2001 add some depth, even perhaps some urgency, to the case for shoring up our democratic institutions. In the end, election 2000 did not prove to be a full-blown crisis of political legitimacy. Although many analysts and legal scholars found the Supreme Court's actions to be shocking, public rage diminished rapidly (except within the black community), and normal rhythms of life and politics were quickly restored. To some considerable degree, this was the case because the outcome of election 2000 did not appear as though it would make much difference to many people. The most widely discussed issues of the electoral campaign after all were the relative merits of different programs for improving education and different prescription drug plans for senior citizens, not exactly issues that would send large numbers of citizens to the barricades. That President Bush has set out since his inauguration to demonstrate that there were major differences between the two candidates is a different matter. But in the decades ahead, in a world that appears less benign, in a nation less certainly prosperous, political cleavages may sharpen. Electoral contests could well become more contentious, more bitter, more substantive, more vital. In such an environment, it will be all the more essential for the rules of democracy to be clear and the rights of the people unambiguous.

Panel Discussion

CARALEY:* Alex, everyone has read your paper. Do you want to give a short summary?

KEYSSAR: What I was asked to do was to reflect, as an historian, on this proposition regarding a constitutional amendment to guarantee the right to vote for presidential electors. I have reflected on it. I have no difficulty offering my support for it. My own views, and I have spoken about this fairly widely in the past, favor an even broader amendment, one which would guarantee the right to vote in all elections in the United States, and in so doing would also obliterate the electoral college. This comes both out of principle and out of my longstanding impossible-ist streak, which for the purposes of the present discussion I will forego. I actually do think that abolishing the electoral college would be a good idea, and as I mention in the paper, I think that the odds of doing that are roughly equal to the odds of Fidel Castro becoming governor of Florida.

CARALEY: You mean you prefer only eliminating people as electors or eliminating the whole electoral vote system of voting?

KEYSSAR: The whole electoral system of voting, the whole deal. Let me try to go over some of the reasoning that I offered behind this, and frankly I think that there are two overwhelming reasons. The first reason for doing this is in effect to bring the Constitution into harmony with the change in political values that has occurred over the last two centuries. In some sense, it's that simple. At the outset when the Constitution was written, whether or not voting was a right was a matter of substantial dispute. I think that most of the Founding Fathers did not believe that voting was a right. Voting was thought of as a privilege. And in the debate that emerged in the late eighteenth century, there was substantial disagreement about whether voting was a right or was a privilege. If it was a right, and I talk about this in the paper, the question was: Was it a right like other rights that should belong to all citizens or was it a right that only belonged to some people, in which case that made it a peculiar kind of right. That produces wonderful locutions in the language over time. For example, in a debate in the 1870s on women's suffrage, one opponent of women's suffrage stood up and said, "voting is not a natural right, it is a conferred right." And somebody stood up to respond, "if it's a conferred right, who conferred it on us?" Those kinds of debates took place throughout the nineteenth and early twentieth centuries.

One could see the intellectual history of suffrage in the United States as a lurching progression, a shift toward the notion that voting is a right and not a privilege and toward the notion that it is a right like most other rights in the sense that is adheres to all citizens. That takes a long time, and in writing

* Demetrios James Caraley, the editor of *Political Science Quarterly*, is the Janet H. Robb Professor of the Social Sciences and professor of political science at Barnard College and the Graduate School of Arts and Sciences at Columbia University.

this portion of the paper, I found myself telescoping a lot of complicated history and thus slipping into a kind of Whig version of American history that my book was written to attack. But the fact is that there was progress and change over the long run as well as a lot of backing and forthing.

The United States got universal suffrage roughly in 1970, which is rather late for the standard bearer of democracy. Even then, I think there are currents in American life and in American society that are less positive about democracy. One of my favorite examples of this is the 1972 presidential election, which some us of here remember. It was the overwhelming victory for George McGovern in Washington, DC and Massachusetts. But in the 1972 election in Massachusetts, which was the most liberal state in the country at the time, there was a rather remarkable referendum on the ballot, which was to remove from the Massachusetts state constitution the prohibition against paupers' voting. That prohibition had effectively become unconstitutional as a result of *Harper v Virginia*, but the language was in the state constitution, and so there was a referendum asking: "Should we remove this prohibition that says that paupers cannot vote?" Well, the proposition passed. But 400,000 people voted against it in Massachusetts in 1972. So I think we have to recognize that this embrace of voting even today is not universal. Still, change has occurred at some critical junctions that I have tried to outline in the paper, and the temper of political thought is quite different in the early twenty-first century society than it was in the late eighteenth century.

The second point that I tried to address, as cued by the organizers of this symposium, was the potential objection to a "right to vote" amendment that might be raised by those claiming to protect states' rights: if we had such a constitutional amendment, it would eliminate the hallowed right of state legislatures to hijack elections. This is, we all know, a very valued state right. But rather than simply poke fun at that, the reflections I give to that as a historian are really twofold. One is that in contrast to the situation at the end of the eighteenth century or the early nineteenth century, we are now fully a nation. There were numerous constitutional amendments proposed between 1810 and 1830 that would have federalized the right to vote. Thomas Hart Benton introduced one every year into Congress, and John Tyler's opposition to it was to say that such a proposition was as if or as though we were a nation and not a compact of states. Well, at this point in our history I am comfortable saying that we are a nation and not a compact of states. And I think most other people accept this as well.

The other thing that the historical background sheds light on is that throughout American history, voting issues have been the subject of more constitutional amendments than any other single subject, occasioning frequent tension between the states and the federal government. With possibly one or 1.5 exceptions, in conflicts between the states and the federal government, the federal government has always been on the side of greater democracy and expanding the right to vote, while the cry of states' rights has almost invariably been a demand to restrict the suffrage and to discriminate in one form or another. The one broad exception was that in part of the nineteenth century, in a very interesting development, a lot of the states got way out ahead of the federal government in granting the right to vote to people who were not citizens. But then they crept back into the fold in the late nineteenth and early twentieth century as they realized that these noncitizens weren't any longer the kinds of folks they wanted to have vote in the first place. The other interesting case about this is the Supreme Court's action and the federal government's stance during and just after the 1842 Dorr War in Rhode Island, when the federal government certainly took an emphatically conservative position. In general the story about voting rights is largely about the South, but not exclusively so, as is revealed by the evolution of Native-American rights in the West. Thus states' rights has generally been a rhetorical shield behind which lay a desire to discriminate: usually to discriminate against people of color.

Let me make two more comments, again about things that are in the paper in a somewhat more coherent form. One is that any amendment of this type is bound to bump into the issue of felons. How you word the amendment will in one form or another play into the debate about whether felons and exfelons should be, are, or ought not be enfranchised. I am not sure one can find a wording that does not either enfranchise people who are currently incarcerated or in postincarceration, or that does not thicken the legal barriers against their enfranchisement by providing a federal constitutional sanction for it. I think that if there were a public debate over this constitutional amendment, the question of felons would come to the fore; Puerto Rico in some places might also emerge. And my reaction to that is to welcome it. That is not a reason to back away from it. It is an issue that needs public debating.

The last thing I would say, and I don't think this is just a rhetorical flourish, is that in the post-September 11 world there's a new measure of urgency about questions of rights and certain questions of politics. I don't think that it is an artificial attachment of one thing to another. Everyone in this room found election 2000 to be a massive crisis. But in the end it really was not much of a crisis. It did not go very deep. It was a legal crisis and a minor political crisis. But the water settled over it very quickly. I think that occurred precisely because there did not appear to be much difference between the two candidates. After all, the single most debated issue in the last weeks of the campaign was exactly which prescription drug plan to have for seniors. That is not an issue that was going to send a lot of people to the barricades when their candidate lost. The whole structure, the way the campaign was conducted really minimized any sense of difference between the candidates. We have learned since then that there was an enormous difference. Moreover, in a world where we feel a sense of threat, in an international environment that may feel substantially less warm and fuzzy, and in an economy which may have less promise of continuous growth, we may start seeing the emergence of a more contentious and conflictual politics in which making the right to vote less ambiguous becomes all the more important.

CARALEY: Yes, and post-September 11, when our government is debating whether to start a potentially large war in the Middle East, that's all the more reason to know who has a right to vote for the person who has most to do in making that kind of decision.

SMITH:* I agree completely with every point in Alex's paper. I am, therefore, glad that he kept it short, because otherwise he might have gone on to say everything that I have to say. But perhaps by making some further points, I can reach some fruitful disagreements with him or, I'm sure, with some of the rest of you.

Alex notes that he would really like to see the electoral college abolished. So would I. During the *Bush v Gore* controversy, I briefly tested the waters of cyberspace to see if there might be some rising public sentiment to do so. I found none, a point to which I will return.

But first let me give my reasons for disliking the electoral college. It is not only that the power to appoint electors actually belongs to the state legislatures, undemocratic as that is in terms of modern notions of democracy. And it's also not only that it apportions electors via a state's number of senators plus representatives and thereby reproduces the least democratic features of Congress, bad as I think that is. I also dislike building state representation into the electoral college, because that system did not simply arise from the desires of small states to balance out the power of big states. It also won support in part from the desire of slave states to balance out the power of free states, because the slave states rightly expected the free states would grow in population more rapidly. So the electoral college was designed to give the slave states disproportionate power in selecting presidents—and it worked. Apart from the two troubled one-term presidencies of the two Adamses, presidents from slave states governed the nation for the first forty-seven years of its existence—the years when slavery was allowed to spread and tighten its cancerous hold on the body politic.

So I see the electoral college as in part an ugly relic of slavery, and I hate that. But, I know that slavery is in the distant past, so that's not a reason to abolish it today. It is probably more prudent to do as Alex and Jim Caraley suggested—to leave the electoral college intact but to establish a constitutional right of citizens to vote for presidential electors. More minimal though this proposal is, it does still raise troubling and important questions that should be raised, and Alex has just identified the key ones. It would raise the question of whether we can and should disenfranchise felons; and let me add some points on this issue. No nation in the world disenfranchises felons to anything like the extent that the United States does. We are at the far extreme in this

* Rogers M. Smith is the Christopher H. Browne Distinguished Professor of Political Science at the University of Pennsylvania.

pattern. And the United States today disenfranchises many more felons than it used to, because over the last thirty years we've added many more criminal laws; we've added disenfranchisement as a penalty for more crimes and have made many more acts into felonies that bring disenfranchisement and incarceration instead of lesser penalties. This recent period represents the second time in our history that we've had a large surge in new criminal laws and heightened incarcerations. The first such period came in the late nineteenth century, and it resulted primarily in the imprisonment and disenfranchisement of large numbers of newly freed and newly enfranchised black men. In our time, of course, matters are very different. The surge in criminalization over the past thirty years has resulted primarily in the imprisonment and disenfranchisement of large numbers of long-freed and newly-enfranchised black men. It should be evident from that description why I think the question of whether we should be doing this is one that definitely merits deep consideration and debate today.

Alex is also right to say that the denial of the franchise in presidential elections to U.S. citizens residing in Puerto Rico would also be called into question by this proposal; and that, too, is a good thing. The history of the debates over what to do with the Spanish American War acquisitions in 1900, the debates over the Foraker Act, which initially structured American colonial governance in Puerto Rico, the debates over the Jones Act of 1917, which gave Puerto Ricans U.S. citizenship over the objections of their leadership, all show that the main reason that this kind of U.S. citizenship did not include voting rights in U.S. elections was that Puerto Ricans were considered culturally and racially unfit for the franchise. Of course, like slavery, that's well in our past. That cannot be the reason why U.S. citizens residing in Puerto Rico do not vote in presidential elections now. But then, what is the reason? That is a question that merits deep consideration, and if this proposal helps spur that discussion, I think that would be a good thing.

But I have to say, even though I think discussing these questions would be valuable and important, I very much fear that if these questions are raised, even this modest, minimal proposal might fail to win the supermajority support needed for a constitutional amendment. I'm afraid, even though we tell ourselves in all sincerity that governing in accordance with racial prejudices belongs to our past, we are still often reluctant to change policies and institutions that we have inherited from those days, including those I've just described, even if they perpetuate many of the old injustices in our own time, as I think they often do.

Since even this modest proposal for a constitutional right to vote in federal elections may well be defeated anyway, let me mention that I would like to see it made slightly less modest. Alex indicates that under this proposal the states would still have leeway to indicate whether the voters choose electors as a bloc in a statewide winner-take-all election or by districts. I'd like the amendment to require that electors be assigned by some system of proportional representation, with the candidate getting a plurality nationwide winning the

White House. I realize that this is a radical addition that would probably make prospects for change even grimmer, so I will understand if no one here wants to go along with it.

But I mention it because the thing I found most discouraging about the election of 2000 and *Bush v Gore* was not that the candidate with fewer votes nationwide took office with the help of the electoral college and the U.S. Supreme Court. The thing that I found most discouraging was that after a few months, nobody much cared. They didn't care enough to want to reform the electoral college. They didn't care enough to be concerned with whether in some way we should curb the power of the Supreme Court. Now, it may have been because the election was essentially a tie, so that this was as good as flipping a coin. Some arbitrary means seemed the best possible under the circumstances. It may have been because the candidates didn't seem all that different anyway, as Alex suggests. Some would dispute that, but it's possible. It may also have been, however, because Americans have gotten used to the idea that our democratic processes are mostly just rituals anyway and that some subset of our mainstream elites ends up governing no matter what. So it's not really worth worrying too much about how they get there, we just worry whether they're doing all right for us or not. And for most Americans, Bush has been doing all right for us; that's all that matters, so we don't need to worry about the election of 2000 and how democratic or undemocratic it may have shown our institutions to be.

Maybe things have to be that way in such a vast country as ours; maybe real democracy, if we're honest, is a pipedream under modern circumstances. But I also think that people don't care too much about whether our democratic processes are really all that democratic, because those processes provide such limited avenues for real democratic participation and efficacy. Therefore, they don't nourish or encourage democratic commitments substantially. I think perhaps if we build an element of proportional representation into presidential voting, even if we keep what I see as the ill-conceived electoral college and even though in the end only one person would get elected president, that change would still encourage the growth of third-party candidacies; for it would provide more visible evidence of their strength, which can encourage them. It also might serve as an example that would help legitimate changes in other electoral systems to make them less biased in favor of the two major parties in other elections. That in turn might mean that with a more robust and diverse party system reflecting more different types of view, more people would really feel represented, would feel that they have a real chance for a voice and an impact in our political system. And more people might think it worthwhile to engage in democratic politics; and then more people might become more committed to democratic values and to the actual realization of them; and more people might get upset if the electorally-registered democratic will were thwarted on occasion and if some citizens were locked out of democratic participation altogether.

If we can't get that kind of more radical reform to affirm and strengthen the reality of our system's professed commitments to democracy, let us at a minimum try to do so by insuring that all citizens gain a constitutional right to vote for president of the United States. What real democratic reason is there not to do so?

CARALEY: Thank you. Linda, do you want to weigh in?

GREENHOUSE:* Yes. I think Bush against Gore was certainly a wake-up call for those of us not in the scholarly community. Until Bush against Gore, I had no idea that I didn't have a direct right to vote. And it's possible, if people reflect back on it, that even short of a constitutional amendment there may be a way of addressing the problem. Remember what happened in Florida, how close the legislature came to trumping the peoples' right to vote. I don't know if it's a practical idea to have debates in state legislatures to bring the popular democracy point to the fore and achieve by legislation, state by state, the kind of guarantee that would be achieved nationwide by an amendment.

Let me make one micropoint also in focusing on the felon issue. One other kind of glaring hole in the franchise that was brought to the fore in Florida was the question of military ballots. If you remember, that was a very tricky issue because there was a lot of game-playing among the Florida electoral apparatus as to how closely to look at the time stamp on the absentee ballots that had been mailed from ships beyond the deadline. There was a debate in the Gore camp over whether to challenge ballots that were, at least facially, invalid. Then the Gore people decided at the end of the day not to do that, because they didn't want to look unfriendly to the military. But that's something that I think, if we're talking national picture, certainly has to be regularized and taken out of the hands of partisan state electoral officials.

CARALEY: But if the state legislatures do it, why can't they change their minds and undo it whenever they feel like it?

GREENHOUSE: I think Alex's point about harmonizing the Constitution with prevailing political and social values also applies there. Once the issue is joined and people are aware of what the issue is, as few were until now, I think it would be, as a political matter, impossible for legislatures to take back this sleeping giant's power.

CARALEY: But the Florida state legislature was about to do just that, was about to choose the Bush electors on its own if Gore came out ahead in the popular vote. So they were going to take back the power to choose electors from the people.

GREENHOUSE: Sure. But what I was proposing would be state-by-state legislation where there would be a state law in the exercise of the legislature's federal constitutional power to determine this. The legislature would give up its power and make it clear that there's no set of circumstances under which what was about to happen in Florida would happen.

* Linda Greenhouse is a Pulitzer Prize-winning Supreme Court correspondent for the *New York Times*.

KEYSSAR: Where do you see the resistance to a federal constitutional amendment coming from?

GREENHOUSE: The problem I see with a constitutional amendment is that it would get very complicated and very encrusted with the wish lists of other groups. I mean, whether we get back to the term limits debate, although that moment, I guess, seems to have passed. Who knows what would come out of the woodwork once there's an amendment process on the floor? A few years ago, when there were lots of various amendments floating around, a couple of blue-ribbon panels were convened. The Century Foundation had one to warn of the dangers in this kind of climate, of quote, "tinkering with the Constitution." I can see some things getting encrusted and more complicated than we'd like to deal with.

SMITH: That would have been an argument against the Fifteenth Amendment and against enfranchising women as well, though, which were both attempted at some degree at the state level.

POMPER:* There's something about this discussion that seems to me off in space. If you take it in its bold terms that there should be a constitutional amendment or there should be language that says Americans should vote for president, or should have the right to vote directly for president, that seems like an obvious proposal. If you put it straight on the table and nothing else, nobody would disagree with it, nobody would have the nerve to disagree with it politically. But, of course, it wouldn't just be that, and Rogers Smith illustrates exactly what would happen. He said, well this is okay, but what I really want is proportional representation of the electoral votes or proportional representation of the direct popular vote; somebody else will want the district system; Arthur Schlesinger will want his particular kind of hybrid. And so, it will not be just that. An amendment that says "the right of the American people to vote for electors shall not be infringed," raises the question, "Who are the American people?" Are they under 18 years old? Are they alien permanent residents? Particularly, are they felons? It seems to me that if you want to do something serious, you ought to, and you don't need a constitutional amendment for this. You need legislation to deal with the largest disenfranchisement in the country.

There are four million Americans who could not vote in 2000 because of the exclusion of exfelons. In Florida, a couple of sociologists have done a wonderful study. In Florida, if exfelons had been enfranchised, Gore would have carried the state by 71,000 votes. We wouldn't have had this conference. You wouldn't have had the grant from Carnegie.

CARALEY: Yes, Gerry. Since I'm the convener I guess I should talk to that. Without some change, I think you could have a political crisis. If this were in the middle of a war, as the elections of 1864 and 1944 were, and

* Gerald Pomper is the Board of Governors Professor Emeritus of Political Science at the Eagleton Institute of Politics at Rutgers University.

one person seemed to be getting the popular vote plurality and there was skullduggery in the ballots in another state headed by a governor who's the brother of the opposing presidential candidate, it wouldn't be accepted as readily as it got accepted when we thought that there was really no difference between Bush and Gore.

KEYSSAR: In any case, I think the felon issue is what is the setting or context. How do you want to bring that issue up into a public debate? It would seem to me, and I'm not saying there are no other ways, that bringing it up in the context of a statement of universal rights may be a good way to do it. The second point is that in many states, you could not do it just by legislation. These things are in state constitutions. The felony exclusions are in state constitutions. You could not simply do it by legislation.

POMPER: May I ask you or Linda Greenhouse a question? There was something I dimly remember in 2000. The Florida constitution says something about "the people shall determine all offices" or something like that. And that raises the prospect that if the Florida legislature had hijacked the election, they might have been sued by somebody, which of course would have gone to the Florida Supreme Court and then ultimately the U.S. Supreme Court. But maybe this problem doesn't even exist in Florida.

KEYSSAR: Florida's constitution opens with a very strong declaration, an affirmation of the right to vote for all public offices. As I recall, that was part of what Larry Tribe was trying to use as the tie breaker in interpreting conflicting statutes: he pointed toward this strong Florida right to vote to which Supreme Court Justice Antonin Scalia responded, "But there is no right to vote under Article II, section I," which trumps the state constitution. I think that's the way that argument evolved.

CARALEY: What about something else? I would not prefer a straight national popular election of the president, because of psychological reasons. I voted for presidential candidates who most of the time lost elections, but they carried either New York, when I was voting in New York, or Connecticut, where I now vote. And that gives me a sense of "Okay, at least I helped carry my state." Am I the only one who gets any kind of gratification out of that? I see Bob Shapiro laughing.

SHAPIRO:* I haven't seen any public opinion data on that in particular. I think it's an interesting question. The question I had for you, Jim, was in framing this question about the amendment were you thinking in terms of broader issues of the definition of who the electorate is, who the voters are as opposed to simply dealing with problems of renegade state legislatures? Because one political solution here is just to think about this in normal incremental political terms and just focus on that as the issue and be silent on all the other kinds of things. With regard to felons, just one small footnote, as

---

* Robert Shapiro is professor of political science and chair of the Department of Political Science at Columbia University.

more elected officials and politicians go to jail, maybe they'll become more concerned about it.

RAKOVE:** I think this issue of the Florida legislature, or any legislature, being able to hijack an election really is a specious one. The Constitution is clear, and federal statutory law is clear, that electors have to be appointed within a certain time and then to vote on a certain day. Notwithstanding these guys, who I really regard as constitutional hookers, who told the Florida legislature that they could go ahead and appoint this slate of electors after 7 November, on the simple face of it that would be a blatantly unconstitutional and illegal action in terms of the text of the Constitution and the statute. So I think it's problematic to ground this proposal on the danger of the Florida scenario, which is unlikely to repeat itself, both in terms of the circumstances and in terms of the existing constitutional and legal norms.

What I think would be more interesting, Alex, and it's a point you develop in your book, is to think about the implications of stating a positive right to vote for the presidency as distinguished from all those amendments, which as you certainly argue in your book, have never been phrased in robust positive terms, but have simply involved the removal of prohibitions or restrictions. Thinking about the democratic implications of expressing a right to vote for the presidency in the most positive terms as possible may not solve the Puerto Rican problem or the problem of felons, but it would represent an interesting advance beyond the way in which these amendments have previously been drafted. This is an interesting idea fraught with all kinds of implications. I'm aware of all of the dangers that arise here. But it would be interesting to see a debate about the basis on which we disenfranchise felons, and also why Puerto Ricans are citizens but can't vote in presidential elections. I think most Americans would not realize Puerto Ricans really are citizens.

CARALEY: Well, they also don't have House members and they don't have Senate members.

PILDES:* I want to express a little skepticism about the constitutional route, because, Alex, when you say that the history of the federal government has been one of the expansion of the suffrage, we have to remember that there's a difference between the political and judicial branches of the federal government. I was reminded of this by a conversation with Linda this morning. Once you constitutionalize the issue, you're doing something other than nationalizing it; you're turning over control of that issue to the courts to a significant extent. And if you look at the history of judicial action with respect to the vote and democracy, it's a pretty mixed history. There is an expansive period of time, but it's been twenty years or so in American history, and there are lots of moments when courts have been very—and I think this is such a moment—aggressive in dampening down democratic processes through constitutional

** Jack Rakove is the Coe Professor of History and American Studies at Stanford University.
* Richard H. Pildes is professor of law at New York University School of Law.

law. I think it's quite easy to anticipate or predict that the courts will bring a kind of ideological conservative sensibility about changes to democracy.

This is going on internationally now. For example, the German Constitutional Court was asked whether the entry into the Maastricht Agreement by Germany violated the right to vote of German citizens. The argument was that there is a constitutional right to vote in the German Constitution. This is a dilution of sovereignty, and the German Court didn't say that this is not a question that the courts ought to address at all; they said that this is a serious issue. This could become problematic. Maastricht itself is not yet the point at which the right to vote has been diluted. But the whole idea that the courts would have anything to do with a judgment about the expansion of the European Union strikes me as a very mistaken path to go down.

Even historically, it's true that when we constitutionalize things like the Fourteenth Amendment, there's a conservative tendency, like the felon issue we're talking about. It becomes embedded as an area that states can continue to address through Section II of the Fourteenth Amendment. Women's suffrage gets taken off the table, in part by the adoption of the Fourteenth Amendment, because that's the first time the word "male" was inserted into the Constitution. Even with respect to the Fourteenth Amendment, there can be countervailing, conservatizing tendencies. When you have mass political movements for change, I think it's a much better way to change political process, because it allows a lot more flexibility and accommodation over time. It keeps issues in a political context, as opposed to licensing courts to address these kinds of issues.

ISSACHAROFF:* Usually for alphabetical reasons, I get to go before Rick and I don't like coming after him. I would say two things, and it follows up on what Rick says. Alex gave one and a half of those reasons already and he was right. I was going through my head and I was thinking *California Democratic Party v Jones, Shaw v Reno*, a number of cases where federal law has intervened to restrict the gambit of state political activity in areas where states gave greater latitude to political accommodations of the will of the majority than the federal courts were willing to read into the Constitution. I am not quite so confident that the federalization will push necessarily in the direction which you want it to push. Beyond that, my primary reaction is that there's always the tendency to fight the last fight and to view the last fight as being the most significant. But if you think about what is missing in the American context from the rights domain with regard to the franchise, I would argue that it's basically tinkering at the margins. It is true that the felon disenfranchisement issue is a significant one. It is true that Puerto Rico has all kinds of complications and that the District of Columbia has complications. But is that really where the main inquiry should be? I think this is a point that I make in my paper—if you think about the distortions of the electoral

* Samuel Issacharoff is the Harold R. Medina Professor in Procedural Jurisprudence at Columbia University Law School.

college in the last election, I don't think the rights claim is particularly salient. I don't think that, for example, in given the structure of the campaign where neither candidate campaigned nor spent money in New York or Texas, two of the three largest states, that the electoral results are very meaningful in terms of who actually won and who had more popular support. It's an artifact of the rules of the game, and if the rules had been changed, they would have campaigned differently. We have no confidence about how that would have come out. What is significant is that the winner-take-all feature of the electoral college division of the electors in each state, even if we have the electoral college and everything else, radically changes the terms of political discourse in this country.

Why in the world did we have an election about prescription drugs in 2000? It is impossible even to remember what the discussion was. And it's certainly impossible to remember why that should have any salience except that everybody knew that the election was going to turn on Florida and Pennsylvania, and those are numbers one and two in terms of elders in their population. So we ran an entire national campaign on what was the narrowest form of sectional interest. Now Rogers makes the point that the electoral college grew out of the sectional interests of the slave holders; we had a repeat of that, not at the rights domain but rather a structural distortion of what should be the way in which the Americans select the president. So I would suggest that the federal route is not necessarily the panacea that it's held out to be. It may be that focusing on this as a question of the expansion of the rights domain really misses the issue of what the actual effect of the electoral college is.

CARALEY: What you spoke about the electoral college requiring winner take all, you didn't mean to say that because not every state requires winner take all.

ISSACHAROFF: No, every state but two requires winner take all.

CARALEY: Right, but that's not in the Constitution.

ISSACHAROFF: No, it's not in the Constitution.

CARALEY: If my memory is correct, it was the Virginia legislature that established winner take all first. I think it was in 1796 so that John Adams would not get a single elector from Virginia. So it was to disenfranchise the minority. But I think basically I agree with you, because the other thing you didn't bring in, except inferentially, is the high cost of television advertising. Because Connecticut, Massachusetts, New York, New Jersey, the only states where I watched television, were certain as to how they would go, I didn't see a single ad for Gore or Bush. So we, now sitting in New York, are being ignored by presidential campaigns. The whole winner take all of the populous states was supposed to give them disportionately large influence by casting a large block of electoral votes to one candidate over the other. This kind of influence has evaporated, because the campaigns have to ration money. They don't have unlimited television money, and they ignore people in states that are deemed not to be in play but certain for one or another of the candidates.

SMITH: I think these are very important considerations. I don't disagree with you at all about the history and the Supreme Court's rule and all that. But, two things: one is that we have come to a point in the system in which constitutionalization is viewed as empowering the courts, but that shouldn't necessarily be the case. To some degree, it's an analytically separate problem if we have overly privileged the courts as opposed to other institutions and democratic politics in saying what the Constitution means. I don't think we should just embrace that feature of the contemporary system, and I agree there are problems with a constitutional rights route. I am most struck by the general lack of any political movement on any of these fronts that we're talking about, and if debating a constitutional amendment were a way to get debates going in democratic processes, that would be a good thing.

CARALEY: Let me try to sum up the thinking of our panel. Everyone believes that every American citizen should have the constitutional right to vote for presidential electors. Some didn't even realize that the Constitution does not now give such a right and that popular voting for electors is dependent on the actions of the various state legislatures. While a few of the colleagues preferred a nationwide, straight, popular election of the president, we did not discuss this with any depth, because everyone agreed that a constitutional amendment trying to eliminate the electoral vote system completely could never be adopted. There was also broad consensus, however, that electors as persons should be taken out of the system and that electoral votes should be assigned by a state according to the popular vote without any further human, discretionary intervention.

Even for this minor change of the system, various participants thought the wording of an amendment would not be easy, because the pro-democratic changes in the Constitution for presidential voting are all worded as prohibitions from depriving the right to vote on the basis of race, gender, or age above eighteen years. There is no language for affirmatively granting the right to vote. Also there was some concern that once a constitutional amendment is being considered, the whole system might be opened up. Anti- rather than pro-democratic language might find itself into the amendment. There was also concern over the denial by states of the right to vote to the substantial numbers of persons convicted of felonies.

We all realized that the Constitution itself does not provide for the winner-take-all system of allocating electoral votes that is used in forty-eight states and the District of Columbia. What the winner-take-all system does is to deny statewide minorities any influence in the outcome of the presidential election. Ordinary state or federal legislation could change that system, but there was no consensus on what should replace it: winner take all by congressional district or proportional vote allocation of electoral votes by congressional district or statewide. . . . Only the last variation would put all states "in play" and not have any written off before the general election campaigns even begin.

Thank you everybody.

Part III:
FROM SEPTEMBER 11 TO IRAQ

American Nationalism and
U.S. Foreign Policy from
September 11 to the Iraq War

PAUL T. McCARTNEY

> The deliberate and deadly attacks which were carried out yesterday against our country were more than acts of terror. They were acts of war. This will require our country to unite in steadfast determination and resolve. Freedom and democracy are under attack. . . . This enemy attacked not just our people, but freedom-loving people everywhere in the world. . . . This will be a monumental struggle of good versus evil. But good will prevail.
>
> —President George W. Bush, 12 September 2001[1]

More than three years have passed since the terrorists of al Qaeda brutally attacked the United States and spurred the country into a new era in its history. When the World Trade Center collapsed into a dusty heap while the nerve center of American military might burned with a passenger jet lodged in its side, a generation of Americans who had not yet been born when President John F. Kennedy was assassinated sadly acquired its own tragic defining moment. Yet, America's preoccupation shifted quickly but divisively toward Iraq, and the surreal intensity of September 11 and its aftermath seems to belong to a different time. While it still remains possible to recall how Americans actually experienced that tragic day, it would be useful to evaluate how Americans came to grips with the terrorist attacks, how their attention was directed seamlessly

---

[1] George W. Bush, "Remarks by the President," 12 September 2001, accessed on the White House website at http://www.whitehouse.gov/news/releases/2001/09/20010912-4.html, 2 October 2001.

PAUL T. McCARTNEY is a visiting professor at the University of Richmond. His book, *Power and Progress: American National Identity, the War of 1898, and the Rise of American Imperialism*, will be published in January 2006. This article is part of broader book project examining the connection between American nationalism and U.S. foreign policy.

to war with Iraq, and how September 11 has more broadly shaped subsequent U.S. policy making. In this paper, I consider the lessons that this dramatic episode holds for helping us to understand the connection between U.S. foreign policy and American nationalism.

More specifically, I argue that enduring nationalist themes provided the basic structure in which Americans organized their comprehension of and reaction to the terrorist attacks. In addition, by employing the legitimating power of nationalism to furnish the "official" interpretation of September 11, President George W. Bush was able to provide a context in which Americans could understand and accept a set of foreign policy goals far broader and more ambitious than a simple response to the immediate attacks would have suggested. The only way to ensure that such atrocities never happen again, Bush decided for the United States, was to change the global context that had made them possible. Changing the world in this way—to suit American interests by making it more consistent with American values—has always been an implicit component of American nationalism. Thus, the terrorist strikes provided a rare clarifying moment in the nation's collective consciousness, when both American national identity and U.S. foreign policy were reinvigorated—separately and in relation to each other—and a national focus and sense of mission, absent since the end of the Cold War, reemerged. Bush's call for a worldwide war against the perpetrators and his relentless characterization of them as evil laid the groundwork in the American consciousness (if not the world's) for his militaristic designs against Saddam Hussein's regime, a policy that was clearly central to his breathtakingly ambitious vision for America's role in the world as described in the administration's formal foreign policy statement, the National Security Strategy.

Both the blending of national identity with U.S. foreign policy in Bush's rhetoric and his manner of enunciating U.S. foreign policy goals in lofty and frequently moralistic terms were consistent with established tradition. Reliably but uneasily, the United States has always maintained both a sweeping identification with the whole of humanity and an insular preoccupation with its own lofty distinctiveness, and it has used this paradoxical combination as the basis for claiming its righteous entitlement to lead the world. National identity and foreign policy are intimately connected in the United States because the former rejects (formally, at least) ethnic or other ascriptive bases of national identity and relies instead on an ideological construction of the nation that insists on the global relevance of the American project. (Many scholars have made a strong case that it is misleading to characterize American national identity in terms of its ideology because of the pervasively ascriptive bases of its laws, politics, and culture. I do not disagree with this position, but argue that racial, ethnic, and other ascriptive characteristics have been interpolated into the American ideology in ways that have left its principles sufficiently intact to evolve along with American culture. In other words, at any given moment, American political principles are expressive of their cultural context, which gives particular form to the ideology's otherwise abstract content. More to the point, the ascriptive dimensions of American national identity have been less relevant to the dynamic that I am describing.)[2] The American style of foreign policy reflects an ideological and cultural interpretation of both the nation and its place in the world, one that posits that the United States enjoys universal significance because it is an archetype of virtue and the locomotive of human progress. This American penchant for ascribing transcendent value to itself and for defining itself as exceptional reflects the influence of intellectual and religious tendencies that flourished under historical circumstances that almost seemed tailored to nurture them and that gained strength as the state became more powerful.[3] It has yielded two conflicting impulses—exemplarism, or the desire to stand apart from the world and serve merely as a model of social and political possibility, and vindicationism, the urge to change the world to make it look and act more like the United States.[4] Bush's foreign policy is vindicationism with a vengeance.

This paper's argument is presented in three sections. In the first, I review the nature and sources of the missionary dimension of American national identity and examine, in particular, its relation to American foreign policy. Second, I analyze President Bush's framing of the terrorist attacks and show how he worked rhetorically toward a clear enunciation of the Bush doctrine. My deconstruction of his speeches will emphasize his insistence on American virtue, values, and power; and it will draw special attention to the civil–religious dimension of his rhetoric—an aspect of American identity that is mistakenly ignored in most foreign policy analyses.[5] Third, I locate the tendencies of subsequent foreign policy emphases within the framework of the Bush doctrine, paying specific attention to the war against Iraq. Finally, I argue that while American universalism remains an appropriate element of American national identity, it can no longer be usefully interconnected with a notion of American exceptionalism that sharply distinguishes Americans from the rest of the world. If the

[2] For the best presentation of this argument, see Rogers Smith, *Civic Ideals: Conflicting Visions of Citizenship in US History* (New Haven, CT: Yale University Press, 1997). On the relationship between race and U.S. foreign policy, see Thomas Ambrosio, *Ethnic Identity Groups and U.S. Foreign Policy* (Westport, CT: Praeger, 2002); Gerald Horne, "Race from Power: U.S. Foreign Power and the General Crisis of 'White Supremacy'" in Michael J. Hogan, ed., *The Ambiguous Legacy: U.S. Foreign Relations in the "American Century"* (New York: Cambridge University Press, 1999), 302–336; and Michael Hunt, *Ideology and U.S. Foreign Policy* (New Haven, CT: Yale University Press, 1987).

[3] Arthur M. Schlesinger, Jr. "America: Experiment or Destiny," *The American Historical Review* 82 (June 1977): 505–522.

[4] This distinction between exemplarism and vindicationism is discussed more fully in works such as Henry Kissinger, *Diplomacy* (New York: Simon and Schuster, 1994), 17–56; H.W. Brands, *What America Owes the World: The Struggle for the Soul of Foreign Policy* (New York: Cambridge University Press, 1998); William W. Cobb, Jr., *The American Foundation Myth in Vietnam: Reigning Paradigms and Raining Bombs* (New York: University Press of America, 1998); Elliot Abrams, ed., *The Influence of Faith: Religious Groups and U.S. Foreign Policy* (Lanham, MD: Rowman & Littlefield, 2001), 1–33; and Edward McNall Burns, *The American Idea of Mission: Concepts of National Destiny and Purpose* (New Brunswick, NJ: Rutgers University Press, 1957).

[5] But see Abrams, *The Influence of Faith.*

broad contours of American national identity cannot be expected easily to change, then its more cosmopolitan elements should receive renewed emphasis in a manner better suited to the country's global stature. Unfortunately, the current administration has done precisely the opposite by stressing the particularities of the American experience and asserting rather than demonstrating the virtue of the American national project. Essentially, the United States relies today simply on superior military power to ground its claims to moral excellence. This is, both morally and politically, treacherous ground on which to stand at a time when the world demands American leadership.

American Nationalism and U.S. Foreign Policy: Exceptionalism and Universalism

Uniquely among the great powers, both the United States and the collective identity of its people were consciously *created*, and with a sense of purpose.[6] During their War of Independence, Americans manifested the conviction that their nationalist revolt against Great Britain was a truly revolutionary episode and that their goal was not only to attain justice for themselves, but also to usher in a new, democratic era in human history.[7] Thomas Paine (though not an American himself) declared for instance, "We have it in our power to begin the world over again,"[8] indicating how, from the very beginning, Americans have believed that their polity represents a new development in human history, a particularistic community of universal significance.[9]

Put another way, American national identity has been premised upon the belief that the nation's binding principles are rooted in qualities and capacities shared by all people, everywhere.[10] On the world stage, though, the United States cannot help but act as a single, discrete entity, however universal its pretensions. It is but one state among many. As a result, U.S. foreign policy frequently tries to have it both ways—to assume that America's national interest and the greater good of mankind are one and the same. This approach has resulted in a self-referential understanding of the norms that are to govern the world. It has also encouraged the hope that someday the world will indeed be universally guided by American principles, even as the United States, as the figurehead and governor of the new order, maintains its right to particularistic

---

[6] Brian Klunk, *Consensus and the American Mission* (Lanham, MD: University Press of America, 1986); William Pfaff, *The Wrath of Nations: Civilization and the Furies of Nationalism* (New York: Simon and Schuster, 1993).

[7] Lawrence J. Friedman, *Inventors of the Promised Land* (New York: Alfred A. Knopf, 1975).

[8] Thomas Paine, "Common Sense" in Nelson F. Adkins, ed., *Common Sense and Other Writings* (New York: Macmillan, 1953). See also, Walter A. McDougall, *Promised Land, Crusader State: America's Encounter with the World Since 1776* (New York: Houghton Mifflin, 1997).

[9] James H. Moorhead, "The American Israel: Protestant Tribalism and Universal Mission" in William R. Hutchison and Hartmut Lehman, eds., *Many Are Chosen: Divine Elections and Western Nationalism* (Minneapolis, MN: Fortress Press, 1994), 145–166.

[10] Hans Kohn, *American Nationalism: An Interpretive Essay* (New York: Macmillan, 1957).

loyalty. Needless to say, this "solution" to the tension between national discreteness and universalist pretension has been regarded by others as crudely arrogant, a fact that Americans have been slow to recognize.

Embedded in Americans' belief in their nation's universal significance is a sense of mission, which sometimes emerges as a crusading mentality. This sense of destiny also reflects American exceptionalism, the conviction that the United States is qualitatively different from—and better than—other states. The objective basis for considering the nation to be exceptional is its ideological nature, "the creed of our political faith," as Thomas Jefferson put it.[11] In the words of Seymour Martin Lipset:

> Becoming American [is] a religious, that is, ideological act. . . . The United States is a country organized around an ideology which includes a set of dogmas about the nature of a good society. Americanism . . . is an "ism" or ideology in the same way that communism or fascism or liberalism are isms. . . . In Europe, nationality is related to community, and thus one cannot become un-English or un-Swedish. Being an American, however, is an ideological commitment. It is not a matter of birth. Those who reject American values are un-American.[12]

The belief that the United States is an exceptional nation defined by a creed is inherently normative. As Daniel Bell argued, exceptionalism means more than simply being "different" from others; every society, indeed every individual, is unique in some way, and there is no great pride to be gotten from that fact.[13] Exceptionalism, therefore, connotes an element of superiority, an intangible but clearly recognizable quality that we can identify in geniuses and other people of extraordinary talent on the individual level, for example, and that is rooted in what is sometimes referred to as the "genius" of America's political organization at the collective level. American exceptionalists note that the United States somehow managed to solve the previously intractable challenge of establishing a political regime that is both stable and free, thus demonstrating its possession of some special quality that other states lacked. In turn, this ennobling discovery entitled Americans to lead other nations so that they might thereby enjoy some of the exemplar's success; even more, it has generally been understood to carry for Americans a *duty*, a peculiar responsibility to lead others and share its self-evidently desirable liberty.[14]

---

[11] Thomas Jefferson, "First Inaugural Address" in Davis Newton Lott, ed., *The Presidents Speak: The Inaugural Addresses of the American Presidents, from Washington to Clinton* (New York: Henry Holt, 1994).

[12] Seymour Martin Lipset, *American Exceptionalism: A Double-Edged Sword* (New York: W.W. Norton, 1996), 18, 31.

[13] Daniel Bell, "The 'Hegelian Secret': Civil Society and American Exceptionalism" in Byron E. Shafer, ed., *Is America Different? A New Look at American Exceptionalism* (Oxford: Clarendon Press, 1991), 46–70.

[14] For potent criticisms of the idea of American exceptionalism, see J. Victor Koschmann, "Review Essay: The Nationalism of Cultural Uniqueness," *American Historical Review* 102 (June 1997): 758–768; Ian Tyrrell, "American Exceptionalism in an Age of International History," *American Historical Review* 96 (October 1991): 1031–1055; and Reinhold Niebuhr, *The Irony of American History* (New York: Charles Scribner's Sons, 1954).

The normative dimension of American national identity builds from two disparate sources. The first, American civil religion, is the religious expression of American nationalism; it imparts to Americans the conviction that their enterprise is of truly transcendent value. The second is the Enlightenment, which not only provided the liberal theory that gave form to the American political system, but also supplied a crucial component of America's global teleological ambition. Each tradition merits brief comment.

America's civil religion allows Americans to express their patriotic sentiments in religious language and vice-versa by imagining that a fundamental consistency exists between their political preferences and the theological imperatives of their faith.[15] Despite the claim that some have made that "it is somewhat misleading . . . to refer to the civil or national religion as a 'common denominator' faith," American civil religion in both style and substance bears the strong imprint of America's religious mainstream.[16] Historically, this has meant that its rhetorical and substantive content has been deeply structured by Protestant beliefs: despite its ecumenism, American civil religion rejoices in the favor of Providence, not Allah or Buddha.

America's civil religion provides a way for the nation to interpret its collective, signature experiences according to the logic of ultimacy. In particular, it has often suggested a special role for the country in millennial history. For example, the two most significant events to give substance to America's civil religion were the Revolutionary War and the Civil War. Each conflict inculcated a strongly redemptive message, the first from the corruption of the Old World, the second from the collective sins of the United States itself.[17] Ernest Lee Tuveson, a religious historian, notes how each war, the second in particular, was regarded at the time as "more than just another war about a moral issue, even if a great one; it was *the* crisis of mankind, even if only one nation was involved."[18] That an internal war could be regarded in apocalyptic terms shows that in American civil religion, the nation-state itself is regarded as figuring prominently and directly in God's broader plan for the human race. Civil religion allows Americans to express in the language of transcendence that the United States is an exceptional country and that the American people have a providential destiny. A certain unshakable confidence attaches to foreign policies that are believed to be not only approved by God, but perhaps even required by His inscrutable plan for mankind; civil religion can subtly impart that

[15] Robert N. Bellah, "Civil Religion in America" in Russell E. Richey and Donald G. Jones, eds., *American Civil Religion* (New York: Harper & Row, 1974), 21–44. See also, Dante Germino, *The Inaugural Addresses of American Presidents: The Public Philosophy and Rhetoric*, with a preface and introduction by Kenneth W. Thompson (New York: University Press of America, 1984).

[16] Conrad Cherry, *God's New Israel: Religious Interpretations of American Destiny*, 2nd ed. (Chapel Hill: University of North Carolina Press, 1998), 11.

[17] See Cherry, *God's New Israel*, 11–12; and Bellah, "Civil Religion," 30–32.

[18] Ernest Lee Tuveson, *Redeemer Nation: The Idea of America's Millennial Role* (Chicago, IL: University of Chicago Press, 1968), 195–196.

aura to American actions. One can understand neither the crusading moral spirit that imbues American nationalism nor the centrality of the sense of American mission to U.S. foreign policy without taking due account of American civil religion.

The Enlightenment (at least a watered-down version of it) was also embedded at the country's founding and came intensively to structure the national consciousness.[19] Its normative political vision encouraged widespread individual freedom in order that under the guidance of science, the human race could progress toward perfection. Although, on one level, the protection of humanity's natural liberty sought by Enlightenment political theorists was regarded as an end unto itself, the ultimate purpose of this freedom was progress. If people were free, then they could attain perfection, both individually and as a race. What this progress required was a break from the past, whose corrupt institutions were not amenable to the development of a scientific, forward-looking worldview. A fresh beginning was needed, with past practices discarded and replaced with a new world order founded on reason. National and religious loyalties were productive of little but superstition and bloodshed; they thus had to be abolished. This was the hope and vision of many Enlightenment thinkers: a new beginning in human history, when an individual's relations with both others and herself would be founded on a new set of principles and values that would enable her at last to become perfect, in conditions of freedom, equality, and justice. It should be pointed out that American Enlightenment thinkers tended to espouse less-robust visions of human perfectibility than their European, especially French, counterparts, and the movement's antireligious posture certainly gained no traction in the United States. Nevertheless, the general worldview of liberal optimism was held in common by American and European thinkers alike, particularly the commitment to progress in freedom.

Given these hopes, it is not difficult to see how Enlightenment thinkers placed special value first on North America, which they regarded as a continental *tabula rasa*, and later on the state that was born there. (Obviously, the slate was not in fact "clean," and the fact that the European settlers could regard it as such indicates the strength of both their racism and their willingness to bend their perception of social realities to make them conform to their idealistic vision. It is beyond the purview of this paper to address the significance of racial particularism in American national identity, but the reader should bear its importance in mind when considering the connection between American national identity and foreign policy, especially when the United States deals with the nonwhites who comprise most of the world's population.) Americans agreed with many Enlightenment precepts, particularly regarding government, and they eagerly subscribed to the Enlightenment's esteem for their mission. As Wilson

---

[19] For what remains the best account of the Enlightenment's importance to American political identity, see Louis Hartz, *The Liberal Tradition in America*, with a new Introduction by Tom Wicker (New York: Harcourt, Brace & Company, 1991).

Carey McWilliams writes, "The new theories were flattering, appealing to the uncertain pride of America. For more than one theorist of the Enlightenment—Herder and Blake, among the still prominent—America was the redemptive land which had escaped European corruptions and recovered the liberty of nature. Free to experiment with the new social and moral teachings, America was 'the first lodge of humanity,' and from her example might arise the freedom and brotherhood of man."[20]

The United States represented in many respects the literal break from the past demanded by the Enlightenment vision, and its existence heartened those who anticipated impatiently humanity's new start. For these optimists on both sides of the Atlantic, the United States promised to be the instrumentality by which man's highest hopes could be realized. Because it lacked both a feudal tradition and an overarching religious establishment, it could quietly and without great convulsions institute a model form of democratic government and society.[21] America's geography and founding moment crystallized in the Enlightenment mind the recognition that this nation presented the ideal opportunity for putting into practice the values of the new era. In this way, the Enlightenment not only encouraged Americans to adopt a liberal form of government, it also contributed to the missionary dimension of their collective identity.

The Idea of American Mission and U.S. Foreign Policy

In practice, American nationalism influences U.S. foreign policy by layering altruism on top of basic, self-interested power-seeking behavior while allowing Americans to believe that their good intentions lack a selfish dimension and are truly, in some objective way, good for others. Americans seek to implant or strengthen democratic governance in other states not only to make other peoples "free" (and however culturally insensitive Americans may be in this desire, articulations of this goal are generally sincere), but also and primarily because doing so expands American power. As the divinely appointed vehicle for attaining lasting human progress, the United States is entitled to interpret for other states their own best interests, which are inevitably found to be consistent with those of the United States. After all, inasmuch as the United States both implements God's purposes and leads the secular progress of mankind, other states logically cannot have legitimate interests that oppose America's. By conceptually merging the U.S. national interest with the improvement of other countries in this way, the idea of American mission allows the United States to enhance its own power on the world stage not by "conquering" other states, but by "liberating" them.

By spreading its core values, the United States advances the new stage in human history whose inauguration was marked by the country's founding. Strength-

---

[20] Wilson Carey McWilliams, *The Idea of Fraternity in America* (Berkeley: University of California Press, 1973), 173.

[21] See Hartz, *The Liberal Tradition*, 3–32.

ening the role of the United States in world affairs is therefore, *ipso facto*, legitimate and good for the world. As Arthur Schlesinger, Jr., wrote, "So the impression developed that in the United States of America the Almighty had contrived a nation unique in its virtue and magnanimity, exempt from the motives that governed all other states. ... [This] brought the republic from the original idea of America as exemplary experiment to the recent idea of America as mankind's designated judge, jury, and executioner."[22] According to American nationalist doctrine, in short, the United States can justifiably increase its power and prestige on the world stage, consistently with its mission, because, unlike any other nation-state, it embodies and promulgates values that all people share, even if they do not know it yet. As the following section will show, President Bush has freshly generated a focused sense of mission through his handling of the terrorist attacks and re-articulation of America's world role. Notably, America's new mission as spelled out by Bush draws significantly from its Protestant roots.

FRAMING THE ATTACKS AND DEFINING THE BUSH DOCTRINE

Such an awesomely powerful experience as that which the nation underwent in September 2001 requires framing and contextualization by one who has the authority to do so. People need help getting their minds around events and circumstances that are otherwise incomprehensible. They need someone to explain to them the meaning of what they are going through, to answer the "why" questions that signature moments provoke. In the United States, it falls to the president to provide this service, and indeed this responsibility lies at the heart of the president's role in American governance. As the figurehead of the nation, the president is understood both to embody and to express its values, character, and purpose, and this status allows the president uniquely to speak both to and for the country as a whole. He is, in fact, expected to do so when conditions warrant.

The president's role as figurehead is also one that confers tremendous power, which he can use to generate support for favored policies.[23] A president's ability to shape public opinion is enhanced during crises because it is then that the American people most urgently cast about for leadership and solutions. It is also magnified in the realm of foreign affairs, where the president's constitutional authority is comparatively greater than in domestic affairs, especially since the Supreme Court's dubious but controlling decision in *U.S. v. Curtiss-Wright*, which asserted (with little basis) that the president's overriding authority in international affairs is rooted in sovereign prerogative rather than a constitutional allocation of power.[24] It is not coincidental, therefore, that the

---

[22] Schlesinger, "America: Experiment or Destiny," 517.

[23] Sam Kernell, *Going Public: New Strategies of Presidential Leadership* (Washington, DC: CQ Press, 1986).

[24] 299 U.S. 304, (1936).

strongest and most meaningful statements regarding American national identity have come from presidents during wartime. September 11 was just the most recent event, like the Civil War or World War II, when Americans looked to their leader to help them understand what they were going through and what it meant for them as a people. It was also an opportunity for the president to seize control of the national agenda and shape the country's grand strategy in foreign policy. In classic fashion, President Bush accomplished both tasks by invoking nationalism and foreign policy in the service of each other.

In addition to providing reassurance, the speeches that Bush gave to the American people during the crucial week and a half between the attacks and his 20 September emergency State of the Union Address had two broad goals. The first was to equate the United States with freedom, compassion, and tolerance, qualities that Bush claimed made the country the target of the "evildoers" enmity. Bush's goal, which he easily achieved, was to define the world in Manichean terms, with the United States symbolizing "good" and its enemies embodying "evil." Doing so provided implicit moral justification for the outcome of his second goal, which was to prepare the public to accept the policy manifestations of the eventual administration response. These two rhetorical strategies worked in tandem, so that in the course of employing emotionally charged and provocatively nationalistic imagery, Bush incrementally introduced to the public the core elements of his antiterrorism and subsequently broader foreign policy agenda.

AMERICA THE FREE, HOME OF COMPASSION AND TOLERANCE

As the quote introducing this paper reveals, President Bush had begun describing the terrorist strike as an attack on freedom as early as 12 September. He elaborated this theme in his remarks at the National Cathedral two days later during a civil–religious ceremony marking the National Day of Prayer and Remembrance (such healing events, charged with religious and nationalist imagery, follow every major national disaster). In this speech/political sermon, Bush declared, "In every generation, the world has produced enemies of human freedom. They have attacked America, because we are freedom's home and defender."[25] In a subsequent press conference, he added that the terrorists "can't stand freedom; they hate what America stands for."[26] These examples can be multiplied, and Bush's steady and unflinching repetition of the assertion that the United States was targeted *because* it represents freedom quickly became assimilated into Americans' understanding of the nature of their foes.

[25] "President's Remarks at National Day of Prayer and Remembrance," 14 September 2001, accessed on the White House website at http://www.whitehouse.gov/news/releases/2001/09/print/20010914-2.html, 2 October 2001.

[26] "Remarks by the President upon Arrival at the South Lawn," 16 September 2001, accessed on the White House website at http://whitehouse.gov/news/releases/2001/09/print/20010916-2.html, 2 October 2001.

In addition to freedom, Bush also identified two other features as being part of the national character—compassion and tolerance—and according to the President, the terrorists attacked them, too. In one of his early speeches, for example, Bush affirmed, "In this trial, we have been reminded, and the world has seen, that our fellow Americans are generous and kind, resourceful and brave."[27] Later, he announced, "We're too great a nation to allow the evil-doers to affect our soul and our spirit. . . . This is a great land. It's a great land, because our people are so decent and strong and compassionate."[28] And in remarks condemning anti-Muslim activities, he declared, "Those who feel like they can intimidate our fellow citizens to take out their anger don't represent the best of America, they represent the worst of humankind, and they should be ashamed of their behavior. This is a great country. It's a great country because we share the same values of respect and dignity and human worth."[29]

Clearly, these expressions of American integrity were intended to reaffirm Americans' sense of worth and to support appropriate private conduct during a volatile period. Any leader in any country will testify to the goodness of his or her nation during a time of trial, and Bush was extraordinarily effective in helping the American people through those dark days. In conjunction with his steadily more militaristic rhetoric and identification of the enemy as evildoers who not only lacked American virtues but specifically attacked the United States because of them, his consistent equation of America with virtuousness served as well to dichotomize the world between those, such as the United States, who are good and those who oppose it, who are evil. In this way, by painting America and its enemies with such a broadly abstract and moralistic brush, Bush left himself no gray areas within which to conduct foreign affairs, one consequence of which is that those who disagree with the United States for any reason are thereby identifying themselves as either evil or, at best, morally flawed. At the time, though, this moralistic language seems to have been what the American people wanted and needed to hear. This tension between the demands of geopolitics and the need for American statesmen to use ideologically charged nationalistic language remains one of the tragic ironies of American politics.

Framing the attack as one motivated by a hatred of freedom and compassion enabled the president to emphasize that America's retaliation would be directed against moral outliers, and not against Islamic countries per se. "We don't view this as a war of religion, in any way, shape or form," he announced, for example. "And for those who try to pit religion against religion, our great nation will stand up and reject that kind of thought. . . . We're going to lead the

[27] "President's Remarks at National Day of Prayer and Remembrance."

[28] "Remarks by the President Supporting Charities," 18 September 2001, accessed on the White House website at http://www.whitehouse.gov/news/releases/2001/09/20010918-1.html, 4 October 2001.

[29] "Remarks by the President at the Islamic Center of Washington, DC," 17 September 2001, accessed on the White House website at http://whitehouse.gov/news/releases/2001/09/ 20010917-11.html, 2 October 2001.

world to fight for freedom, and we'll have Muslim and Jew and Christian side by side with us."[30] This was an important point to make, and Bush did both the country and American nationalism a great service when he praised the Islamic faith.[31] Of course, these comments were made necessary by ugly incidents from around the country in which Muslim Americans and Arab Americans (and even a South Asian Sikh) were targeted by some of their white, Christian compatriots, who seemed to believe that September 11 marked the beginning of a religious war. The suggestion of holy war had also been reinforced by one of Bush's own comments, in which he said, "This crusade, this war on terrorism is going to take a while."[32] To be fair to the President, it is almost certain that he did not have the capital "C" Crusades in mind when he made that off-the-cuff remark. As our earlier discussion of the idea of American mission should make clear, a "crusading" spirit has always attached itself to American foreign policy, and it is reasonable to assume that Bush used the term in that sense. On the other hand, it is revealing that Bush did not consider how his Islamic audience would have interpreted his use of the word "crusade," coming as it did from an avowed Christian fundamentalist in response to an attack by Muslim individuals.

Indeed, given civil religion's prominence in America's nationalist mythos, it is not at all surprising that both Muslims and many non-Muslims, including Europeans of all stripes, have believed that America's war against terrorism has had a Christian dimension. The National Day of Prayer and Remembrance, after all, was held in a Christian house of worship, and the symbolism of the President preaching literally from the altar communicated far more about the religious center of gravity in the American nation than did his subsequent pleas for tolerance. As one might expect, moreover, his comments on this occasion were particularly evocative of civil–religious imagery, as his closing remarks indicate: "On this national day of prayer and remembrance, we ask almighty God to watch over our nation, and grant us patience and resolve in all that is to come. . . . May He bless the souls of the departed. May He comfort our own. And may He always guide our country. God bless America."[33] Of course, the President could not have done otherwise than lead this service even if he had been so inclined, and his sermon was ecumenical and deeply appreciated by Americans of all faiths. Nevertheless, the substance of his comments there and elsewhere during the first few days and weeks after the attacks reaffirmed the civil–religious dimension of American nationalism and helped the nation to take comfort in the belief that despite suffering apparent retribution for unnamed sins, they were, in fact, a good and noble people whose values and bearing still enjoyed divine favor.

[30] "Remarks by the President at Photo Opportunity with House and Senate Leadership," 19 September 2001, accessed on the White House website at http://whitehouse.gov/news/releases/2001/09/20010919-8.html, 5 August 2002.
[31] "Remarks by the President at Islamic Center."
[32] "Remarks by the President Upon Arrival at the South Lawn."
[33] "President's Remarks at National Day of Prayer and Remembrance."

Bush's civil–religious fervor, it should be further pointed out, did not emerge spontaneously during the postattack climate of jingoistic mourning. Rather, it would be more accurate to say that September 11 created a particularly acute context within which Bush's already well-developed nationalism could find both ready articulation and an unusually receptive audience. Clear evidence of his pre–September 11 religious nationalism, for example, peppers his inaugural address, as when he perorated, "We are not this story's author, who fills time and eternity with his purpose."[34] Yet, it would be mistaken to understate the powerful role that the attacks themselves played in not only clarifying American nationalism but also in merging it with American foreign policy. If anything, September 11 roused Bush's righteous patriotism and gave it focused meaning and purpose.

DEVELOPING THE DOCTRINE

In the chaos of September 11 and its aftermath, the desire for vengeance understandably surged through Americans' veins. In his address to the nation on the night of the attacks, therefore, Bush plainly stated: "The United States will hunt down and punish those responsible for these cowardly acts," adding, "The resolve of our great nation is being tested. But make no mistake: We will show the world that we will pass this test."[35] From the very outset, then, it was obvious that the United States would use force to strike back at those who viciously murdered its innocent civilians, and no state would have been expected to do otherwise. Given the fact that the actual perpetrators were dead, however, the question was, who to go after?

On 13 September, Bush gave his first hint of an answer when he announced that *"those who helped or harbored the terrorists* will be punished—and punished severely. The enormity of their evil demands it."[36] The following day at the national prayer service, Bush ratcheted up the moralism in his rhetoric, and in the process, he expanded the range of potential targets. "Our responsibility to history is already clear: to answer these attacks and rid the world of evil."[37] On 17 September, he clarified his moralism somewhat:

> We are planning a broad and sustained campaign to secure our country and *eradicate the evil of terrorism*. . . . Great tragedy has come to us, and we are meeting it with the best that is in our country, with courage and concern for others. Because this is America. This is who we are. This is what our enemies hate and have attacked. And this is why we will prevail.

[34] "President George W. Bush's Inaugural Address," 20 January 2001, accessed on the White House website at http://whitehouse.gov/news/inaugural-address.html, 23 September 2003.

[35] "Remarks by the President upon Arrival at Barksdale Air Force Base," 11 September 2001, accessed on the White House website at http://www.whitehouse.gov/news/releases/2001/09/20010911.1-html, 2 October 2001.

[36] "Presidential Proclamation: National Day of Prayer and Remembrance for the Victims of the Terrorist Attacks on September 11, 2001," 13 September 2001, accessed on the White House website at http://www.whitehouse.gov/news/releases/2001/09/20010913-7.html, 2 October 2001 (emphasis added).

[37] "President's Remarks at National Day of Prayer and Remembrance."

(Bush was explicit in extending the object of the American response beyond the immediate perpetrators when he said, "After all, our mission is not just Osama bin Laden, the al Qaeda organization. Our mission is to battle terrorism and to join with freedom-loving people."[38])

In just a few days, then, the President succeeded in forcefully reassuring the American people that they were great, strong, and good and that they would punish with force those who had made them suffer. But in his moral posturing and nationalistic fervor, he also promised them more: the United States would not only punish the network behind the nefarious suicide pilots, it would also eradicate terrorism itself. Further, the United States would target not only terrorists but also those who aid them. Thus, when at last he felt prepared to articulate fully the country's formal response to the terrorist attacks, President Bush had already prepared the American people to accept what needed to be done and to believe that the country's response would reflect the essential spirit of American national identity. But in seizing the opportunity to refashion the national mission, he also left America's options extremely open-ended. In this way, he spelled out a strategy that went far beyond what a narrow tailoring to the proximate causes of September 11 would have suggested. The result is what we now call the Bush doctrine.

THE BUSH DOCTRINE: FIRST DRAFT

Bush devoted a substantial portion of his 20 September emergency State of the Union Address, in which he first spelled out his doctrine, to identifying America's new enemies. In particular, he named al Qaeda and the Taliban regime as the objects of immediate concern, and he made some very specific requests of the latter if it were not to risk facing American military might.[39] As we now know, the Taliban refused these demands, and the United States removed it from power in Afghanistan. When he had previously defined the enemy more broadly than these two groups, Bush had identified states that harbor or support terrorism as "hostile regimes," but in this address, he went further: "Every nation in every region now has a decision to make," he intoned. "Either you are with us or you are with the terrorists." Like any great moral issue, apparently, America's global war on terror could not tolerate neutrality.[40]

Blending his new "with-us-or-against-us" posture with traditional, universalist constructions of American nationalism, Bush then described the new war on terror as one to be waged for the good of mankind. "This is not, however, just

---

[38] "Remarks by the President to Employees at the Pentagon," 17 September 2001, accessed on the White House website at http://whitehouse.gov/news/releases/2001/09/20010917-3.html, 4 October 2001 (emphasis added).

[39] George W. Bush, "President Bush's Address on Terrorism before a Joint Meeting of Congress: Transcript," 21 September 2001, accessed on *New York Times on the Web* at www.nytimes.com/2001/09/21/national/21BTEX.html, 21 September 2001.

[40] Ibid.

America's fight," he claimed. "And what is at stake is not just America's freedom. This is the world's fight, this is civilization's fight, this is the fight of all
who believe in progress and pluralism, tolerance and freedom." In this way,
Bush both transformed an attack against one country into an attack on the "civilized" world—a suggestion of collective security that he acknowledged in a
passing reference to NATO[41]—and cemented the globally Manichean perspective that he had been encouraging since the attacks.

Interpolated within these descriptions of American national identity and
the enemy that opposed it were suggestions about what exactly the country
would do to win the "war." Most important was his hint that the use of military
force was imminent, and that it would be directed against terrorists wherever
they happened to be. In addition, he promised to "starve terrorists of funding"
and to use "every means of diplomacy, every tool of intelligence, every instrument of law enforcement" to destroy the terrorist networks. He would nurture
a multilateral coalition to achieve this end, which would be bound not only by
shared values but also by a shared vulnerability to terrorism. Bush also announced the creation of the Office of Homeland Security, indicating the new
priority of the government's bureaucracies.

Ultimately, Bush framed the conflict against terrorism as implicating the
world's destiny. On one side were al Qaeda and other "enemies of freedom,"
who had the goal of "remaking the world and imposing [their] radical beliefs
on people everywhere." On the other side was the United States, with its own
ideas about how the world should look:

> As long as the United States is determined and strong, this will not be an age of
> terror. This will be an age of liberty here and across the world. . . . In our grief and
> anger, we have found our mission and our moment. Freedom and fear are at war.
> The advance of human freedom, the great achievement of our time and the great
> hope of every time, now depends on us. Our nation, this generation, will lift the
> dark threat of violence from our people and our future. We will rally the world to
> this cause by our efforts, by our courage. . . . Freedom and fear, justice and cruelty,
> have always been at war. And we know that God is not neutral between them.[42]

This earliest incarnation of the Bush doctrine thus held that the United
States would use military force against terrorists of global reach and against the
states that harbor them. It would also engage in a multilateral strategy of freez-
ing financial assets and sharing intelligence in pursuit of the goal of a global
freedom built in America's image. These were fairly specific priorities, albeit
broadly framed, and they responded to the assault of September 11. As we have
since witnessed, though, Bush's broadly dichotomous language has proven to
be as important to his foreign policy objectives as these concrete proposals, and
the logic behind the rhetoric has spawned a comprehensive vision that builds
on this post–September 11 groundwork even as it defines a radical new blue-
print for international relations and America's role in them.

[41] Ibid.
[42] Ibid.

FINALIZING THE DOCTRINE: FROM NYC TO BAGHDAD AND BEYOND

Since Bush first enunciated his doctrine in September 2001, he has added two significant dimensions to it. The first is his association with the "enemy" of those who develop weapons of mass destruction (WMDs). He first alluded to this threat in his United Nations speech of 9 November 2001—less than two months after the terrorist attacks and long before Iraq was on most people's radar screens—when he warned, "Civilization itself, the civilization we share, is threatened."[43] Bush more formally incorporated these actors into the Bush doctrine by memorably uttering, during his annual State of the Union address in January 2002, "States like these [he mentioned specifically Iran, Iraq, and North Korea], and their terrorist allies, constitute an axis of evil, arming to threaten the peace of the world."[44] Bush's use of this by-now notorious phrase was premised on these states' desire to develop WMDs, a dubious criterion for such severe moral evaluation (especially when one considers that the United States itself has developed many such weapons), but one that Americans were prepared to accept as long as it somehow related to terrorism. Bush continued to stress the centrality of WMDs to his antiterror agenda throughout the year following the terrorist attacks, and by seamlessly integrating this concern into his post–September 11 doctrine, he normatively and conceptually tied his subsequent Iraq policy into the deep structure of America's global posture. In March, for example, Bush stressed that "Men with no respect for life must never be allowed to control the ultimate instruments of death."[45] He repeated the new mantra a month later: "And for the long-term security of America and civilization itself, we must confront the great threat of biological and chemical and nuclear weapons in the hands of terrorists or hostile regimes. . . . History has called us to these responsibilities and we accept them. America has always had a special mission to defend justice and advance freedom around the world."[46]

The second major development in the Bush doctrine, preemption, laid the groundwork for Bush's Iraq policy even more forcefully. In a major foreign policy statement, his graduation speech at West Point on 1 June 2002, President Bush spelled out America's new policy. As one of the most important recent addresses on U.S. foreign policy, this speech merits particular attention. In it, Bush was unusually clear in articulating the rationale for America's preemption

---

[43] George W. Bush, "Text: President Bush Addresses the U.N.," 10 November 2001, accessed on *The Washington Post Online* at www.washingtonpost.com/wp-srv/nation/specials/attacked/transcripts/bushtext_111001, 10 November 2001.

[44] George W. Bush, "Prepared Text: The State of the Union Address," 29 January 2002, accessed on *The Washington Post Online* at http://washingtonpost.com/wp-srv/onpolitics/transcripts/sou012902.html, 29 January 2002.

[45] "Remarks by the President on the Six-Month Anniversary of the September 11th Attacks," 11 March 2002," accessed on the White House website at http://www.whitehouse.gov/news/releases/2002/03/20020311-1.html, 5 August 2002.

[46] "President Promotes Compassionate Conservatism," 30 April 2002, accessed on the White House website at http://www.whitehouse.gov/news/releases/2002/04/20020430-5.html, 5 August 2002.

(or, more accurately, *prevention*) policy: "We cannot defend America by hoping for the best. ... If we wait for threats to fully materialize, we will have waited too long. ... We must take the battle to the enemy, disrupt his plans, and confront the worst threats before they emerge."[47] By explicitly advocating the violation of one of international society and law's most fundamental norms, that against external aggression, while simultaneously eschewing the need for international approval, Bush moved the United States considerably closer to an unambiguously unilateralist posture. The United States, he communicated through this policy, would not be bound by the same rules as other states. His rationale was American exceptionalism ("The twentieth century ended with a single surviving model of human progress," he claimed at one point), but the real basis of his position was American power.[48] Nevertheless, he argued, because the United States represents universal moral values, other states should not regard this posture as dangerous to them—unless they are on the wrong side of the moral coin: "Because the war on terror will require resolve and patience, it will also require firm moral purpose. In this way our struggle is similar to the Cold War ... [and] moral clarity was essential to our victory in the Cold War. Moral truth is the same in every culture, in every time, and in every place. ... We are in a conflict between good and evil, and America will call evil by its name."[49]

THE BUSH DOCTRINE, FULLY FORMED: THE NATIONAL SECURITY STRATEGY

All of the elements of Bush's vision for America's global role came together in the National Security Strategy (NSS), which was released on 20 September 2002.[50] This document systematically laid out the administration's vision for America's place in the world, and it contained no surprises. Indeed, each section of the strategy was introduced with an excerpt from one or another previous speech—some of which have also been quoted here. In the NSS, Bush asserted the universality of American values and the inherent entitlement of the United States to establish the conditions according to which international relations should operate. As G. John Ikenberry put it, "It is a vision in which sovereignty becomes more absolute for America even as it becomes more conditional for countries that challenge Washington's standards of internal and external behavior."[51] Noting the country's military and economic advantage

---

[47] "Remarks by the President at 2002 Graduation Exercise of the United States Military Academy," 1 June 2002, accessed on the White House website at http://www.whitehouse.gov.news/releases/2002/06/20020601-3.html, 5 August 2002.

[48] Ibid.

[49] Ibid.

[50] For the best analysis of this document, see Edward Rhodes, "The Imperial Logic of Bush's Liberal Agenda," *Survival* (Spring, 2003): 131–154.

[51] G. John Ikenberry, "America's Imperial Ambition," *Foreign Affairs* 81 (September/October 2002): 44–60.

over both its actual and its potential competitors, the NSS made clear that both American interests and human progress depended on the continuation of this power gap: "Today, the United States enjoys a position of unparalleled military strength and great economic and political influence. . . . We will maintain the forces sufficient to support our obligations, and to defend freedom. Our forces will be strong enough to dissuade potential adversaries from pursuing a military build-up in hopes of surpassing, or equaling, the power of the United States."[52] Unabashedly, the NSS defended this posture by reference to "a distinctly American internationalism that reflects the union of our values and our national interests." It continued, "The aim of this strategy is to help make the world not just safer but better."[53] In this way, and throughout the document, as the following synopsis will demonstrate, both the exceptionalism and the universalism of American national identity were consistently invoked to frame and legitimate—and in many cases, in fact, to constitute—the stated foreign policy interests. The NSS is the official statement of the Bush doctrine, and its vision is startling in its scope.

Repeating an argument first made in the West Point address, the strategy argued that the world was at a turning point and that a new era in international politics was dawning: "Today, the international community has the best chance since the rise of the nation-state in the seventeenth century to build a world where great powers compete in peace instead of continually prepare for war. Today, the world's great powers find ourselves on the same side—united by common dangers of terrorist violence and chaos. . . . We are also increasingly united by common values."[54] Bush envisioned a central role for the United States in the building and maintenance of this world order and found justification for this position in its universalism: "Freedom is the non-negotiable demand of human dignity; the birthright of every person—in every civilization. . . . Today, humanity holds in its hands the opportunity to further freedom's triumph over [its] foes. The United States welcomes our responsibility to lead in this great mission."[55]

The specific actions outlined in the NSS that would help to make concrete these grandiose sentiments include the following: support "human dignity"; strengthen antiterrorism alliances; defuse regional conflicts; eliminate the threat of WMDs; enhance free markets and free trade; "expand the circle of development by opening societies and building the infrastructure of democracy"; develop multilateral agendas; and upgrade the military.[56] It is worth taking a moment here to refer to some of the language used in the NSS to frame a few of these objectives as a way of demonstrating the moralistic and nationalistic logic of the Bush doctrine. Regarding the goal of "Champion[ing] Aspirations for Hu-

[52] George W. Bush, "Full Text: Bush's National Security Strategy," 1, 22–23.
[53] Ibid., 3.
[54] Ibid., 2.
[55] Ibid., 3.
[56] Ibid., 3–4.

man Dignity," for instance, the NSS noted that "the United States must defend liberty and justice because these principles are right and true for all people everywhere. . . . Embodying lessons from our past and using the opportunity we have today, the national security strategy of the United States must start from these core beliefs and look outward for possibilities to expand liberty."[57] The war on terrorism, moreover, was treated not simply as a security threat: "In the war against global terrorism, we will never forget that we are ultimately fighting for our democratic values and way of life. Freedom and fear are at war."[58] And in promoting its economic vision, Bush reminded readers that "The concept of 'free trade' arose as a moral principle even before it was a pillar of economics."[59]

Many elements of the strategy seemed to be directed specifically at justifying the by-then clearly developing war against Iraq. In particular, the NSS undertook a painstaking explanation about how both WMDs and preemption were central components of America's broader foreign policy vision. The NSS tied the two concerns together in a manner that clearly argued that the primary indicator of whether the United States would find itself obligated to intervene in a given state was the type of regime that ruled it. Of immediate concern were "a small number of rogue states that, while different in important ways, share a number of attributes." Rogue states sponsor terrorism, ignore international law, threaten their neighbors, "brutalize their own people and squander their national resources for the personal gain of the rulers." They strive to acquire WMDs "to be used as threats" and "reject basic human values and hate the United States and everything for which its stands."[60] Unmistakably, Iraq satisfied these criteria. The NSS insisted that preemption was the only viable policy for dealing with rogue states because they were destabilizing and unpredictable, unlike America's previous adversary, the Soviet Union. Furthermore, given these characteristics during a time marked by the threat of global terrorism and the capacity of modern technology, preemption, properly applied, included preventive action aimed at eliminating threats before they became manifest.[61]

In the NSS, therefore, we can see how Bush carried forward on the current of American nationalism September 11's urgent posture and began applying it indirectly to Iraq. Certainly, the NSS was not meant to serve merely as a justification for the evolving Iraq policy, but it did spell out evocatively why an American invasion was justified by the logic of both interests and values.

THE WAR AGAINST IRAQ

The NSS presents a broad vision for U.S. foreign policy, and many of its stated goals are both commendable and consistent with the nobler strands of Ameri-

[57] Ibid., 4–5.
[58] Ibid., 7.
[59] Ibid., 14.
[60] Ibid., 10.
[61] Ibid., 11–12.

can political thought and practice. Who could argue, after all, with defending human dignity or helping to defuse regional conflicts? Nevertheless, the statement too conveniently provides a coherent framework for justifying what was by then the obvious focus of the administration: regime change in Iraq. Rumors of the administration's intentions regarding Iraq had been circulating for some time before the release of the NSS (according to Richard Haas, the director of the policy planning staff at the State Department, the decision was set by early July).[62] When President Bush formally dispelled these rumors by unconditionally confirming them, he chose to make his announcement in a speech to the United Nations on 12 September 2002—just after the first anniversary of September 11. (The first clear statement from the administration stating that it had designs on Saddam Hussein actually came from Vice President Dick Cheney, in his speech to the National Convention of the Veterans of Foreign Wars on 26 August 2002. The 12 September 2002 speech was the first statement offered by the President himself.[63]) If the timing was insufficient to convey the symbolic merging of the Iraq agenda with the more general response to September 11, his rhetoric eliminated any lingering doubts.

In his 12 September 2002 speech, Bush sought to argue systematically that Iraq was in violation of several international laws and that the world community must respond vigorously to the challenge this situation represented. Although it is not the purpose of this paper to explore the machinations leading up to the war or to assess the validity of the war itself, it is pertinent to excerpt here some of the key speeches surrounding the war to show how Bush not only mingled it into the emotional viscera of September 11, but also legitimated it according to the nationalist themes detailed above. In his 2002 UN speech, for instance, Bush insisted:

> With every step the Iraqi regime takes toward gaining and deploying the most terrible weapons, our own options to confront the regime will narrow. And if an emboldened regime were to supply these weapons to terrorist allies, then the attacks of September 11 would be a prelude to far greater horrors. ... We must choose between a world of fear and a world of progress. We cannot stand by and do nothing while dangers gather. We must stand up for our security and for the permanent rights and hopes of mankind. By heritage and by choice, the United States of America will make that stand. And, delegates to the United Nations, you have the power to make that stand as well.[64]

A few weeks later, on 7 October 2002, Bush made his pitch directly to the American people from the Cincinnati Union Terminal. In his speech, he de-

[62] Nicholas Lemann, "How It Came to War," *The New Yorker* (31 March 2003): 36–40, 39.

[63] See Richard Cheney, "Full Text: In Cheney's Words," 26 August 2002, accessed on *New York Times Online* at http://www.nytimes.com/2002/08/26/international/middleeast/26WEB-CHENEY.html, 26 August 2002.

[64] George W. Bush, "Text: Bush's Speech to the U.N. on Iraq," 12 September 2002, accessed on *New York Times Online* at http://www.nytimes.com/2002/09/12/politics/12AP-PTEX.html, 12 September 2002.

tailed various atrocities the Hussein regime had committed upon the Iraqi people as a way of demonstrating its evil character. Several times, Bush referred explicitly to the terrorist attacks of September 11, at one point even linking Saddam's regime to the al Qaeda terrorist network—a connection that has never been convincingly proven and that has always been the weakest component of the administration's case for war.

In these and other speeches, Bush and other members of his administration pleaded that war would only be a last resort and that all sides hoped that a peaceful resolution could be found to the suddenly urgent crisis surrounding Hussein's alleged development of WMDs. From the moment that Iraq supplanted Afghanistan as the focus of the administration and of public discourse, however, it appeared obvious that there would be war. Bush therefore needed to convince the American people—and possibly the world, although that audience seemed secondary—that war's sacrifice was both necessary and honorable. The Bush doctrine performed this task. As noted, Bush consistently and repeatedly referred to September 11 in his Iraq speeches, thus reinforcing in Americans' minds a protean connection between the two, and in his major speeches touching on the topic, he made sure to recur to the nationalist imagery that he had already commandeered in the service of his doctrine.

In his 2003 State of the Union of Address, for example, Bush transitioned from his summary of the immediate administration response to September 11 to his discussion of Iraq by providing a summary of twentieth-century U.S. foreign policy that celebrated a noble superpower saving the world from evil. Bush's conclusion of the address—the time when presidents reliably invoke great and woolly abstractions to characterize the nation—employed such classically nationalist themes in a way that clearly implicated their relevance to U.S. foreign policy:

> Americans are a resolute people, who have risen to every test of our time. Adversity has revealed the character of our country, to the world, and to ourselves. America is a strong nation, and honorable in the use of our strength. We exercise power without conquest, and sacrifice for the liberty of strangers. Americans are a free people, who know that freedom is the right of every person and the future of every nation. The liberty we prize is not America's gift to the world, it is God's gift to humanity. We Americans have faith in ourselves but not in ourselves alone. We do not claim to know all the ways of Providence, yet we can trust in them, placing our confidence in the loving God behind all of life, and all of history. May He guide us now, and may God continue to bless the United States of America.[65]

Throughout his speeches surrounding the Iraq war, Bush not only relied on God to justify his actions, he also claimed that the United States was ushering in a new, more democratic era. On 26 February 2003, for example, he justified the looming war by claiming:

---

[65] George W. Bush, "State of the Union Address," 28 January 2003, accessed on *New York Times Online* at http://www.nytimes.com/2003/01/28/politics/28CND-TEXT1.html, 28 January 2003.

The world has a clear interest in the spread of democratic values, because stable and free nations do not breed the ideologies of murder. They encourage the peaceful pursuit of a better life. . . . A new regime in Iraq would serve as a dramatic and inspiring example of freedom for other nations in the region. . . . By the resolve and purpose of America, and of our friends and allies, we will make this an age of progress and liberty. Free people will set the course of history, and free people will keep the peace of the world.[66]

Finally, having thus characterized America's mission to Iraq and the world, it was only to be expected that Bush would celebrate the conclusion of the "main part" of the hostilities by declaring, "In this battle, we have fought for the cause of liberty, and for the peace of the world." Bush wrapped his characterization of the war in nationalist imagery that not only referred to American history and values, but also hinted that service to America is akin to service to God:

Our commitment to liberty is America's tradition—declared at our founding, affirmed in Franklin Roosevelt's Four Freedoms, asserted in the Truman Doctrine and in Ronald Reagan's challenge to an evil empire. We are committed to freedom in Afghanistan, in Iraq and in a peaceful Palestine. The advance of freedom is the surest strategy to undermine the appeal of terror in the world. . . . American values and American interests lead in the same direction: We stand for human liberty. . . . Those we lost were last seen on duty. Their final act on this Earth was to fight a great evil and bring liberty to others.[67]

There is little reason to doubt that President Bush, as a leader whose obvious nationalism colors his perspective of global affairs, ever doubted that American security (filtered through the experience of September 11) and the peace and liberty of the world are coterminous.

DISCUSSION AND CONCLUSION

Clearly, President Bush has mastered the art of marshalling nationalist symbolism in support of his foreign policy vision. This skill is both useful and problematic, for while American national identity has proven to be remarkably durable, current events suggest that it has become in some ways dangerously obsolete. Inasmuch as the United States is now at the center of the international system,[68] it can no longer find moral self-justification in being untainted by a corrupt world that it has been chosen to lead out of the dark ages, as historically it has liked to believe. Rather, it is essential that the United States accept that its relationship with the international order has changed since the early days of the

[66] George W. Bush, "President Discusses the Future of Iraq," 26 February 2003, accessed on the White House website at http://www.whitehouse.gov/news/releases/2003/02/20030226-11.html, 24 May 2003.

[67] George W. Bush, "President Bush Announces Combat Operations in Iraq Have Ended," 1 May 2003, accessed on the White House website at http://whithouse.gov/news/releases/2003/05/20030501-15.html, 24 May 2003.

[68] Stephen G. Brooks and William C. Wohlforth, "American Primacy in Perspective," *Foreign Affairs* 81 (July/August 2002): 20–33.

republic when the core elements of American national identity were first set in place. In particular, traditional claims to moral distinctiveness must be abandoned. Unless its multilateral and nation-building dimensions—the cosmopolitan shadows of American national identity—are re-emphasized and strengthened, American universalism will continue to spawn a self-deceiving and increasingly dangerous paternalism. By this I do not mean to argue that American norms are flawed or that liberalism is not, on balance, preferable to its chief competitors. In general, Americans have accomplished many good things, both in terms of establishing liberal democracy as the norm for domestic governance and in regard to fostering a more stable and prosperous international community. Rather, it is the missionary disposition, the smug "holier-than-thou" character of American nationalism that must change. Simply put, it is time that Americans shed their self-identity as an exceptional people and accept instead their mature identity as integrated global citizens.[69]

Part of what is at stake is what Joseph Nye calls American "soft power," or the ability of the United States to influence global affairs without coercion by relying only on the attraction of its norms and success.[70] The very existence of American soft power demonstrates that American nationalism does, in fact, have a noble side, which most of the world's societies have recognized at some point or other.[71] Indeed, international norms today closely resemble those that the United States claims to champion. The world may not yet be at Francis Fukuyama's "End of History," but international law and current world opinion each rests inordinately on the same liberal democratic norms that the United States promulgates.[72] This global situation suggests that claims to American universalism are less fatuous than anti-American demonstrators have been prone to argue; freedom, as Woodrow Wilson and Bush each claimed for his own purposes, certainly does have a global appeal. The challenge confronting Americans as they enter a "new world order" will be to disentangle this recognition from the belief that only the moral agency of the United States can lead to the realization of humanity's promise.[73]

The methods that the United States employed to achieve its goals between September 11 and the Iraq war, however, have generally perpetuated the globally unpopular, chauvinistic, and ultimately dangerous tendencies of American nationalism while undercutting those aspects of the American experience that other peoples have found attractive. Because America's new foreign policy di-

---

[69] On this point, see Henry Nau, *At Home Abroad: Identity and Power in American Foreign Policy* (Ithaca, NY: Cornell University Press, 2002).

[70] Joseph Nye, *The Paradox of American Power: Why the World's Only Superpower Can't Go It Alone* (New York: Oxford University Press, 2002).

[71] Geir Lundestad, "'Empire By Invitation' in the American Century" in Michael J. Hogan, ed., *The Ambiguous Legacy: US Foreign Relations in the "American Century"* (New York: Cambridge University Press, 1999), 52–91.

[72] Thomas M. Franck, "The Emerging Right to Democratic Governance," *American Journal of International Law* 86 (January 1992): 46–91.

[73] See Graham T. Allison, Jr. and Robert P. Beschel, Jr., "Can the United States Promote Democracy?" *Political Science Quarterly* 107 (Spring 1992): 81–98.

rection was spurred by an attack on American soil, which itself has become interwoven into the national mythos, militarism has become among the most pronounced features of the country's global posture. Unilateral militarism is a strategy that not only casts American exceptionalism in an ugly light but also belies, or at the very least distorts, claims to American universalism. Given the fact that as this paper shows, American nationalist rhetoric has been a fixture in Bush's foreign policy speeches, an unavoidable consequence is that the militaristic tactics employed by the administration will color the world's perceptions of American norms and identity. This result is both unfortunate and unnecessary.

A substantial source of the Bush doctrine's moral difficulties is rooted in its—and, more generally, American nationalism's—problematic association of a distinct political community with higher values. Consider the concept "freedom," for example, which Bush has relied heavily upon to define the United States. Any abstract term such as freedom can only have a substantive meaning that is determined in part by its cultural context. In the United States, the meaning of the term "freedom" has evolved as American notions of justice have changed over time, as any casual reading of the history of any particular constitutional right amply demonstrates.[74] When one associates such a general concept with any particularistic community or practice in the way that both President Bush and, more generally, American nationalism have related the United States to freedom and human dignity, the effect is not only to endow the community with the esteemed qualities of the abstraction, but also to define the principle according to the imperfections of the community. In the new age of American imperialism, as Bush insists on corrupting American principles with a casual prioritization of the country's strength, he risks rendering American principles meaningless. Virtue can only be buried under so much hypocrisy before it loses its moral force. It would be a profound shame if the United States were to squander its opportunity to help spread democracy in a meaningful and systematic way by employing means whose logic so clearly contradicts the ends.[75]

Today, after a century in which the American mission to spread the nation's values and ideals abroad enjoyed obvious success, the United States is exceptional only in the preponderance of its power. Precisely because the United States has succeeded in abetting the spread of democracy, it is no longer ideologically exceptional, and because it is now deeply networked into the international system, it cannot eschew the ordinary requirements of geopolitical participation, as it once was able to do (although its involvement in world affairs was always greater than the myth of early American isolationism maintains). The values that Americans have always claimed to represent must be viewed not as *descriptions* of American identity, but as ideals to which the nation must

[74] See Eric Foner, *The Story of American Freedom* (New York: W.W. Norton & Co., 1998).

[75] See Rhodes, "The Imperial Logic of Bush's Liberal Agenda"; and John Gerard Ruggie, "Third Try at World Order? America and Multilateralism after the Cold War," *Political Science Quarterly* 109 (Autumn 1994): 553–570.

aspire, not only domestically, but also in its relations with the rest of the world. If the United States is in some way a literal embodiment of the values that it esteems, then it is no longer accountable to the standards those values represent. Instead, its practices become definitive of the standards to which others are to be held accountable. When one considers the deep flaws of this (or any other) state, the implications of this normative matrix become quite worrisome.

There is another, more practical reason for abandoning exceptionalism: the Manichean streak, rooted in American exceptionalism, that can lurk beneath the surface of American nationalism is unwise in international relations because it distracts policy makers from the messy realities of global politics. Realist theorists of international relations, beginning with E.H. Carr, have made it abundantly clear that pursuing black-and-white ideals at the expense of proximate, accessible political goals is not only unwise but also, ultimately, destructive. Unfortunately, September 11's moral "clarification" on this point was, once again, counterproductive because the terrorist attacks naturally invited a fiercely binary view of the world and America's role in it. The logic that the Bush doctrine has tapped into goes something like this: inasmuch as the United States embodies what is good and just, to oppose its interests is *ipso facto* to define oneself as evil. This stance is especially ill-suited to America's current world stature, and it risks encouraging both ideological backlash and great-power balancing. Thus, as he finds himself increasingly tempted to ignore world opinion as he defines America's new world role, Bush would do well to recall Senator J. William Fulbright's insight:

> Power tends to confuse itself with virtue and a great nation is peculiarly susceptible to the idea that its power is a sign of God's favor, conferring upon it a special responsibility for other nations—to make them richer and happier and wiser, to remake them, that is, in its own shining image. Power confuses itself with virtue and tends to take itself for omnipotence. Once imbued with the idea of mission, a great nation easily assumes that it has the means as well as the duty to do God's work. The Lord, after all, surely would not choose you as His agent and then deny you the sword with which to work his will.[76]

Scholars in the post–Cold War era have frequently argued that the United States must redefine the national interest so that it can conform more productively to new global realities.[77] What this paper's arguments suggest is that the national interest will not—cannot—change unless and until the national identity upon which it rests also changes. The tragic flaw of the Bush doctrine is that it draws on a model of American nationalism that has become outdated. In that sense, the tragedy is not only Bush's, but also our own.

---

[76] J. William Fulbright, *The Arrogance of Power* (New York: Random House, 1966), quoted in Cherry, *God's New Israel*, 328.

[77] See Allison and Beschel, "Can the United States Promote Democracy?"; Nau, *At Home Abroad*; Nye, *The Paradox of American Power*; Ruggie, "Third Try at World Order."

Deciding on War Against Iraq:
Institutional Failures

LOUIS FISHER

Following the swift U.S. military victory in Iraq, teams of experts conducted careful searches to discover the weapons of mass destruction that President George W. Bush offered as the principal justification for war. It was his claim that these weapons represented a direct and immediate threat. Months after the president announced victory, little evidence has been found nor is there much reason to expect anything significant to emerge. Stories began to circulate that perhaps the Bush administration had deceived allies, Congress, and the American public.

It is quite late to play the innocent, to express shock at troubling new disclosures. For over a year, the administration supplied a steady stream of unreliable statements. At no time did it make a persuasive, credible, or consistent case for war. Much of its rationale was exploded on a regular basis by the press. The campaign for war was dominated more by fear than facts, more by assertions of what might be, or could be, or used to be, than by what actually existed. Those who now felt duped had not been paying attention.

Month after month, the administration released claims that were unproven. In preparing for war in that manner, it should come as no surprise that plans for a stable, functioning Iraqi civil society seemed to be an afterthought. Having proved itself skilled in military combat, the Bush administration failed to address predictable looting and violence. After Afghanistan, it should have been obvious that a military victory must be followed quickly by a secure environment and visible reconstruction efforts. For its part, Congress seemed incapable of analyzing a presidential proposal and protecting its institutional powers. The decision to go to war cast a dark shadow over the health of U.S. political

LOUIS FISHER is senior specialist in separation of powers at the Congressional Research Service of the Library of Congress. He is the author of many books, including *Presidential War Power* and *Congressional Abdication on War and Spending*.

institutions and the celebrated system of democratic debate and checks and balances.

The dismal performances of the executive and legislative branches raise disturbing questions about the capacity and desire of the United States to function as a republican form of government. Americans are supposed to do more than salute the flag. The pledge of allegiance is to something much more fundamental. Consider the words: "I pledge allegiance to the flag of the United States of America, and to the republic for which it stands." A republic means giving power to the people through their elected representatives, trusting in informed, legislative deliberation rather than monarchical edicts, and keeping the war power in Congress instead of transferring it to the president. Fed unreliable information from the administration, democratic deliberation becomes shallow and vacuous. Lose what it means to be a republic, and the flag stands for nothing.

It is tempting for the Bush administration and its supporters to dismiss opposition to the war in Iraq as primarily leftist and antiwar, inspired by those who insist on international—not unilateral—solutions. That misses the point. After September 11, Americans were united in supporting military action against the terrorist structures in Afghanistan. If no other country had offered us support, Bush could have acted singlehandedly against al Qaeda and the Taliban with full public approval. He would have enjoyed the same public backing had he used military force against any other country or group responsible for September 11. Americans are willing to use force, and use it unilaterally, when necessary to defend the nation. Past and current opposition to the war in Iraq is of the administration's own making, nourished by statements that lacked credibility.

Patriotism is not indiscriminate flag-waving at each and every war. Citizens stand ready to sacrifice lives and fortunes for national security. At the same time, they oppose wars that cause needless deaths, including one's sons and daughters, and regard it a public duty to confront government officials who urge war without justifying it. Military force demands solid evidence that a threat is imminent and war is unavoidable. It is on that ground that the Bush administration and its allies—here and abroad—failed a fundamental democratic test.

A MUDDLED EXPLANATION

David Frum, after a little more than a year as a speechwriter in the Bush White House, offered some insights into the process of policy making at the highest levels. Frum tells us that Bush "hated repetition and redundancy."[1] Frum is convinced that if Bush had read that sentence, he would have deleted the words "and redundancy." Still, Bush never tired of repeating that a link existed between Iraq and al Qaeda, even if the evidence remained tenuous and unpersua-

[1] David Frum, *The Right Man* (New York: Random House, 2003), 48.

sive. Bush said it so often that most of the public came to believe it was true. In this area, he liked both repetition and redundancy.

One of Frum's draft speeches contained the phrase, "I've seen with my own eyes." Bush used his marking pen to add in the margin a sarcastic "DUH." Such experiences convinced Frum that Bush "insisted on strict linear logic."[2] There is much to be said for that. Bush's performance in the 2000 presidential campaign consisted of straight, simple talk, with an impressive ability to connect with an audience. Al Gore's delivery was much more convoluted, leaving listeners uncertain about the destination of his thoughts. Comparatively, Bush was a model of clarity.

Why did Bush, in advocating military action against Iraq, abandon "strict linear logic?" His speeches were filled with strained arguments and dramatic claims that could not be substantiated. Presentations were cloudy, repetitive, and lacking in credibility. It shouldn't have been difficult to make a plausible case for war and stick with it. Bush could have said: "Saddam Hussein has used chemical weapons against his own people. I don't want him in a position to use chemical agents again, possibly along with biological and nuclear weapons. Nor will I give him any potential for transferring such weapons to terrorists from other countries. I will do everything in my power to prevent another attack like September 11. To survive as a nation, we must be willing to act in advance."

Those themes appear in Bush's speeches and statements, but his rationale for war was confused by poorly reasoned statements and claims of Iraqi programs that rested on nonexistent facts. The administration seemed content to throw anything out to see if it would stick. That is the record from August 2002 to the present.

Looking at "All Options"

When the administration first began talking about war against Iraq, White House Spokesman Ari Fleischer cautioned on a number of occasions that President Bush was not rushing into war. Instead, he was described as a deliberate man who carefully studied all options. On 21 August 2002, President Bush called himself "a patient man. And when I say I'm a patient man, I mean I'm a patient man, and that we will look at all options, and we will consider all technologies available to us and diplomacy and intelligence."[3] With such statements Bush seemed to move with great care and circumspection.

A war plan, Americans were told, was not "on the President's desk."[4] At that same press conference on 21 August, Bush noted that "there is this kind of intense speculation that seems to be going on, a kind of a—I don't know how you would describe it. It's kind of a churning—." Secretary of Defense Donald

[2] Ibid.

[3] *Weekly Compilation of Presidential Documents*, 38: 1393–1394 (21 August 2002).

[4] Elizabeth Bumiller, "U.S. Must Act First to Battle Terror, Bush Tells Cadets," *New York Times*, 2 June 2002.

Rumsfeld, standing next to him, supplied the missing word: "frenzy." Bush agreed. The country was too preoccupied, he said, with military action against Iraq.

Yet, within five days, the administration switched to a frenzied mode. Vice President Dick Cheney delivered a forceful speech that offered a single option: going to war. He warned that Saddam Hussein would "fairly soon" have nuclear weapons, and that it would be useless to seek a Security Council resolution requiring Iraq to submit to weapons inspectors. Hussein's threat, Cheney said, made preemptive attack against Iraq imperative.[5] The press interpreted his speech as "ruling out anything short of an attack."[6] Newspaper editorials concluded that Cheney's speech "left little room for measures short of the destruction of Saddam Hussein's regime through preemptive military action."[7] On 6 September, two reporters for the *Washington Post* noted the abrupt transition: "this week's frenzy of attention to Iraq was entirely generated by a White House whose occupants returned from the August recess anxious and ready to push the debate to a new level."[8] What happened to the options carefully being weighed by Bush?

In that first month, the administration was not yet walking lock-step. Secretary of State Colin Powell, in a 1 September interview with the BBC, recommended that weapons inspectors should return to Iraq as a "first step" in resolving the dispute with Iraq. Ari Fleischer, asked whether Powell's statement revealed a conflict within the administration, labored to convince reporters that Cheney and Powell agreed on fundamentals: "that arms inspectors in Iraq are a means to an end, and the end is knowledge that Iraq has lived up to its promises that it made to end the Gulf War, that it has in fact disarmed, that it does not possess weapons of mass destruction."[9] However, Cheney had already announced that Iraq *did* possess weapons of mass destruction.

On 3 September, Senate Minority Leader Trent Lott (R-MS) acknowledged the disarray within the administration: "I do think that we're going to have to get a more coherent message together."[10] Asked whether he was comfortable with the White House's presentation of the case for war against Iraq, he responded gamely: "I'd like to have a couple more days before I respond to that."[11] Such frankness must have made it easier for the administration to support Lott's replacement for majority leader, Bill Frist.

---

[5] Elizabeth Bumiller and James Dao, "Cheney Says Peril of a Nuclear Iraq Justifies Attack," *New York Times*, 27 August 2002.

[6] Dana Milbank, "Cheney Says Iraqi Strike Is Justified," *Washington Post*, 27 August 2002.

[7] "Mr. Cheney on Iraq" (Editorial), *Washington Post*, 27 August 2002.

[8] Dan Balz and Dana Milbank, "Iraq Policy Shift Follows Pattern," *Washington Post*, 6 September 2002.

[9] Dana Milbank, "No Conflict on Iraq Policy, Fleischer Says," *Washington Post*, 3 September 2002.

[10] Alison Mitchell and David E. Sanger, "Bush to Put Case for Action in Iraq to Key Lawmakers," *New York Times*, 4 September 2002.

[11] Helen Dewar and Mike Allen, "Senators Wary About Action Against Iraq," *Washington Post*, 4 September 2002.

"Regime Change"

The meaning of "regime change" changed from week to week. On 4 April 2002, in an interview with a British television network, Bush said: "I made up my mind that Saddam needs to go. . . . The policy of my Government is that he goes. . . . [T]he policy of my Government is that Saddam Hussein not be in power."[12] That was vintage Bush: clear, straight talk. On 1 August, he stated that the "policy of my Government . . . is regime change—for a reason. Saddam Hussein is a man who poisons his own people, who threatens his neighbors, who develops weapons of mass destruction."[13] Without equivocation, Hussein had to go.

The commitment to regime change and offensive war changed abruptly when President Bush addressed the United Nations on 12 September. After cataloguing Saddam Hussein's noncompliance with Security Council resolutions, apparently building a case for regime change and military operations, Bush then laid down five conditions for a peaceful resolution. If Iraq wanted to avoid war, it would have to immediately and unconditionally pledge to remove or destroy all weapons of mass destruction, end all support for terrorism, cease persecution of its civilian population, release or account for all Gulf War personnel, and immediately end all illicit trade outside the oil-for-food program.[14] The underlying message: If Iraq complied with those demands, Saddam Hussein could stay in power.

On 21 October, after Congress had passed the Iraq resolution, Bush again said that Hussein could stay. He announced that if Hussein complied with every UN mandate, "that in itself will signal the regime has changed."[15] An exquisite sentence, with overtones of Bill Clinton, much like a magic trick where you ask: "Could you do that again, only this time more slowly?" Saddam Hussein could now stay in office if he changed.

Belittling Inspections

After the 12 September UN speech, offering peace to Iraq if it complied with the five demands, Iraq agreed four days later to unconditional inspections. Given Iraq's record since 1991, there was good cause to be skeptical of its promises. But the response should have been to test Iraq's sincerity by sending inspection teams there to learn on the ground whether it would give full access to buildings and presidential palaces. Instead, the administration began to make light of inspections. Pentagon spokeswoman Victoria Clarke warned that

---

[12] *Weekly Compilation of Presidential Documents*, 38: 573 (4 April 2002).

[13] Ibid., 1295.

[14] Ibid., 1532.

[15] David E. Sanger, "Bush Declares U.S. Is Using Diplomacy to Disarm Hussein," *New York Times*, 22 October 2002.

inspections would be difficult if not impossible to carry out.[16] If so, why have Bush go to the UN and place that demand on Iraq and the Security Council?

On 26 September, during a campaign speech in Houston, Texas, Bush delivered the standard litany of offenses committed by Saddam Hussein, but added, perhaps carelessly: "this is a guy that tried to kill my dad at one time."[17] The comment made some wonder whether the impulse for war reflected careful considerations of national security or was instead a "family grudge match."[18] The administration offered many reasons for war, often going beyond concerns about weapons of mass destruction. Senator Paul Sarbanes (D-MD) questioned the claims by Secretary Colin Powell that Iraq, to avoid military action, would have to comply with a number of UN resolutions, including one directed against prohibited trade. Sarbanes asked: "Are we prepared to go to war to make sure they comply with U.N. resolutions on illicit trade outside the oil for food program? Will we take military action or go to war in order to make them release or account for all Gulf War personnel whose fate is still unknown? Would we do that?"[19] No answer was forthcoming.

The administration seemed unprepared or unwilling to distinguish between fundamental reasons and less consequential considerations. All became interchangeable, forming a mass here, separating into parts there. Missing throughout this process was integrity. Senator Richard Lugar (R-IN) criticized the undifferentiated laundry list of charges against Saddam Hussein, such as brutality toward his own people. In conversations with top officials of the administration, Lugar was satisfied that they recognized that such conduct could not justify a U.S. war.[20] In public statements, however, the administration—including President Bush—treated all these charges with the same seriousness. Whatever seemed to work was tried.

Why the zigs and zags? Going to war is a serious enterprise and calls for consistency, clarity, and coherence. It is supposed to be reasoned deliberation. In an op-ed piece in the *Washington Post* on 11 October 2002, Michael Kinsley acknowledged that ambiguity can be useful in dealing with other nations. Sending mixed signals can keep an enemy off balance. Yet, Kinsley concluded: "the cloud of confusion that surrounds Bush's Iraq policy is not tactical. It's the real thing. And the dissembling is aimed at the American citizenry, not at Saddam Hussein." Kinsley said that arguments that "stumble into each other like drunks are not serious. Washington is abuzz with the 'real reason' this or that subgroup of the administration wants this war."[21] Even after the military victory in April 2003, people are still asking the same question: "Why did we go to war?"

[16] Todd A. Purdum and David Firestone, "Chief U.N. Inspector Backs U.S., Demanding Full Iraq Disclosure," *New York Times*, 5 October 2002.

[17] *Weekly Compilation of Presidential Documents*, 38: 1633 (26 September 2002).

[18] Mike Allen, "Bush's Words Can Go to the Blunt Edge of Trouble," *Washington Post*, 29 September 2002.

[19] Todd S. Purdum, "The U.S. Case Against Iraq; Counting Up the Reasons," *New York Times*, 1 October 2002.

[20] David E. Sanger and Carl Hulse, "Bush Appears to Soften Tone on Iraq Action," *New York Times*, 2 October 2002.

[21] Michael Kinsley, "War for Dummies," *Washington Post*, 11 October 2002.

Legal Authority

Initially the administration concluded that President Bush did not need authority from Congress to mount an offensive war against Iraq. The White House Counsel's office gave a broad reading to the President's power as Commander in Chief and argued that the 1991 Iraq resolution provided continuing military authority to the President, transferring the authority neatly from father to son.[22] In an article for *Legal Times*, I detailed why those arguments were forced and unconvincing.[23] The Framers made the president Commander in Chief, not a monarch.

The White House claimed that Congress, by passing the Iraq Liberation Act of 1998, had already approved U.S. military action against Iraq for violations of Security Council resolutions.[24] That argument was empty. The statute begins by itemizing a number of congressional findings about Iraq: invasion of Iraq and Kuwait, the killing of Kurds, using chemical weapons against civilians, and other offenses. It supported, as a legally nonbinding "sense of Congress," efforts to remove Saddam Hussein from power and replace him with a democratic government. The law states that none of its provisions "shall be construed to authorize or otherwise speak to the use of United States Armed Forces (except as provided in section 4(a)(2)) in carrying out this Act."[25] That section authorized up to $97 million in military supplies to Iraqi opposition groups as part of the transition to democracy in Iraq. By its explicit terms, the statute did not authorize war.

Ari Fleischer announced that Bush "intends to consult with Congress because Congress has an important role to play."[26] Yet, for Bush and his aides to merely "consult" with Congress would not meet the needs of the Constitution. No doubt policy making works better when the president consults with lawmakers, but consultation is not a substitute for receiving statutory authority to go to war. Congress is a legislative body that discharges its constitutional duties by passing statutes to authorize and define national policy. It exists to legislate and legitimate, particularly for military and financial commitments. Only congressional authorization of a war against Iraq would satisfy the Constitution.

BRINGING CONGRESS ON BOARD

For one reason or another, Bush decided in early September 2002 to seek authorization from Congress. On several Sunday talk shows broadcast on 8 September, administration officials abandoned the unilateralist rhetoric and began

---

[22] Mike Allen and Juliet Eilperin, "Bush Aides Say Iraq War Needs No Hill Vote," *Washington Post*, 26 August 2002.

[23] Louis Fisher, "The Road to Iraq," *Legal Times*, 2 September 2002, 34.

[24] "Bush Rejects Hill Limits on Resolution Allowing War," *Washington Post*, 2 October 2002.

[25] 112 Stat. 3181, §8 (1998).

[26] Ron Fournier, "White House Lawyers Give Bush OK on Iraq," *Washington Times*, 26 August 2002.

building a case for a broad coalition. Cheney, having advocated preemptive strikes against Iraq a few weeks earlier, now embraced an entirely different strategy: "We're working together to build support with the American people, with the Congress, as many have suggested we should. And we're also, as many have suggested we should, going to the United Nations."[27]

The Rush to War

Although the administration had debated going to war against Iraq ever since September 11, Congress was expected to act quickly. According to one newspaper story, White House officials "have said that their patience with Congress would not extend much past the current session."[28] The message to Congress was now: Get on board or we'll leave without you. The administration wanted Congress to pass an authorizing resolution before it adjourned for the November elections. National Security Adviser Condoleeza Rice said that President Bush wanted lawmakers to approve the resolution before leaving town, adding that Bush "thinks it's better to do this sooner rather than later."[29]

What was so urgent? Senator Robert C. Byrd (D-WV) deplored "the war fervor, the drums of war, the bugles of war, the clouds of war—this war hysteria has blown in like a hurricane."[30] What could explain the shift from a relaxed policy in August to a "frenzied" demand a month later? White House Chief of Staff Andrew Card gave an interesting reason for waiting until September to advocate military action against Iraq: "from a marketing point of view, you don't introduce new products in August."[31] Was this another careless, flippant remark, or an inadvertent disclosure of the truth?

Bush could not rely on the precedents established by his father. In 1990, after Iraq had invaded Kuwait, the administration did not ask Congress for authority before the November elections. Instead, it first went to the Security Council and requested a resolution to authorize military operations, which passed on 29 November. Only in January 1991, after lawmakers returned, did they debate and pass legislation to authorize war against Iraq.

For reasons that were never explained, Congress in 2002 had to act pell-mell. In an op-ed piece that supported the administration's strategy, former Secretary of State George Shultz argued that the "danger is immediate." Iraq's making of weapons of mass destruction "grows increasingly difficult to counter with each passing day."[32] Thoughtful deliberation was pushed to the side in fa-

[27] Mike Allen, "War Cabinet Argues for Iraq Attack," *Washington Post*, 9 September 2002.
[28] David Firestone and David E. Sanger, "Congress Now Promises to Hold Weeks of Hearings About Iraq," *New York Times*, 6 September 2002.
[29] Mike Allen, "War Cabinet Argues for Iraq Attack," *Washington Post*, 9 September 2002.
[30] *Congressional Record*, 148: S8966 (daily edition, 20 September 2002).
[31] Dana Milbank, "Democrats Question Iraq Timing," *Washington Post*, 16 September 2002.
[32] George P. Shultz, "Act Now: The Danger Is Immediate: Saddam Hussein Must Be Removed," *Washington Post*, 6 September 2002.

vor of hyperventilation. Senate Majority Leader Tom Daschle (D-SD) suggested that Bush would have an easier time getting congressional support if he first gained Security Council approval, but the administration would brook no delays.[33] Congress had to act first. There was no constitutional requirement for Congress to wait until the Security Council met and voted, but acting in the months before the November elections placed lawmakers in a subordinate position.

Disarray by Democrats

Democrats, unable to develop a counterstrategy, appeared to favor a prompt vote on the Iraq resolution to get that issue off the table. It was reported that Senator Daschle hoped to expedite action on the Iraq resolution "to focus on his party's core message highlighting economic distress before the November midterm elections."[34] Senator John Edwards (D-NC) counseled quick action: "In a short period of time, Congress will have dealt with Iraq and we'll be on to other issues."[35]

This approach had multiple drawbacks, both moral and practical. Could Democrats credibly authorize a war merely to draw attention to their domestic agenda? That seems unconscionable. As noted by Senator Mark Dayton (D-MN), trying to gain "political advantage in a midterm election is a shameful reason to hurry decisions of this magnitude."[36] Second, voting on the Iraq resolution could never erase the White House's advantage in controlling the headlines, if not through the Iraq resolution then through ongoing, cliffhanging negotiations with the UN Security Council. Third, although these Democrats said they wanted to put the issue of war against Iraq behind them, it would always be in front.

Legislative action before the November elections invited partisan exploitation of the war issue. Several Republican nominees in congressional contests made a political weapon out of Iraq, comparing their "strong stand" on Iraq to "weak" positions by Democratic campaigners. Some of the key races in the nation appeared to turn on what candidates were saying about Iraq.[37] Because of the steady focus on the war, Democrats were unable to redirect the political agenda to corporate crime, the state of the stock market, and the struggling economy.[38]

[33] Bradley Graham, "Cheney, Tenet Brief Leaders of Hill on Iraq," *Washington Post*, 6 September 2002.

[34] David Firestone, "Liberals Object to Bush Policy on Iraq Attack," *New York Times*, 28 September 2002.

[35] Dana Milbank, "In President's Speeches, Iraq Dominates, Economy Fades," *Washington Post*, 25 September 2002.

[36] Mark Drayton, "Go Slow on Iraq," *Washington Post*, 28 September 2002.

[37] Jim VandeHei, "GOP Nominees Make Iraq a Political Weapon," *Washington Post*, 18 September 2002.

[38] Dana Milbank, "Democrats Question Iraq Timing," *Washington Post*, 16 September 2002.

The partisan flavor intensified when President Bush, in a speech in Trenton, New Jersey on 23 September, said that the Democratic Senate "is more interested in special interests in Washington and not interested in the security of the American people."[39] That was a stunning charge, invoking national security to brand Democrats as corrupt, if not traitorous. Recognizing that it might have stepped over the line, the administration quickly explained that Bush's remark was delivered in the context of the legislative delay on the Department of Homeland Security, but Democrats faulted Bush for using the war as leverage in the House and Senate races.[40]

After the Trenton speech, Democrats could have announced that Bush had so politicized and poisoned the debate on the Iraq resolution that it could not be considered with the care and seriousness it deserved. Daschle, in particular, could have used his position as Senate Majority Leader to delay a vote until after the elections. Perhaps he lacked the votes in the Senate Democratic Caucus to prevail. If he failed to rally his troops, he would have highlighted his weakness as a leader and advertised the divisions within his own ranks. In the end, however, as evidenced by the vote on the Iraq resolution, Senate Democrats were divided anyway. Several Senate Democrats criticized Daschle for working too closely with Bush on the Iraq resolution and getting nothing in return. Bush's comments on 23 September, they said, made it look like Daschle was being "played for a fool."[41]

UNSUBSTANTIATED EXECUTIVE CLAIMS

Bush and other top officials invited members of Congress to sessions where they would receive confidential information about the threat from Iraq, but the lawmakers said they heard little that was new. After one of the briefings, Senator Bob Graham (D-FL) remarked: "I did not receive any new information."[42] House Minority Whip Nancy Pelosi (D-CA), who also served as ranking Democrat on the House Intelligence Committee, announced that she knew of "no information that the threat is so imminent from Iraq" that Congress could not wait until January to vote on an authorizing resolution.[43] None of the charges against Iraq in Bush's address to the UN was new. After a "top secret" briefing by Defense Secretary Rumsfeld in a secure room in the Capitol, Senator John McCain (R-AZ) soon rose and walked out, saying, "It was a joke."[44]

[39] *Weekly Compilation of Presidential Documents*, 38: 1598 (23 September 2002).

[40] Carl Hulse and Todd S. Purdum, "Daschle Defends Democrats' Stand on Security of U.S.," *New York Times*, 26 September 2002.

[41] Jim VandeHei, "Daschle Angered by Bush Statement," *Washington Post*, 26 September 2002.

[42] Mike Allen and Karen DeYoung, "Bush to Seek Hill Approval on Iraq War," *Washington Post*, 5 September 2002.

[43] Jim VandeHei and Juliet Eilperin, "Democrats Unconvinced on Iraq War," *Washington Post*, 11 September 2002.

[44] Jim VandeHei, "Iraq Briefings: Don't Ask, Don't Tell," *Washington Post*, 15 September 2002.

A Link Between Iraq and al Qaeda?

The administration tried repeatedly to establish a connection between Iraq and al Qaeda, but the reports could never be substantiated. On 25 September, Bush claimed that Saddam Hussein and al Qaeda "work in concert."[45] On the following day, he claimed that the Iraqi regime "has longstanding and continuing ties to terrorist organizations, and there are [al Qaeda] terrorists inside Iraq."[46] Ari Fleischer tried to play down Bush's remark, saying he was talking about what he feared *could* occur.[47] Why weren't Bush and his press secretary able to speak from the same page? Did the ties and links exist, as Bush claimed, or were they merely future possibilities?

Senator Joseph Biden (D-DE), who attended a classified briefing that talked about the relationship between Iraq and al Qaeda, said that credible evidence had not been presented.[48] There was some evidence of possible al Qaeda activity in the northeastern part of Iraq—the community of Ansar al-Islam—but that was Kurdish territory made semiautonomous because of American and British flights over the no-fly zones. Saddam Hussein wasn't in a position to do anything about Ansar. Besides, members of al Qaeda are present in some sixty countries. Presence alone does not justify military force.

Allies in Europe, active in investigating al Qaeda and radical Islamic cells, could find no evidence of links between Iraq and al Qaeda. Interviews with top investigative magistrates, prosecutors, police, and intelligence officials could uncover no information to support the claims by the Bush administration. Investigative officials in Spain, France, and Germany, after dismissing a connection between Iraq and al Qaeda, worried that a war against Iraq would increase the terrorist threat rather than diminish it.[49]

On 27 September, Secretary Rumsfeld announced that the administration had "bulletproof" evidence of Iraq's links to al Qaeda. He said that declassified intelligence reports, showing the presence of senior members of al Qaeda in Baghdad in "recent periods," were "factual" and "exactly accurate." However, when reporters sought to substantiate his claim, officials offered no details to back up the assertions. Having claimed bulletproof support, Rumsfeld admitted that the information was "not beyond a reasonable doubt." That's quite a definition of bulletproof. Senator Chuck Hagel (R-NE) told Secretary of State Powell: "To say, 'Yes, I know there is evidence there, but I don't want to tell you any more about it,' that does not encourage any of us. Nor does it give the American public a heck of a lot of faith that, in fact, what anyone is saying is true."[50]

[45] *Weekly Compilation of Presidential Documents*, 38: 1619 (25 September 2002).

[46] Ibid., 1625.

[47] Mike Allen, "Bush Asserts That Al Qaeda Has Links to Iraq's Hussein," *Washington Post*, 26 September 2002.

[48] Karen De Young, "Unwanted Debate on Iraq-Al Qaeda Links Revived," *Washington Post*, 27 September 2002.

[49] Sebastian Rotella, "Allies Find No Links Between Iraq, Al Qaeda," *Los Angeles Times*, 4 November 2002.

[50] Eric Schmitt, "Rumsfeld Says U.S. Has 'Bulletproof' Evidence of Iraq's Links to Al Qaeda," *New York Times*, 28 September 2002.

In his speech to the nation on 7 October, on the eve of the congressional vote, President Bush said that Iraq "has trained Al Qaida members in bomb-making and poisons and deadly gases."[51] Intelligence officials, however, played down the reliability of those reports.[52] After the vote, the administration promoted a story about Mohamed Atta, the leader of the September 11 attacks, meeting with an Iraqi intelligence officer in Prague in April 2001. Yet, this assertion was also without foundation: Czech President Vaclav Havel and the Czech intelligence service said that there was no evidence that the meeting ever took place. Central Intelligence Agency (CIA) Director George Tenet told Congress that his agency had no information that could confirm the meeting.[53]

On 11 February 2003, Secretary Powell cited an audiotape believed to be of Osama bin Laden as evidence that he was "in partnership with Iraq."[54] The tape contained no such evidence. It specifically criticized "pagan regimes" and the "apostasy" practiced by socialist governments like Iraq. In a military contest between the United States and Iraq, the tape certainly supported Iraq, but that is hardly evidence of partnership. As much as al Qaeda detests Iraq, it detests the United States more. In an op-ed for the *Washington Post* on 13 February, Richard Cohen wondered why Powell had to "gild the lily. The case for war is a good one." He reminded Powell that in the war against Vietnam, the U.S. government's exaggerations and decisions eventually "lost the confidence of the people." The Bush administration, Cohen said, had a habit of tickling the facts and expunging caveats, doubts, and conditional clauses from the record.[55] An editorial in the *New York Times* warned that there was "no need for the administration to jeopardize its own credibility with unproved claims about an alliance between Iraq and Al Qaeda."[56]

Nevertheless, on 1 May 2003, while standing on the deck of the *Abraham Lincoln* carrier to announce military victory over Iraq, Bush announced: "We've removed an ally of Al Qaida."[57] With repetition and redundancy, an unsubstantiated claim has an excellent chance of sticking.

Weapons of Mass Destruction

The administration kept a steady drumbeat for war, releasing various accounts to demonstrate why Iraq was an imminent threat. On 7 September, President

[51] *Weekly Compilation of Presidential Documents*, 38: 1717 (7 October 2002).

[52] Karen De Young, "Bush Cites Urgent Iraqi Threat," *Washington Post*, 8 October 2002.

[53] James Risen, "Prague Discounts An Iraqi Meeting," *New York Times*, 21 October 2002; James Risen, "How Politics and Rivalries Fed Suspicions of a Meeting," *New York Times*, 21 October 2002; Peter S. Green, "Havel Denies Telephoning U.S. on Iraq Meeting," *New York Times*, 23 October 2002.

[54] Dan Eggen and Susan Schmidt, "Bin Laden Calls Iraqis to Arms," *Washington Post*, 12 February 2003.

[55] Richard Cohen, "Powellian Propaganda?" *Washington Post*, 13 February 2003.

[56] "Elusive Qaeda Connections" (Editorial), *New York Times*, 14 February 2003.

[57] *Weekly Compilation of Presidential Documents*, 39: 517 (1 May 2003).

Bush cited a report by the International Atomic Energy Agency (IAEA) that the Iraqis were "6 months away from developing a weapon. I don't know what more evidence we need."[58] More evidence was indeed needed because the report Bush referred to didn't exist.[59] It would seem embarrassing for a president to be that far from the truth. Shouldn't some White House aide get kicked out the door for making Bush look ill-informed? There were no such embarrassments and no such casualties.

In his 7 October speech, President Bush claimed that satellite photographs "reveal that Iraq is rebuilding facilities at sites that have been part of his nuclear program in the past."[60] The administration decided to declassify two before-and-after photos of the Al Furat manufacturing facility.[61] This "declassification" was interesting: the administration regularly complained about leaks of sensitive documents to the media, but if classified information seemed to bolster the administration's case, it quickly became public. Five busloads of 200 reporters descended on the site and received a ninety-minute tour by Iraqi generals. The reporters found few clues to indicate a weapons program.[62]

True, a quick visit by reporters meant little. They had neither time nor expertise to explore all the buildings and examine them carefully. But it is equally true that satellite photos are unable to penetrate buildings and analyze their interiors. Only a ground search by experienced inspectors could do that. When the UN inspection teams reached Iraq in November, they could find no evidence of a nuclear weapons program at Al Furat or anywhere else in Iraq.[63]

The Bush administration claimed that Iraq had bought aluminum tubes and planned to use them to enrich uranium to produce nuclear weapons. Specialists from UN inspection teams concluded that the specifications of the tubes were consistent with tubes used for rockets. The tubes could have been modified to serve as centrifuges for enriching uranium, but the modifications would have had to be substantial. Moreover, there was no evidence that Iraq had purchased materials needed for centrifuges, such as motors, metal caps, and special magnets.[64]

On 5 February 2003, in his statement to the UN Security Council, Secretary Powell laid out his case for going to war against Iraq, citing what he considered to be evidence of weapons of mass destruction. With little evidence of a nuclear weapons program, he emphasized that Iraq had mobile production facilities

---

[58] Ibid., 38: 1518.

[59] Dana Milbank, "For Bush, Facts Are Malleable," *Washington Post*, 22 October 2002.

[60] *Weekly Compilation of Presidential Documents*, 38: 1718 (7 October 2002).

[61] "Al Furat Manufacturing Facility, Iraq," *Washington Post*, 8 October 2002.

[62] John Burns, "Iraq Tour of Suspected Sites Gives Few Clues on Weapons," *New York Times*, 13 October 2002.

[63] "Nuclear Inspection Chief Reports Finding No New Weapons," *New York Times*, 28 January 2003.

[64] Michael R. Gordon, "Agency Challenges Evidence Against Iraq Cited by Bush," *New York Times*, 10 January 2003; Joby Warrick, "U.S. Claim on Iraqi Nuclear Program Is Called Into Question," *Washington Post*, 24 January 2003.

"used to make biological agents."[65] In a matter of months, he said, these mobile facilities "can produce a quantity of biological poison equal to the entire amount that Iraq claimed to have produced in the years prior to the Gulf War."[66] After hostilities were over, U.S. forces discovered two mobile labs in Iraq, but it is uncertain what they had been used for.[67] A 28 May 2003 report by the intelligence community found nothing definitive.

Plagiarism and Fabrication

The British government released a nineteen-page report entitled "Iraq: Its Infrastructure of Concealment, Deception and Intimidation," posting it on No. 10 Downing Street's web site. It appeared to be a thorough analysis prepared by the British intelligence agencies. In fact, the report had its own problems with concealment and deception. In February 2003, the British government admitted that much of the report had been lifted from magazines and academic journals, some of it verbatim. Spelling and punctuation errors in the originals were faithfully reproduced in the government's report. Although the government claimed that the report contained "up-to-date details of Iraq's network of intelligence and security," much of it was based on an article by a postgraduate student who focused on events a dozen years old, in the 1990–1991 period.[68] After defending the report, the British government in June 2003 conceded that including the student's article was "regrettable."[69]

In his State of the Union message on 28 January 2003, President Bush said that the British government "has learned that Saddam Hussein recently sought significant quantities of uranium from Africa."[70] Two points deserve mention. First, "sought" is not the same as "bought." More seriously, the British government relied on evidence that its intelligence agencies thought unreliable. The documents turned out to be not only unreliable but actually a fabrication. The forged documents contained crude errors that undermined their credibility.[71] As one U.S. official admitted: "We fell for it."[72] The significant point is not an

[65] Michael Dobbs, "Powell Lays Out Case Against Iraq," *Washington Post*, 6 February 2003.

[66] Ibid.

[67] Walter Pincus and Michael Dobbs, "Suspected Bioweapon Mobile Lab Recovered," *Washington Post*, 7 May 2003; "A Suspected Weapons Lab Is Found in Northern Iraq," *New York Times*, 10 May 2003; Judith Miller, "Trailer is a Mobile Lab Capable of Turning Out Bioweapons, a Team Says," *New York Times*, 11 May 2003; Judith Miller and William J. Broad, "U.S. Analysts Link Iraq Labs to Germ Arms," *New York Times*, 21 May 2003.

[68] Sarah Lyall, "Britain Admits That Much of Its Report on Iraq Came From Magazines," *New York Times*, 8 February 2003; Glenn Frankel, "Blair Acknowledges Flaws in Iraq Dossier," *Washington Post*, 8 February 2003.

[69] Jane Wardell, "Blair Aide Concedes Error on Iraq Dossier," *Washington Post*, 26 June 2003.

[70] *Weekly Compilation of Presidential Documents*, 39: 115 (28 January 2003).

[71] Joby Warrick, "Some Evidence on Iraq Called Fake," *Washington Post*, 8 March 2003.

[72] Ibid.

unfortunate mistake but rather the willingness of the administration to exploit and go public with any information no matter how tenuous and suspect.

CONGRESS FOLDS

There was little doubt that President Bush would gain approval for military action in the Republican House. The question was whether the vote would divide along party lines. Some of the partisan issue blurred when House Minority Leader Dick Gephardt (D-MO) broke ranks with many in his party and announced support for a slightly redrafted resolution. He said, "We had to go through this, putting politics aside, so we have a chance to get a consensus that will lead the country in the right direction."[73] Of course, politics could not be put aside. Even when leaders of the two parties and the two branches appealed for nonpartisan or bipartisan conduct, their comments were generally viewed as calculated to have some partisan benefit. Gephardt's interest in running for the presidency was well known, as was Daschle's and several other members of Congress. Democratic Senators John Edwards and Joseph Lieberman, both interested in a 2004 bid for the presidency, endorsed the Iraq resolution. Senator John Kerry, about to announce his bid for the presidency, initially expressed doubts about the resolution but later voted for it.[74] One Democratic lawmaker concluded that Gephardt, by supporting Bush, had "inoculated Democrats against the charge that they are antiwar and obstructionist."[75]

Why were Democrats so anxious about being seen as antiwar? There was no evidence that the public in any broad sense supported immediate war against Iraq. A *New York Times* poll published on 7 October 2002 indicated that 69 percent of Americans believed that Bush should be paying more attention to the economy. Although support was high for military action (with 67 percent approving U.S. military action against Iraq with the goal of removing Hussein from power), when it was asked, "Should the U.S. take military action against Iraq fairly soon or wait and give the U.N. more time to get weapons inspectors into Iraq?" 63 percent preferred to wait. To the question "Is Congress asking enough questions about President Bush's policy toward Iraq?" only 20 percent said too many, while 51 percent said not enough. Asked whether Bush was more interested in removing Hussein than weapons of mass destruction, 53 percent said Hussein and only 29 percent said weapons.[76]

[73] "For Gephardt, Risks and a Crucial Role," *Washington Post*, 3 October 2002.
[74] Dan Balz and Jim VandeHei, "Democratic Hopefuls Back Bush on Iraq," *Washington Post*, 14 September 2002.
[75] David E. Rosenbaum, "United Voice on Iraq Eludes Majority Leader," *New York Times*, 4 October 2002.
[76] Adam Nagourney and Janet Elder, "Public Says Bush Needs to Pay Heed to Weak Economy," *New York Times*, 7 October 2002.

A *Washington Post* story on 8 October described the public's enthusiasm for war against Iraq as "tepid and declining."[77] Americans gave Bush the benefit of the doubt but were not convinced by his arguments. Because of those doubts, "support could fade if the conflict in Iraq becomes bloody and extended."[78] These public attitudes led the *New York Times* to wonder: "Given the cautionary mood of the country, it is puzzling that most members of Congress seem fearful of challenging the hawkish approach to Iraq."[79]

The vote on the Iraq resolution could never be anything other than a political decision, probably the most important congressional vote of the year. Inescapably and legitimately it called for a political judgment. Lawmakers would be voting on whether to commit as much as $100 billion or $200 billion to a war stretching over a period of years. Their actions would stabilize or destabilize the Middle East, strengthen or weaken the war against terrorism, enhance or debase the nation's prestige. Politics would always be present, as would partisan calculations and strategy.

When the House International Relations Committee reported the resolution, it divided thirty-one to eleven. Democrats on the committee split ten to nine in favoring it. Two Republicans, Jim Leach of Iowa and Ron Paul of Texas, opposed it. The forty-seven-page committee report consists of only five pages of text analyzing the resolution.[80] President Bush's speech to the UN occupies another five pages. Twenty-one pages are devoted to an administration document called "A Decade of Deception and Defiance: Saddam Hussein's Defiance of the United Nations" (12 September 2002). It was prepared as a background paper for Bush's speech to the UN. Some of it describes what was supposedly the administration's main concern: the development of weapons of mass destruction. Other sections focused on conditions in Iraq that, while deplorable, could hardly justify war: Iraq's refusal to allow visits by human rights monitors; the expulsion of UN humanitarian relief workers; violence against women; child labor and forced labor; the lack of freedom of speech and press; and refusal to return to Kuwait state archives and museum pieces.

A key section of the report reads: "The Committee hopes that the use of military force can be avoided. It believes, however, that providing the President with the authority he needs to use force is the best way to avoid its use. A signal of our Nation's seriousness of purpose and its willingness to use force may yet persuade Iraq to meet its international obligations, and is the best way to persuade members of the Security Council and others in the international community to join us in bringing pressure on Iraq or, if required, in using armed force against it."[81] Thus, the legislation would decide neither for nor against war. That judgment, which the Constitution places in Congress, would now be left in the hands of the President.

[77] Dana Milbank, "With Congress Aboard, Bush Targets a Doubtful Public," *Washington Post*, 8 October 2002.

[78] Ibid.

[79] "A Nation Wary of War" (Editorial), *New York Times*, 8 October 2002.

[80] H. Rept. No. 107–721, 107th Cong., 2d Sess. (2002).

[81] Ibid., 4–5.

The Tonkin Gulf Precedent

Acting as it did, the House International Relations Committee both authorized military force and hoped it would not be necessary. That kind of straddling reminds one of the Tonkin Gulf resolution of 1964, which Congress passed almost unanimously, with only two dissenting votes in the Senate. Passage of this resolution was not an endorsement of war either. Instead, members of Congress thought that by offering broad, bipartisan support to President Lyndon B. Johnson, war with North Vietnam could be avoided. Like the Iraq resolution, the legislative vote in 1964 was neither for war nor against it.

During Senate debate on the Tonkin Gulf resolution, Gaylord Nelson reviewed the statements by his colleagues and noticed that "every Senator who spoke had his own personal interpretation of what the joint resolution means." He found that "there is no agreement in the Senate on what the joint resolution means."[82] To clarify the intent of the resolution, he offered an amendment to state that President Johnson would seek "no extension of the present military conflict" and that "we should continue to attempt to avoid a direct military involvement in the southeast Asian conflict." Senator J. William Fulbright, floor manager of the resolution, refused to accept the amendment because it would force the two Houses to go to conference to resolve the differences between the versions passed by each chamber. Fulbright didn't want Congress taking another week or so to clarify the resolution. Nevertheless, he felt satisfied that Nelson's amendment expressed "fairly accurately what the President has said would be our policy, and what I stated my understanding was as to our policy." Fulbright believed that the resolution "is calculated to prevent the spread of the war, rather than to spread it."[83] What counts, however, is not what lawmakers say during debate but what the president does with broad statutory authority. The military expansion that began in February 1965 led to the deaths of 58,000 Americans and several million in Southeast Asia.

Congressional debate in 2002 contains some similarities and differences to the Tonkin Gulf resolution. The House passed the Iraq resolution, 296–133, compared to the unanimous House vote in 1964. Yet, the resolutions are virtually identical in transferring to the president the sole decision to go to war and determine its scope and duration. In each case, lawmakers chose to trust in the president, not in themselves. Instead of acting as the people's representatives and preserving the republican form of government, they gave the president unchecked power.

Senate Action

After the House vote in 2002, Senate Majority Leader Daschle announced his support for the resolution. Although he suggested that senators might "go back and tie down the language a little bit more if we can," he insisted that "we have

[82] *Congressional Record*, 110: 18458 (1964).
[83] Ibid., 18462.

got to support this effort. We have got to do it in an enthusiastic and bipartisan way."[84] Why the need for enthusiasm and bipartisanship? Why wasn't the argument on the merits? Placing trust in the president or calling for bipartisanship are not proper substitutes for analyzing the need for military force against another country. Senator Kerry, who had earlier raised substantive arguments against going to war against Iraq, now accepted presidential superiority over Congress: "We are affirming a president's right and responsibility to keep the American people safe, and the president must take that grant of responsibility seriously."[85] With that kind of reading of constitutional authority, Congress had little role other than to offer words of encouragement and support to a president who already seemed to possess all the constitutional authority he needed to act singlehandedly. Far from being a coequal branch, Congress was distinctly junior varsity. It no longer functioned as an authorizing body. Its task was simply to endorse what the president had already decided.

A similar position appears in Daschle's statement that "it is important for America to speak with one voice at this critical moment."[86] Comparable statements were made by senators in 1964, when they endorsed the Tonkin Gulf resolution. Why should legislators consider agreement with the president more important than conscientious and individual allegiance to their constitutional duties? The Framers counted on collective judgment, the deliberative process, and checks and balances. All of that is lost when lawmakers decide to join with the president and subordinate their positions to his. A member of Congress takes an oath to support and defend the Constitution, not the president. The experience with the Tonkin Gulf resolution demonstrated that unity and lockstep decision making do not assure wise policy.

This issue played out in other contexts. During debate on the Department of Homeland Security, Senator Daschle said he intended "to give the President the benefit of the doubt." His Democratic colleague, Robert Byrd, took sharp exception: "I will not give the benefit of the doubt to the President. I will give the benefit of the doubt to the Constitution."[87] Byrd watched the congressional debate drift from an initial willingness of lawmakers to analyze issues and weigh the merits to wholesale legislative abdication to the President. To Byrd, the fundamental question of why the United States should go to war was replaced by "the mechanics of how best to wordsmith the President's use-of-force resolution in order to give him virtually unchecked authority to commit the nation's military to an unprovoked attack on a sovereign nation." Having followed the arguments presented by Bush and after questioning the top executive branch

---

[84] John H. Cushman, Jr., "Daschle Predicts Broad Support for Military Action Against Iraq," *New York Times*, 7 October 2002.

[85] Helen Dewar and Juliet Eilperin, "Iraq Resolution Passes Test, Gains Support," *Washington Post*, 10 October 2002.

[86] Jim VandeHei and Juliet Eilperin, "House Passes Iraq War Resolution," *Washington Post*, 11 October 2002.

[87] *Congressional Record*: 148; S9187, S9188 (daily edition, 25 September 2002).

officials responsible for crafting the resolution, Byrd did not find the threat from Iraq "so great that we must be stampeded to provide such authority to this president just weeks before an election."[88]

Republican Senators Lugar, Hagel, and Arlen Specter (PA), after raising serious questions about the Iraq resolution, decided by 7 October to support it.[89] On 10 October, the Senate voted seventy-seven to twenty-three for the resolution. The only Republican voting against the resolution was Lincoln Chafee of Rhode Island. An Independent, James Jeffords of Vermont, also voted No.

A MILITARY, NOT A POLITICAL, VICTORY

The United States triumphed militarily over Iraq in less than a month, but with deep, long-term costs to constitutional government. The euphoria and celebrations at home were strange. No one doubted that U.S. forces would prevail over an Iraq that lacked an air force and had few ground troops willing to fight. It is understandable that great pride would be placed in the American men and women who put their lives at stake in Iraq and accomplished their military mission. But the issue was never whether the United States would win the war. It was whether war was necessary and what would happen in Iraq and the region after military operations had ceased.

Congress failed to discharge its constitutional duties when it passed the Iraq resolution. Instead of making a decision about whether to go to war and spend billions for a multiyear commitment, it transferred those legislative judgments to the President. Legislators washed their hands of the key decisions to go to war and for how long. Congress should not have voted on the resolution before the election, which colored the votes and the political calculations. Voting under that pressure benefited the President.

It would have been better for Congress as an institution and for the country as a whole to first wait for President Bush to request the Security Council to authorize inspections in Iraq. Depending on what the Security Council did or did not do, and on what Iraq agreed or did not agree to do, Congress could then have debated whether to authorize war. Having learned what the Security Council and Iraq actually did, rather than speculate on what they might do, Congress would have been in the position to make an informed choice. Instead, it voted under partisan pressures, with inadequate information, and thereby abdicated its constitutional duties to the President. Congress suffered a loss, as did popular control and the democratic process.

In the end, Congress had two models to choose from. It could have acted after the election, as it did in 1990–1991, or it could have acted in the middle of an election, as in 1964. The first would have maintained the integrity of the legislative institution by minimizing partisan tactics and scheduling legislative

---

[88] Robert C. Byrd, "Congress Must Resist the Rush to War," *New York Times*, 10 October 2002.
[89] Helen Dewar, "Armey, Lugar Reverse Stand on Resolution," *Washington Post*, 8 October 2002.

debate after the Security Council voted. The second would have placed Congress in a position of voting hurriedly without the information it needed and with information it did receive (the two "attacks" in Tonkin Gulf) of dubious quality. In 2002, Congress picked the Tonkin Gulf model. There may be times when Congress might have to authorize war in the middle of an election. The year 2002 wasn't one.

DOCTORING INTELLIGENCE REPORTS

The failure thus far to find weapons of mass destruction in Iraq has raised a serious question: Did the Bush administration deliberately misread or misrepresent intelligence reports to exaggerate the nature of the Iraqi threat? This charge assumes that reports prepared by the intelligence agencies are professionally crafted when presented to administration officials and that distortions begin at that point. Yet, the reports from the intelligence agencies might already have been manipulated.

Consider the CIA report of October 2002, "Iraq's Weapons of Mass Destruction Programs." It was released at a critical time when Congress was considering whether to authorize military operations. On 2 October, President Bush announced a bipartisan agreement on a joint resolution to authorize armed force against Iraq. He stated that Iraq "has stockpiled biological and chemical weapons."[90] In his address to the nation on 7 October, from Cincinnati, he said that Iraq "possesses and produces chemical and biological weapons."[91]

These remarks reflected an analysis prepared by the Central Intelligence Agency. The unclassified version, available on the CIA's web site (www.cia.gov), states unequivocally: "Baghdad has chemical and biological weapons. . . ." The impact of any report depends on its opening line. Readers are apt to skim the rest. Yet, the detailed analytical section that follows contradicts the flat assertion, providing statements that are much more cautious and qualified:

- "Iraq has the ability to produce chemical warfare (CW) agents within its chemical industry. . . ."
- "Iraq probably has concealed precursors, production equipment, documentation, and other items necessary for continuing its CW effort."
- "Baghdad continues to rebuild and expand dual-use infrastructure that it could divert quickly to CW production."
- "Iraq has the capability to convert quickly legitimate vaccine and biopesticide plants to biological warfare (BW) production and already may have done so."

None of the statements in the analytical section support the striking claim in the first paragraph of the CIA report and in Bush's statements to the nation.

---

[90] *Weekly Compilation of Presidential Documents*, 38: 1670 (2 October 2002).
[91] Ibid., 1716.

The same gap between the front material and the internal analysis appears in a 28 May 2003 publication on mobile labs, jointly authored by the CIA and the Defense Intelligence Agency (DIA). Entitled "Iraqi Mobile Biological Warfare Agent Production Plans," the analysis can be found on CIA's web site. The first sentence asserts: "Coalition forces have uncovered the strongest evidence to date that Iraq was hiding a biological warfare program." The analysis within the report offers no evidence for that claim.

The purpose of the mobile labs remains under study. The CIA/DIA report concedes that some of the features of the labs "are consistent with both bioproduction [of BW agents] and hydrogen production" for artillery weather balloons. Clearly, much more analysis is necessary. What is evident now is that intelligence analysts prepared a report, complete with caveats and qualifications, and someone came along and put a screamer up front. Was the classified report more professional and nuanced? When it was decided to put an unclassified version on the web site, did someone think it important—with public consumption in mind—to select a more dramatic, eye-catching lead?

On 18 June 2003, Deputy Defense Secretary Paul Wolfowitz appeared before the House Armed Services Committee, where Rep. Gene Taylor (D-MS) asked whether the intelligence about the threat from Iraq's weapons was wrong. Taylor said he voted for the Iraq resolution because of the administration's warning that Iraq had weapons of mass destruction. He now told Wolfowitz: "A person is only as good as his word. This nation is only as good as its word. And if that's the reason why we did it—and I voted for it—then we need some clarification here." Wolfowitz replied: "If there's a problem with intelligence . . . it doesn't mean that anybody misled anybody. It means that intelligence is an art and not a science."[92]

That modest tone was absent during the debate on the Iraq resolution. The administration treated intelligence as a science, yielding certitude, not doubt. The position was not merely that Iraq had weapons of mass destruction in the past. Bush, Cheney, Rumsfeld, and other top administration officials insisted that Iraq currently had that capability, particularly chemical and biological weapons. According to their analysis, the threat was imminent, not in the future.

Congress should not allow any president to dictate the timing of a vote on war. Democracy depends on laws, but much more on trust. Constitutions and statutes are necessarily general in scope, placing a premium on judgment and discretion. Without confidence in what public officials say and do, laws are easily twisted to satisfy private ends. Leaders who claim to act in the national interest may, instead, pursue personal or partisan agendas. The opportunity for harm is especially great in the field of national security. Approximately $40 billion in secret funds are spent by the U.S. intelligence community. Its mission is to supply reliable analysis for policy makers, both executive and legislative,

[92] Walter Pincus and Dana Priest, "Lawmakers Begin Iraq Intelligence Hearings," *Washington Post*, 19 June 2003.

including whatever caveats and qualifications are appropriate. When those reports are doctored, either before they leave the agency or afterwards, government is likely to blunder. In an age of terrorism, especially after September 11, the public needs full trust in the integrity of its elected leaders and in the intelligence agencies that guide crucial decisions. For all the sophistication of the U.S. political and economic system, if trust is absent, so is popular control. The United States cannot install democracy abroad if it lacks it at home.

CONCLUSIONS

U.S. political institutions failed in their constitutional duties when they authorized war against Iraq. The Bush administration never presented sufficient and credible information to justify statutory action in October 2002 and military operations in March 2003. Statements by executive officials were regularly punctured by press disclosures. The call to war demands a careful marshaling of evidence to build public confidence. The record of the Bush administration on warmaking created distrust of the spoken word and the declassified document. For its part, Congress failed to insist on reliable arguments and evidence before passing the Iraq resolution. There was no need for Congress to act when it did. Instead of passing legislation to authorize war, members of Congress agreed to compromise language that left the decisive judgment with the President. Placing the power to initiate war in the hands of one person was precisely what the Framers hoped to avoid when they drafted the Constitution.

Rather than proceed with deliberation and care, the two branches rushed to war on a claim of imminent threat that lacked credibility. The Bush administration never made a convincing case why the delay of a few months would injure or jeopardize national security. By acting hastily and without just cause, the administration did damage to what President Bush highlighted in his 12 September 2002 address: the relevance of the United Nations. Unwilling to wait an extra month or two to allow UN inspectors to continue their work, the Bush administration missed an opportunity to attract the support of other nations. In place of a multinational effort to remove Saddam Hussein and rebuild Iraq, the United States finds itself six months after the invasion almost solely responsible for an occupation that has uncertain goals, heavy costs, and open-ended duration.

Misperceptions, the Media,
and the Iraq War

STEVEN KULL
CLAY RAMSAY
EVAN LEWIS

The Iraq war and its aftermath have raised compelling questions about the capacity of the executive branch to elicit public consent for the use of military force and about the role the media plays in this process. From the outset, the Bush administration was faced with unique challenges in its effort to legitimate its decision to go to war. Because the war was not prompted by an overt act against the United States or its interests, and was not approved by the UN Security Council, the Bush administration argued that the war was necessary on the basis of a potential threat. Because the evidence for this threat was not fully manifest, the Bush administration led the public to believe that Iraq was developing weapons of mass destruction (WMD) and providing substantial support to the al Qaeda terrorist group. The challenge for the administration was later intensified when the United States occupied Iraq and was unable to find the expected corroborating evidence.

From the outset the public was sympathetic to the idea of removing Saddam Hussein, though only a small minority of Americans was ready to go to war with Iraq without UN Security Council approval.[1] The majority was inclined to believe that Iraq had a WMD program and was supporting al Qaeda. However,

---

[1] Asked in a Chicago Council on Foreign Relations poll in June 2002 about their position on invading Iraq, 65 percent said the United States "should only invade Iraq with UN approval and the support of its allies"; 20 percent said "the US should invade Iraq even if we have to go it alone"; and 13 percent said "the US should not invade Iraq."

STEVEN KULL is the director of the Program on International Policy Attitudes (PIPA), a joint program of the Center on Policy Attitudes and the Center for International and Security Studies at Maryland, and a faculty member at the School of Public Affairs, University of Maryland.
CLAY RAMSAY is the director of research at PIPA.
EVAN LEWIS is a research associate at PIPA.

most were not persuaded that the case was strong enough to justify taking action unilaterally. The majority preferred to continue looking for more decisive evidence through the UN inspection process and to continue seeking the support of the UN Security Council.[2]

Nevertheless, when the President decided to go to war, the majority of the public expressed support. More significantly, when the United States failed to find the expected evidence that would corroborate the administration's assumptions that prompted the war, the majority continued to support the decision to go to war.[3]

This polling data raises the question of why the public has been so accommodating. Did they simply change their views about the war despite their earlier reservations? Or did they in some way come to have certain false beliefs or misperceptions that would make going to war appear more legitimate, consistent with pre-existing beliefs?

A variety of possible misperceptions could justify going to war with Iraq. If Americans believed that the United States had found WMD in Iraq or had found evidence that Iraq was providing support to al Qaeda, then they may have seen the war as justified as an act of self-defense even without UN approval. If Americans believed that world public opinion backed the United States going to war with Iraq, then they may have seen the war as legitimate even if some members of the UN Security Council obstructed approval.

Of course, people do not develop misperceptions in a vacuum. The administration disseminates information directly and by implication. The press transmits this information and, at least in theory, provides critical analysis. One's source of news or how closely one pays attention to the news may influence whether or how misperceptions may develop.

To find out more about the possible role of misperceptions in public support for the Iraq war, and the role of the media in this process before and during the war, the Program on International Policy Attitudes (PIPA) conducted a series of polls with the polling firm Knowledge Networks (KN). From January through May 2003, a more limited set of questions was asked in four different polls. Later, Knowledge Networks developed a more systematic set of questions that was included in a series of three polls, conducted from June through

---

[2] In August 2002, 55 percent thought Iraq "currently has weapons of mass destruction," and 39 percent thought Iraq is trying to develop these weapons but does not currently have them (CNN/USA Today). On al Qaeda, Newsweek asked in September 2002, "From what you've seen or heard in the news ... do you believe that Saddam Hussein's regime in Iraq is harboring al Qaeda terrorists and helping them to develop chemical weapons, or not?" Seventy-five percent said yes. Yet, in a 24–25 February 2003 CBS News poll, only 31 percent agreed that "Iraq presents such a clear danger to American interests that the United States needs to act now"; 64 percent agreed that "the US needs to wait for approval of the United Nations before taking action against Iraq," and 62 percent said that "the United States should wait and give the United Nations inspectors more time."

[3] From May through November 2003, the Program on International Policy Attitudes/Knowledge Networks (PIPA/KN) has found a declining majority of 68 percent to 57 percent saying "the US made the right decision ... in going to war with Iraq."

September, with a total of 3,334 respondents. These results were combined with the findings from four other polls, conducted from January through May, for a total data set of 8,634 respondents. In addition, relevant polling data from other organizations were analyzed, including polls that asked questions about possible misperceptions.

The polls were fielded by Knowledge Networks using its nationwide panel. Panel members are recruited through standard telephone interviews with random digit dialing (RDD) samples of the entire adult population and subsequently provided internet access. Questionnaires are then administered over the Internet to a randomly selected sample of the panel.[4]

This article first explores the degree of pervasiveness of misperceptions, particularly the following three: that since the war U.S. forces have found Iraqi WMD in Iraq; that clear evidence has been found that Saddam Hussein was working closely with al Qaeda; and that world public opinion was in favor of the United States going to war with Iraq. Second, it analyzes the relationship between the holding of these misperceptions and support for the Iraq war by using multivariate regression analysis to compare the strength of this factor with a range of other factors. Third, it analyzes the relationship between the holding of misperceptions and the respondent's primary news source. Fourth, it evaluates the relationship between attention to news and the level of misperceptions. Fifth, it analyzes misperceptions as a function of political attitudes, including intention to vote for the President and party identification. A binary logistic regression analysis including misperceptions and eight other factors provides a ranking of factors by power. The article concludes with an analysis of the various factors that could explain the phenomenon of misperceptions, including administration statements and media reporting.

MISPERCEPTIONS RELATED TO THE IRAQ WAR

In the run-up to the war with Iraq and in the postwar period, a significant portion of the American public has held a number of misperceptions[5] relevant to the rationales for going to war with Iraq. While in most cases only a minority has had any particular misperception, a strong majority has had at least one key misperception.

Close Links between Iraq and al Qaeda

Both before and after the war, a substantial portion of Americans have believed that evidence of a link between Iraq and al Qaeda existed. Before the

---

[4] For more information about this methodology, see the Appendix or go to www.knowledgenetworks. com/ganp.

[5] Herein the term "misperceptions" is not used to refer to controversial beliefs about what U.S. intelligence has been able to infer, such as the belief that Saddam Hussein was directly involved in September 11. The term is limited to noncontroversial perceptions such as whether actual weapons or actual evidence have in fact been *found*. The misperception related to world public opinion is established based on polling data discussed later.

TABLE 1

Evidence of Link between Iraq and al Qaeda
(percentages)

Is it your impression that the US has or has not found clear evidence in Iraq that
Saddam Hussein was working closely with the al Qaeda terrorist organization?

	8–9/03	7/03	6/03	(6/03–9/03)
US has	49	45	52	48
US has not	45	49	43	46
(No answer)	6	6	5	6

Source: Program on International Policy Attitudes/Knowledge Networks.

war, in the January PIPA/KN poll, 68 percent expressed the belief that Iraq played an important role in September 11, with 13 percent even expressing the belief that "conclusive evidence" of Iraq's involvement had been found. Asked in June, July, and August-September (Table 1), large percentages (45 to 52 percent) said they believed that the United States had "found clear evidence in Iraq that Saddam Hussein was working closely with the al-Qaeda [*sic*] terrorist organization."

Harris Interactive in June and August asked, "Do you believe clear evidence that Iraq was supporting al Qaeda has been found in Iraq or not?" In June, 48 percent said that clear evidence had been found, with just 33 percent saying that it had not and 19 percent saying they were not sure. Despite intensive discussion of the issue in the press, in August the numbers were essentially the same: 50 percent believed evidence had been found, 35 percent believed that it had not been, and 14 percent were unsure.

Weapons of Mass Destruction

Before the war, overwhelming majorities believed that Iraq had WMD. Though it now appears likely that this belief was incorrect, it does not seem appropriate to call this a misperception because it was so widespread at the time, even within the intelligence community.

However, a striking misperception occurred after the war, when the United States failed to find any WMD or even any solid evidence of a WMD program. PIPA/KN first asked in May whether respondents thought that the United States has or has not "found Iraqi weapons of mass destruction" in Iraq, and 34 percent said the United States had (another 7 percent did not know). In June, Harris Interactive subsequently asked, "Do you believe clear evidence of weapons of mass destruction has been found in Iraq or not?" and 35 percent said that it had.

PIPA/KN asked again in late June—during a period with much discussion in the press about the absence of WMD—and found that the percentage hold-

TABLE 2

Existence of Weapons of Mass Destruction in Iraq
(percentages)

Since the war with Iraq ended, is it your impression that the US has or has not found Iraqi weapons of mass destruction?

	9/03	7/03	6/03	3/03	(6/03–9/03)
US has	24	21	23	34	22
US has not	73	76	73	59	75
(No answer)	3	3	4	7	3

Source: Program on International Policy Attitudes/Knowledge Networks.

ing this belief had dropped to 23 percent. This number then stayed roughly the same in July and early September. In late July, NBC/*Wall Street Journal* asked whether the United States has been successful in "finding evidence of weapons of mass destruction," and 22 percent said that it had. Harris asked again in mid-August and found 27 percent saying that evidence of WMD had been found (Table 2).

Americans have also incorrectly believed that Iraq actually *used* WMD in the recent war with the United States. PIPA/KN asked respondents whether "Iraq did or did not use chemical or biological weapons in the war that had just ended." In May, 22 percent of respondents said that it had. In mid-June, ABC/*Washington Post* presented a slightly adapted version of the question and found 24 percent said that that they thought it had. When asked by PIPA/KN again in August-September, the percentage saying that Iraq had used such weapons slipped only slightly to 20 percent.

World Public Opinion

A key factor in American public support for going to war with Iraq has been its international legitimacy. Right up to the period immediately before the war, a majority favored taking more time to build international support. A key question, then, is how the public perceived world public opinion on going to war with Iraq.

PIPA/KN polls have shown that Americans have misperceived world public opinion on the U.S. decision to go to war and on the way that the United States is generally dealing with the problem of terrorism. This has been true during and after the war and applies to perceptions about world public opinion as a whole, European public opinion, and public opinion in the Muslim world.

In March 2003, shortly after the war started, PIPA/KN asked respondents "how all of the people in the world feel about the US going to war with Iraq." Respondents perceived greater support for the war than existed at the time or has existed since.[6] Only 35 percent perceived correctly that the majority of

[6] Gallup International conducted two international polls (in January and April-May 2003) and Pew Research Center conducted one (in April-May 2003), which included poll questions that directly measured support or opposition to the Iraq war. In the three polls taken together, fifty-six countries were

TABLE 3

World Opinion about the U.S. Decision to Go to War
(percentages)

Thinking about how all the people in the world feel about the US going/having gone to war with Iraq, do you think	9/03	7/03	6/03	3/03	(6/03–9/03)
The majority of people favor it	27	24	25	31	25
The majority of people oppose it	38	42	41	35	41
Views are evenly balanced	33	30	32	31	31
(No answer)	2	4	2	3	3

Source: Program on International Policy Attitudes/Knowledge Network.

people opposed the decision. Thirty-one percent expressed the mistaken assumption that views were evenly balanced on the issue, and another 31 percent expressed the egregious misperception that the majority favored it. Asked again in June, July, and August-September, these views changed very little (Table 3).

Perceptions have been a bit more accurate when it comes to perceiving European public opinion, but still there are widespread misperceptions. Asked in June and August-September, nearly half (48 to 49 percent) correctly said that the "majority of people oppose the United States having gone to war." But 29 to 30 percent believed incorrectly that views are evenly balanced, and 18 percent believed that the majority even favors it.[7]

A substantial number of Americans also misperceive attitudes in the Islamic world toward U.S. efforts to fight terrorism and its policies in the Middle East. Respondents were asked in August-September whether they thought "a majority of people in the Islamic world favor or oppose U.S.-led efforts to fight terrorism." A plurality of 48 percent incorrectly assumed that a majority of Islamic people favors U.S.-led efforts to fight terrorism, while 46 percent assumed that they do not. When asked whether respondents thought "a majority of people in the Islamic world think U.S. policies in the Middle East make the region more or less stable," 35 percent incorrectly assumed that the majority of people

---

surveyed. The January Gallup International poll asked, "Are you in favor of military action against Iraq: under no circumstances; only if sanctioned by the United Nations; unilaterally by America and its allies?" Of the thirty-eight countries polled (including twenty European countries), not a single one showed majority support for unilateral action, and in nearly every case the percentage was very low. When asked, "If military action goes ahead against Iraq, do you think [survey country] should or should not support this action?" in thirty-four of the thirty-eight countries polled (seventeen out of twenty in Europe), a majority opposed having their country support this action. In April-May, the Pew Global Attitudes Survey asked respondents in eighteen countries how they felt about their country's decision to participate or not participate in "us[ing] military force against Iraq." Among the thirteen countries that had not participated, in every case, a large to overwhelming majority approved of the decision. For the three countries that contributed troops, in the United Kingdom and Australia, a majority approved; in Spain, a majority was opposed. For the two countries that had allowed the United States to use bases, in Kuwait, the majority approved; in Turkey, the majority was opposed. For full results, see www.gallup-international.com and www.people-press.org.

[7] Ibid.

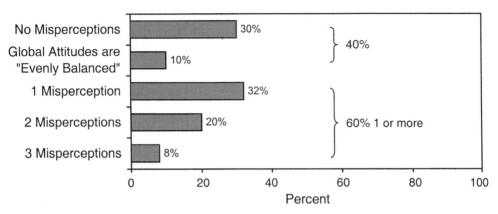

FIGURE 1
Percentage Having Key Misperceptions:
Evidence of Links to al Qaeda, WMD Found, and World Public Opinion Favorable

Composite of Polls Conducted June-September 2003

Source: Program on International Policy Attitudes/Knowledge Networks, October 2003.

in the Islamic world feel that U.S. policies make the region more stable, while 60 percent perceived attitudes correctly.[8]

Combined Analysis

Most specific misperceptions are held by a minority of respondents. However, this does not tell us if these misperceptions are held by the same minority or if large percentages have at least one misperception. To find out, we repeated three key perception questions over three polls, conducted in June, July, and August-September with 3,334 respondents.

The three key perception questions used were the ones that found the most egregious misperceptions, and to qualify as a misperception the most extreme form of the misperception was used. These were the beliefs:

- Clear evidence that Saddam Hussein was working closely with al Qaeda has been *found.*
- Weapons of mass destruction have been *found* in Iraq.
- World public opinion *favored* the United States going to war with Iraq.

To determine the pervasiveness of misperceptions, we focused on the 1,362 respondents who heard all three of the perception questions.

Misperceptions were not limited to a small minority that had repeated misperceptions. A majority of 60 percent had at least one of these three unambiguous misperceptions, and only 30 percent had no misperceptions (Figure 1). An-

[8] The Pew Global Attitudes survey in summer 2002 and May 2003 asked in seven countries with primarily Muslim populations (Turkey, Indonesia, Pakistan, Lebanon, Jordan, Kuwait, and Morocco, plus the Palestinian Authority): "Which of the following phrases comes closer to your view? I favor

other 10 percent had the more modest misperception that world public opinion was evenly balanced between support and opposition to the Iraq war.

MISPERCEPTIONS AND SUPPORT FOR WAR

The misperceptions about the war appear to be highly related to attitudes about the decision to go to war, both before and after the war. In every case, those who have the misperception have been more supportive of the war. As the combined analysis of the three key misperceptions will show, those with none of the key misperceptions have opposed the decision while the presence of each additional misperception has gone together with sharply higher support.

Close Links to al Qaeda

Before the war, those who believed that Iraq was directly involved in September 11 showed greater support for going to war even without multilateral approval. In the January PIPA/KN poll, among those who wrongly believed that they had "seen conclusive evidence" that "Iraq played an important role in September 11 attacks," 56 percent said they would agree with a decision by the President to proceed to go to war with Iraq if the UN Security Council refused to endorse such an action. Among those who said they had not seen such evidence but still believed that Iraq was involved in September 11, 42 percent said they would support such a decision. Among those who said they had not seen such evidence and were not convinced that it was true, only 9 percent said they would agree with such a decision.

In the February PIPA/KN poll, support for going to war was high among those who believed that Saddam Hussein was directly involved in September 11 but was progressively lower as the perceived link between Iraq and al Qaeda became more tenuous. Among those who believed that Iraq was directly involved in September 11, 58 percent said they would agree with the President deciding to go to war with Iraq even without UN approval. Among those who believed that Iraq had given al Qaeda substantial support but was not involved in September 11, support dropped to 37 percent. Among those who believed that a few al Qaeda individuals had contact with Iraqi officials, 32 percent were

the US-led efforts to fight terrorism, or I oppose the US-led efforts to fight terrorism." In six of the eight cases, strong majorities ranging from 56 to 85 percent in summer 2002, and rising to 67 to 97 percent in May 2003, said they opposed "US-led efforts to fight terrorism." In only one case—Kuwait in May 2003—did a majority say they favored U.S. efforts. In the case of Pakistan, a plurality of 45 percent opposed U.S. efforts in the summer of 2003, rising to 74 percent in May 2003. In May 2003, respondents were asked: "Do you think US policies in the Middle East make the region more stable or less stable?" In six of the eight cases, majorities said that U.S. policies in the Middle East make the region less stable. These majorities ranged from 56 percent in Lebanon to 91 percent in Jordan. In Pakistan, 43 percent said U.S. policies make the Middle East less stable, but another 43 percent said U.S. policies either "made no difference" (12 percent) or that they did not know (31 percent). In Kuwait, a 48 percent plurality said U.S. policies made the Middle East more stable.

FIGURE 2
Support for War and Misperception of Evidence of Iraqi Links to al Qaeda

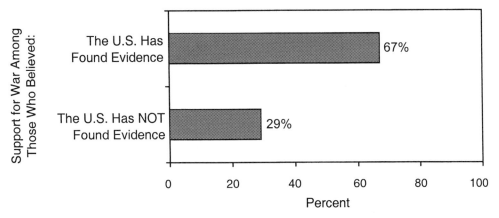

Composite of Polls Conducted June-September 2003

Source: Program on International Policy Attitudes/Knowledge Networks, October 2003.
Note: The question also offered respondents the option of saying that they did not know if going to war was the best thing to do, but that they nonetheless supported the President. Here and in comparisons discussed later, we have limited our analysis to those who took an unequivocal position in favor or against the decision to go to war.

supportive, while just 25 percent expressed support among those who believed that there was no connection.

During the war, Americans who supported the war also said that the supposed link was a major reason for supporting the decision to go to war. An April poll for *Investor's Business Daily* and the *Christian Science Monitor* asked the 72 percent who said they supported the war to rate the importance of a number of reasons for their support. "Iraq's connection with groups like Al-Qaeda" was rated as a major reason by 80 percent.

After the war, nearly half of the respondents mistakenly believed that clear evidence that Saddam Hussein was working closely with al Qaeda had been found. PIPA/KN found a strong relationship between the belief that evidence of such links has been found and support for the decision to go to war. Combining data from June through September, among those with the misperception, 67 percent held the view that going to war was the best thing to do, while only 29 percent expressed support among those who did not have the misperception (Figure 2). Among those without the misperception, 52 percent said it was the wrong decision.

Just as before the war, in the postwar period there was also a strong relationship between beliefs about the nature of the connection between al Qaeda and Iraq and support for the war. Among those who believed that Saddam Hussein was directly involved in September 11, 69 percent said going to war was the best thing to do. Among those who believed that Iraq had given al Qaeda substantial support but was not involved in September 11, approval dropped

FIGURE 3
Support for the War and Misperception that Iraqi WMD Found

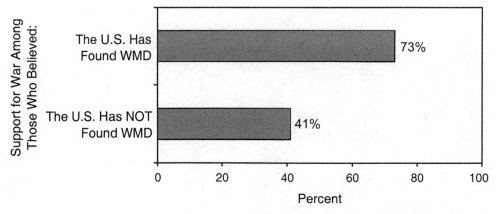

Support for War Among
Those Who Believed:

Composite of Polls Conducted May-September 2003

Source: Program on International Policy Attitudes/Knowledge Networks, October 2003.

to 54 percent. Among those who believed that a few al Qaeda individuals had contact with Iraqi officials, 39 percent were supportive, while just 11 percent expressed support among those who believed that there was no connection. Among those who believed that there was no connection, 73 percent thought that going to war was the wrong decision.

Weapons of Mass Destruction

The mistaken beliefs that WMD have been found in Iraq, or that Iraq used WMD in the war, have been highly related to support for the decision to go to war. Consolidating all respondents asked by PIPA/KN in four polls conducted from May through September, among those who believed that WMD have been found, 73 percent thought that going to war was the best decision (Figure 3). Among those who did not have this misperception, only 41 percent held this view.

Similarly, consolidating two polls conducted in May and August-September, among those who believed that Iraq had used chemical and biological weapons in the war, 64 percent said they thought going to war was the best thing to do. Among those who did not have this belief, only 48 percent thought it was the best thing to do.

World Public Opinion

Perceptions of world public opinion on going to war with Iraq have been significantly related to support for the war. This has been true during and after the war.

In the PIPA/KN poll conducted in late March, shortly after the onset of the war, among those who wrongly believed that the majority of the people in the

FIGURE 4
Views of World Public Opinion and Support for War During and After the War

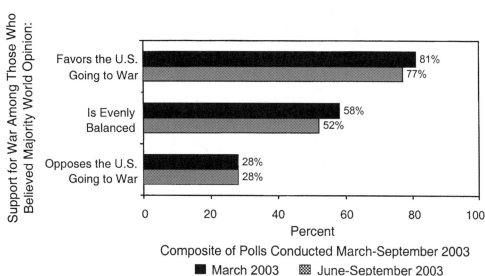

Source: Program on International Policy Attitudes/Knowledge Networks, October 2003.

world favored the United States going to war with Iraq, an overwhelming 81 percent said they agreed with the President's decision to go to war with Iraq, despite his failure to garner UN Security Council approval. Among those who—also incorrectly—believed that views were evenly balanced on this question, 58 percent said they agreed. Among those who correctly believed that the majority of people opposed it, only 28 percent said they agreed with the President's decision. When polled after the war (May-September) the pattern was basically the same, though a different question was used to measure support for the war (Figure 4).

Combined Analysis

To determine the cumulative strength of the relationship between various misperceptions and support for the war, we analyzed those who had been asked all of the three key misperception questions—whether evidence of links between Iraq and al Qaeda have been found, whether WMD have been found in Iraq, and whether world public opinion favored the United States going to war with Iraq—in three polls conducted from June through September. These polls revealed a strong cumulative relationship (Figure 5).

Multivariate Analysis

To determine how strong a factor misperceptions are in predicting support for the war as compared to other factors, a binary logistic regression analysis was

FIGURE 5

Cumulative Effect of Having Key Misperceptions on Support for the War

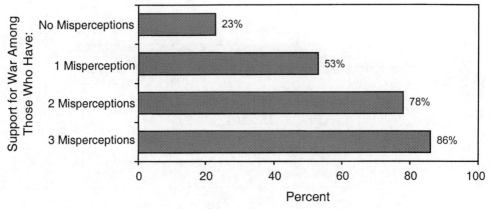

Composite of Polls Conducted June-September 2003

Source: Program on International Policy Attitudes/Knowledge Networks, October 2003.
Note: Misperceptions included were that clear evidence of Iraq-al Qaeda links have been found, WMD have been found, and world public opinion favored the Iraq war.

performed together with eight other factors. Four of the factors were demographic: gender, age, household income, and education. Two other categorical factors were party identification and intention to vote for the President in the next election as opposed to an unnamed Democratic nominee. In addition, there were the factors of how closely people follow events in Iraq and their primary news source. The odds ratio statistic was used to determine the relative likelihood that respondents would support the war. Support for the war was defined as the respondent saying that he or she thought the war was the right decision and the best thing to do, not that he or she was just supporting the President. For this analysis, the number of respondents was 1,219.

When all respondents with one or more of the three key misperceptions were put into one category and compared to those with none of these misperceptions, the presence of misperceptions was the most powerful predictor of support for the war, with those misperceiving being 4.3 times more likely to support the war than those who did not misperceive. The second most powerful predictor was the intention to vote for the President, with those intending to vote for the President being 3 times more likely to support the war than those who planned to vote for the Democratic nominee. Those who intended to vote for the Democratic nominee were 1.8 times less likely to support the war. All other factors were far less influential. Those who followed the news on Iraq very or somewhat closely were 1.2 times more likely to support the war than those who followed it "not very closely" or "not at all." Men were 1.5 times more likely to support the war than women. Those with higher incomes were very slightly more likely to support the war. All other factors were insignificant, including education and age. Party identification by itself would be predictive, but when intention to vote for the President is included, party identification also becomes insignificant.

To determine the cumulative strength of misperceptions as a predictor of war support, the smaller sample that received all of the three key misperceptions questions was analyzed. Respondents were divided into four categories of no misperceptions, exactly one misperception, exactly two misperceptions, and all three misperceptions. Those with just one misperception were 2.9 times more likely to support the war, rising to 8.1 times more likely among those with exactly two misperceptions and to 9.8 times more likely among those with all three misperceptions. In this sample, all other factors remain essentially unchanged, with those intending to vote for the President being 2.8 times and men 1.5 times more likely to support the war. Those intending to vote for the Democratic nominee were 1.6 times less likely to support the war. Attention to news coded as a binary form, however, became insignificant while remaining significant as a continuous variable.

When the three key misperceptions are treated as separate factors, there is wide variation in their power to predict support for the war. By far, the strongest is the perception of world public opinion, with those who perceive the world public opinion as approving of the war being 3.3 times more likely to support the war themselves. Those with the perception that evidence of links to al Qaeda have been found were 2.5 times more likely to support the war, and those who perceived that evidence of WMD have been found were 2.0 times more likely.

Misperceptions as a Function of Source of News

The widespread presence of misperceptions naturally raises the question of whether they are to some extent a function of an individual's source of news. To find out, in three different PIPA/KN polls conducted in June, July, and August-September, an aggregate sample of 3,334 respondents was asked, "Where do you tend to get most of your news?" and offered the options of "newspapers and magazines" or "TV and radio." Overall, 19 percent said their primary news source was print media, while 80 percent said it was electronic. Respondents were then asked, "If one of the networks below is your primary source of news please select it. If you get news from two or more networks about equally, just go on to the next question." The networks offered were ABC, CBS, NBC, CNN, Fox News, PBS, and NPR. Because the PBS and NPR viewers were such a small percentage, we combined them into one category of public networks. In the case of ABC, CBS, and NBC, we do not know how many people primarily got their news from local affiliates and how many from national news shows. Likewise, we do not know if all of those who said that they got their news from

TABLE 4

Frequency of Misperceptions per Respondent: WMD Found, Evidence of al Qaeda Link, and World Majority Support for War
(percentages)

Number of misperceptions per respondent	Fox	CBS	ABC	CNN	NBC	Print Media	NPR/PBS
None of the three	20	30	39	45	45	53	77
One or more misperception	80	71	61	55	55	47	23

Source: Program on International Policy Attitudes/Knowledge Networks.

Fox News primarily got their news from the national cable news network and how many from local Fox affiliates.[9]

The same respondents were also asked about their perceptions, with 1,362 respondents receiving all three key perception questions and 3,334 respondents receiving at least one of them—that is, whether evidence of close links between Iraq and al Qaeda has been found, whether WMD have been found in Iraq, and whether world public opinion approved of the United States going to war with Iraq.

COMBINED ANALYSIS

Because it provides the best overview of the relationship between media sources, this article first analyzes the relationship between media sources and the presence of multiple misperceptions to explore the variation in the level of misperceptions according to the respondents' news source. Afterward, it analyzes the variance for specific misperceptions.

An analysis of those who were asked all of the key three perception questions does reveal a remarkable level of variation in the presence of misperceptions according to news source. Standing out in the analysis are Fox and NPR/PBS, but for opposite reasons. Fox was the news source whose viewers had the most misperceptions. NPR/PBS are notable because their viewers and listeners consistently held fewer misperceptions than respondents who obtained their information from other news sources. Table 4 shows this clearly. Listed are the breakouts of the sample according to the frequency of the three key misperceptions (that is, the beliefs that evidence of links between Iraq and al Qaeda has been found, that WMD have been found in Iraq, and that world public opinion approved of the United States going to war with Iraq) and their primary news source. In the audience for NPR/PBS, there was an overwhelming majority who did not have any of the three misperceptions, and hardly any had all three.

---

[9] Numbers for those naming a network as their primary news source were as follows: Fox, 520; CBS, 258; CNN, 466; ABC, 315; NBC, 420; NPR/PBS, 91. All findings in this section were statistically significant at the $p < 0.05$ level, except where noted.

TABLE 5

*Average of Three Misperception Rates among Viewers and
Listeners: WMD Found, Evidence of al Qaeda Link,
and World Majority Support for War
(percentages)*

News Source	Average Rate per Misperception
Fox	45
CBS	36
CNN	31
ABC	30
NBC	30
Print Media	25
NPR/PBS	11

Source: Program on International Policy Attitudes/Knowledge Networks.

To check these striking findings, the data were analyzed a different way by using the larger sample of 3,334 who had answered at least one of the three questions just mentioned. For each misperception, it was determined how widespread it was in each media audience, and then for each media audience this frequency was averaged for the three misperceptions. Table 5 shows the averages from lowest to highest. Again, the Fox audience showed the highest average rate of misperceptions (45 percent) while the NPR/PBS audience showed the lowest (11 percent).

Close Links to al Qaeda

The same pattern in the distribution of misperceptions among the news sources was obtained in the cases of each specific misperception. When asked whether the United States has found "clear evidence in Iraq that Saddam Hussein was working closely with the al-Qaeda terrorist organization," among the combined sample for the three-month period, 49 percent said that such evidence had been found (Table 6). This misperception was substantially higher among those who get their news primarily from Fox, 67 percent. Once again the NPR/PBS audience was the lowest at 16 percent.

TABLE 6

*Viewers' Beliefs on Whether the United States Has Found
Evidence of an al Qaeda-Iraq Link
(percentages)*

Clear Evidence of al Qaeda Link	NBC	CBS	ABC	Fox	CNN	NPR/PBS	Print Media
US has found	49	56	45	67	48	16	40
US has not found	45	41	49	29	47	85	58

Source: Program on International Policy Attitudes/Knowledge Networks.

TABLE 7

Perception that the United States Has or Has Not Found WMD
(percentages)

Weapons of Mass Destruction	NBC	CBS	ABC	Fox	CNN	NPR/PBS	Print Media
US has found	20	23	19	33	20	11	17
US has not found	79	75	79	64	79	89	82

Source: Program on International Policy Attitudes/Knowledge Networks.

Variations were much more modest on the perception that Iraq was directly involved in September 11. As discussed, the view that Iraq was directly involved in September 11 is not a demonstrable misperception, but it is widely regarded as fallacious by the intelligence community. In this case, the highest level of misperceptions was in the CBS audience (33 percent) followed by Fox (24 percent), ABC (23 percent), NBC (22 percent), and CNN (21 percent). Respondents who got their news primarily from print media (14 percent) and NPR or PBS (10 percent) were less likely to choose this description.

Combining the above group with those who had the less egregious but still unproven belief that Iraq gave substantial support to al Qaeda, the pattern was similar. Among CBS viewers, 68 percent had one of these perceptions, as did 66 percent of Fox viewers, 59 percent of NBC viewers, 55 percent of CNN viewers, and 53 percent of ABC viewers. Print readers were nearly as high at 51 percent, while NPR/PBS audiences were significantly lower at 28 percent.

Weapons of Mass Destruction

When respondents were asked whether the United States has "found Iraqi weapons of mass destruction" since the war had ended, 22 percent of all respondents over June through September mistakenly thought this had happened. Once again, Fox viewers were the highest with 33 percent having this belief. A lower 19 to 23 percent of viewers who watch ABC, NBC, CBS, and CNN had the perception that the United States has found WMD. Seventeen percent of those who primarily get their news from print sources had the misperception, while only 11 percent who watch PBS or listen to NPR had it (Table 7).

World Public Opinion

Respondents were also asked to give their impression of how they think "people in the world feel about the US having gone to war with Iraq." Over the three-month period, 25 percent of all respondents said, incorrectly, "the majority of people favor the US having gone to war" (Table 8). Of Fox watchers, 35 percent said this. Only 5 percent of those who watch PBS or listen to NPR misperceived world opinion in this way. As usual, those who primarily get their

TABLE 8

World Public Opinion on the United States Going to War
(percentages)

Majority of people in world . . .	NBC	CBS	ABC	Fox	CNN	NPR/PBS	Print Media
Favor US going to war in Iraq	20	28	27	35	24	5	17

Source: Program on International Policy Attitudes/Knowledge Networks.

news from print media were the second lowest, with 17 percent having this misperception.

Numerous respondents also chose the option of saying that in world public opinion, views are evenly balanced between favoring and opposing going to war—a misperception, though less egregious. Combining those who said views were evenly balanced with those who assumed that the majority favored the Iraq war—a more inclusive definition of misperception—the same pattern obtained. Fox viewers had the highest level of misperceiving (69 percent) and NPR/PBS the lowest (26 percent). The others also formed a familiar pattern: CBS viewers at 63 percent, ABC at 58 percent, NBC at 56 percent, CNN at 54 percent, and print media at 45 percent.

The same question was asked about European opinion. Perceptions of European views are more accurate among the U.S. public: only 17 percent thought there had been majority support among Europeans for the war. Over the three months, CBS viewers most frequently misperceived European opinion (24 percent); Fox viewers were second (20 percent). The NPR/PBS audience and those relying on printed media were lowest, both at 13 percent.

If one adds together those who thought there was European majority support with those who thought views in Europe were evenly balanced, 47 percent misperceived European opinion; CBS viewers were highest at 56 percent, NBC and Fox viewers were next at 52 percent and 51 percent respectively, while the NPR/PBS audience was lowest at 29 percent. ABC viewers and those using print sources were tied for second lowest at 41 percent.

The Effect of Variations in Audiences

The question thus arises of whether the variation in misperceptions is a function of variations in the demographics or political attitudes of the audience. Some audiences varied according to education, party identification, and support for the President. However, as is evident in the regression analysis, when all of these factors are analyzed together, the respondent's primary source of news is still a strong and significant factor; indeed, it was one of the most powerful factors predicting misperceptions.

MISPERCEPTIONS AS A FUNCTION OF LEVEL OF ATTENTION TO NEWS

It would seem reasonable to assume that misperceptions are due to a failure to pay attention to news and that those who have greater exposure to news would have fewer misperceptions. All respondents were asked, "How closely are you following the news about the situation in Iraq now?" For the summer as a whole (June, July, August-September), 13 percent said they were following the news very closely, 43 percent somewhat closely, 29 percent not very closely, and 14 percent not closely at all.

Strikingly, overall, there was no relation between the reported level of attention to news and the frequency of misperceptions. In the case of those who primarily watched Fox, greater attention to news modestly *increased* the likelihood of misperceptions. Only in the case of those who primarily got their news from print did misperceptions decrease with lower levels of attention, though in some cases this occurred for CNN viewers as well.

The most robust effects were found among those who primarily got their news from Fox. Among those who did not follow the news at all, 42 percent had the misperception that evidence of close links to al Qaeda has been found, rising progressively at higher levels of attention to 80 percent among those who followed the news very closely. For the perception that WMD have been found, those who watched very closely had the highest rate of misperception at 44 percent, while the other levels of attention were lower, though they did not form a clear pattern (not at all, 34 percent; not very, 24 percent; somewhat, 32 percent). Among those who did not follow the news at all, 22 percent believed that world public opinion favored the war, jumping to 34 percent and 32 percent among those who followed the news not very and somewhat closely, respectively, and then jumping even higher to 48 percent among those who followed the news very closely.

With increasing attention, those who got their news from print were less likely to have all three misperceptions. Of those not following the news closely, 49 percent had the misperception that evidence of close links has been found, declining to 32 percent among those who followed the news very closely. Those who did not follow the news at all were far more likely to misperceive (35 percent) that WMD had been found than the other levels (not very, 14 percent; somewhat, 18 percent; very, 13 percent). Twenty-five percent of those who did not follow the news at all had the misperception that world public opinion favored the war, dropping to 16 percent for all other categories.

CNN viewers showed slightly, but significantly, lower levels of misperception on finding WMD and world public opinion at higher levels of attention, though not on evidence of links to al Qaeda.

MISPERCEPTIONS AS A FUNCTION OF POLITICAL ATTITUDES

Not surprisingly, political attitudes did play a role in the frequency of misperceptions. The intention to vote for the President was highly influential. Party

FIGURE 6
Support for President and Frequency of Misperceptions

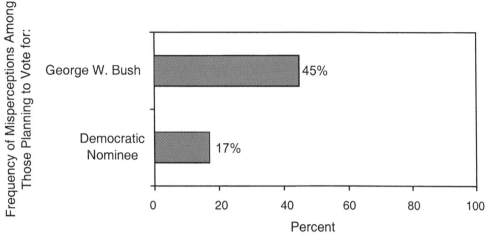

Composite of Polls Conducted June-September 2003

Source: Program on International Policy Attitudes/Knowledge Networks, October 2003.

identification was also influential; however, this effect disappeared after controlling for intention to vote for the President.

Intention to Vote for the President

The polls of June, July, and August-September all included a question, placed near the end, asking whether the respondents thought they would vote for Bush or for the Democratic nominee in the presidential election (Figure 6). In all cases, the responses were very similar to those in numerous other polls at the same time—and showed either a slight edge for Bush or a statistical tie. Only 10 percent did not answer the question. When Bush supporters and supporters of a Democratic nominee are compared, it is clear that supporters of the President are more likely to have misperceptions than are those who oppose him. Multivariate analysis indicates that intention to vote for the President is the single most powerful predictor of misperceptions.

Taking the averages of the percentage that had each of the three key misperceptions—evidence of al Qaeda links found, WMD found, and world public opinion favors war—those who said they would vote for the President were far more likely to misperceive. On average, those who would vote for the President held misperceptions 45 percent of the time, while those who say they will vote for a Democrat held misperceptions, on average, 17 percent of the time (Figure 6).

Looking at the specific cases, in response to the question "Has the US found clear evidence Saddam Hussein was working closely with al-Qaeda?" a strikingly large 68 percent of Bush supporters believed that the United States has found such evidence. On the other side, an equally striking 66 percent of supporters of a Democratic nominee knew that such evidence has not been found. When asked to characterize the relationship between the previous Iraqi government and al Qaeda given four choices, 29 percent of Bush supporters said, "Iraq was directly involved in the 9/11 attacks." Only 15 percent of Democratic supporters chose this description.

Only minorities of either Bush supporters or supporters of a Democratic nominee believe that the United States has found evidence of WMD in Iraq. However, three times as many Bush supporters as Democrat supporters hold this misperception. Thirty-one percent of Bush supporters think the United States has found such evidence, while only 10 percent of Democrat supporters think this.

When asked, "How do you think the people of the world feel about the US having gone to war with Iraq?" Bush supporters were more than three times more likely than supporters of a Democratic nominee to believe that "the majority of people favor the US having gone to war." Thirty-six percent of Bush supporters had this misperception, while only 11 percent of Democratic supporters did.

The PIPA/KN polls asked the same question about Europe, on which misperceptions are less widespread among Americans. Twenty-six percent of Bush supporters mistakenly thought that a majority of Europeans favored the war, while only 7 percent of supporters of a Democratic nominee believed this.

Party Identification

Republicans are also more likely than Democrats or independents to have misperceptions. However, when the analysis controls for support for the President, this party difference largely disappears. For example, among Bush supporters, Republicans, Democrats, and independents were similarly likely to believe that the United States has found clear evidence that Saddam Hussein was working closely with al Qaeda (pro-Bush Republicans, 68 percent; pro-Bush Democrats, 77 percent; pro-Bush independents, 67 percent). On whether the United States has found evidence of WMD, the same pattern among Bush supporters was present (31 percent of pro-Bush Republicans believing such evidence has been found, 29 percent of pro-Bush Democrats believing this, and 29 percent of pro-Bush independents believing this). The same pattern appeared in all cases tested.

RELATIVE STRENGTH OF VARIOUS FACTORS RELATED TO LEVEL OF MISPERCEPTION

To determine which factors had the most power to predict the likelihood of misperceiving, we performed a binary logistic regression analysis, together with eight other factors. Four of the factors were demographic: gender, age, household income, and education. Two other categorical factors were party identification and intention to vote for the President in the next election, as opposed to an unnamed Democratic nominee. In addition, we included the factors of how closely people follow events in Iraq and what their primary news source was. The odds ratio statistic was used to determine the likelihood that respondents would have misperceptions.

In the regression analysis, the most powerful factor was the intention to vote for President Bush. As compared to those who intended to vote for the Democratic nominee or were undecided, those who intended to vote for the President were 2.9 times more likely to believe that close links to al Qaeda have been found, 3.0 times more likely to believe that WMD had been found, and 2.6 times more likely to believe that world public opinion was favorable to the war. Overall, those who intended to vote for the President were 3.7 times more likely to have at least one of these misperceptions.

The second most powerful factor was one's primary source of network news. Analysis shows the factor to be highly significant, but assessing each network is difficult. Though several networks are significant, others are not. To determine the relative importance of each network as a primary source of news, another regression was performed, treating each network as a binary variable and comparing each network's respondents to other respondents. When this analysis is performed, having Fox, CBS, or NPR/PBS as one's primary news source emerges as the most significant predictor of a particular misperception and of misperceptions in general.

To determine the overall importance of one factor to another, a comparison of statistical measures is necessary.[10] Overall, Fox viewing has the greatest and most consistent predictive power in the analysis on a variety of these statistical measures. Table 9 presents the results.

Fox is the most consistently significant predictor of misperceptions. Those who primarily watched Fox were 2.0 times more likely to believe that close links to al Qaeda have been found, 1.6 times more likely to believe that WMD had been found, 1.7 times more likely to believe that world public opinion was favorable to the war, and 2.1 times more likely to have at least one misperception. Interestingly, when asked how the majority of people in the world feel about the war, if the response "views are evenly balanced" is included as a misperception along with "favor," only Fox is a significant predictor of that misperception.

Those who primarily watched CBS were 1.8 times more likely to believe that close links to al Qaeda have been found, 1.9 times more likely to believe that world public opinion was favorable to the war, and 2.3 times more likely to have at least one misperception. However, they were not significantly different on beliefs about the uncovering of WMD.

On the other hand, those who primarily watched PBS or listened to NPR were 3.5 times less likely to believe that close links to al Qaeda have been

---

[10] PIPA compared two statistical measures, the Wald statistic and the difference in the −2 log likelihood if the factor is removed from the analysis.

TABLE 9

Significant Variances in Misperceptions by Primary News Source

	Primary Media Source	Odds/Ratio	N
US has found WMD	Fox	1.6	361
(N = 2,202)	CBS*	1.4	182
	NPR/PBS*	−1.3	53
US has found clear evidence of	Fox	2.0	366
Iraqi link to al Qaeda	CBS	1.8	188
(N = 2,202)	NPR/PBS	−3.5	59
Majority of world favors US	Fox	1.7	294
having gone to war with Iraq	CBS	1.9	168
(N = 1,827)	NPR/PBS	−5.6	55
At least one misperception	Fox	2.1	414
(N = 2,506)	CBS	2.3	213
	NPR/PBS	−3.8	66

Source: Program on International Policy Attitudes/Knowledge Networks.
* Not statistically significant at the 0.05 level. All other media sources did not vary significantly. For data, please contact the authors.

found, 5.6 times less likely to believe that world public opinion was favorable to the war, and 3.8 times less likely to have at least one misperception. However, they were not significantly different on the issue of WMD.

Level of attention to news was not a significant factor overall, with the exception of those who primarily got their news from Fox. This is consistent with the finding that Fox viewers were more likely to misperceive the more closely they followed events in Iraq. Multiplicative variables were derived for each network by multiplying attention to news by each network dummy variable. A multivariate analysis was performed on misperceptions in which each new combined network-attention level variable was added to the previous model. The results show that Fox viewers are the only ones to be significantly more likely to misperceive with higher levels of attention to news.

The third most powerful factor was intention to vote for the Democratic nominee. As compared to those who intended to vote for President Bush or were undecided, those who intended to vote for the Democratic nominee were 2.0 times less likely to believe that close links to al Qaeda have been found and 1.8 times less likely to believe that world public opinion was favorable to the war. Overall, those who intended to vote for the Democratic nominee were 1.8 times less likely to have at least one of these misperceptions, but did not quite achieve significance on the WMD question.

The fourth most powerful factor was education. Those who had no college, as compared to those had at least some college, were 1.3 times more likely to believe that close links to al Qaeda have been found and 1.4 times more likely to have at least one misperception, but did not quite achieve significance on the other misperceptions.

Age was a very weak factor, with older people being very slightly less likely to misperceive. All other factors—gender, party identification (when intention to vote for the President was included), level of attention to news, and income—were not significant. In a separate analysis, region of the country was included and also not found to be significant.

ANALYSIS

These data lead to the question of why so many Americans have misperceptions that appear to be having a significant impact on attitudes about the Iraq war and why these misperceptions vary according to one's source of news and political attitudes. This analysis starts with possible explanations based on exogenous factors and then moves inward.

The first and most obvious reason that the public had so many of these misperceptions is that the Bush administration made numerous statements that could easily be construed as asserting these falsehoods. On numerous occasions the administration made statements strongly implying that it had intelligence substantiating that Iraq was closely involved with al Qaeda and was even directly involved in the September 11 attacks. For example, in his 18 March 2003 Presidential Letter to Congress, President Bush explained that in going to war with Iraq he was taking "the necessary actions against international terrorists and terrorist organizations, including those nations, organizations, or persons who planned, authorized, committed, or aided the terrorist attacks that occurred on September 11, 2001."[11] When Secretary of State Colin Powell addressed the UN Security Council on 5 February 2003, he presented photographs that were identified as al Qaeda training camps inside Iraq, leaving unclear the fact that the camp in question was in the northern part of Iraq, not under the control of the central Iraqi government.[12] Administration figures continued to refer to the purported meeting between Mohammed Atta and an Iraqi official in Prague even after U.S. intelligence agencies established that Atta was in fact in the United States at the time.[13] More recently, on 14 September 2003, Vice President Richard Cheney made the following ambiguous statement: "If we're successful in Iraq . . . so that it's not a safe haven for terrorists, now we will have struck a major blow right at the heart of the base, if you will, the geographic base of the terrorists who have had us under assault now for many years, but most especially on 9/11."[14] Sometimes the association has been established by inserting a reference to September 11 that is a non sequitur and

[11] President George W. Bush, "Presidential Letter," 18 March 2003, available at http://www.whitehouse.gov/news/releases/2003/03/20030319-1.html.

[12] Secretary Colin L. Powell, "Remarks to the United Nations," New York City, 5 February 2003, available at http://www.state.gov/secretary/rm/2003/17300.htm, 12 October 2003.

[13] Dana Priest and Glenn Kessler, "Iraq, 9/11 Still Linked By Cheney," *Washington Post*, 29 September 2003.

[14] Vice President Richard Cheney, "Meet the Press," 14 September 2003.

then simply moving on, or implying that the connection is so self-evident that it does not require explanation. For example, President Bush's own remarks at his press conference of 28 October 2003 could appear to reinforce multiple misperceptions:

> The intelligence that said he [Saddam Hussein] had a weapon system was intelligence that had been used by a multinational agency, the U.N., to pass resolutions. It's been used by my predecessor to conduct bombing raids. It was intelligence gathered from a variety of sources that clearly said Saddam Hussein was a threat. And given the attacks of September the 11th—it was—you know, we needed to enforce U.N. resolution (sic) for the security of the world, and we did. We took action based upon good, solid intelligence. It was the right thing to do to make America more secure and the world more peaceful.[15]

Here the listener could mistakenly interpret the President's comments as meaning that the same intelligence that determined the United States' policy on war had been accepted as correct by the UN Security Council in its deliberations and that the September 11 attacks, a UN Security Council resolution, and the choice to invade Iraq all followed a logical progression ("given the attacks of September the 11th—it was—you know").

In any case, it is quite clear that the public perceived that the administration was asserting a strong link between Iraq and al Qaeda, even to the point of Iraqi direct involvement in September 11. When PIPA/KN asked in June, "Do you think the Bush administration did or did not imply that Iraq under Saddam Hussein was involved in the September 11th attacks?" 71 percent said that it had.

The administration also made statements that came extremely close to asserting that WMD were found in postwar Iraq. On 30 May 2003, President Bush made the statement, ". . . for those who say we haven't found the banned manufacturing devices or banned weapons, they're wrong. We found them."[16]

Another possible explanation for why the public had such misperceptions is the way that the media reported the news. The large variation in the level of misperceptions does suggest that some media sources may have been making greater efforts than others to disabuse their audiences of misperceptions they may have had so as to avoid feeling conflict about going or having gone to war. Of course, the presence or absence of misperceptions in viewers does not necessarily prove that they were caused by the presence or absence of reliable reporting by a news source. Variations in the level of misperceptions according to news source may be related to variations in the political orientations of the audience. However, when political attitudes were controlled for the variations

---

[15] Full transcript: "Bush Defends Foreign Policy," *Washington Post*, online edition, 28 October 2003, available at http://www.washingtonpost.com/ac2/wp-dyn?pagename=article&node=&contentId=A29127-2003Oct28&notFound=true.

[16] Mike Allen, "Bush: 'We Found' Banned Weapons; President Cites Trailers in Iraq as Proof," *Washington Post*, 31 May 2001.

between the networks and the same attitudes still obtained, it suggests that differences in reporting by media sources were playing a role.

There is also evidence that in the run-up to, during, and for a period after the war, many in the media appeared to feel that it was not their role to challenge the administration or that it was even appropriate to take an active pro-war posture. Fox News' programming on the war included a flag in the left-hand corner and assumed the Defense Department's name for the war: "Operation Iraqi Freedom." When criticized in a letter for taking a pro-war stance, Fox News' Neil Cavuto replied, "So am I slanted and biased? You damn well bet I am. . . . You say I wear my biases on my sleeve? Better that than pretend you have none, but show them clearly in your work."[17] Interestingly, even CBS News, which tends to have a more liberal reputation, seemed to think along these lines. CBS anchor Dan Rather commented in a 14 April 2003 interview with Larry King, "Look, I'm an American. I never tried to kid anybody that I'm some internationalist or something. And when my country is at war, I want my country to win. . . . Now, I can't and don't argue that that is coverage without a prejudice. About that I am prejudiced."[18]

A study of the frequencies of pro-war and anti-war commentators on the major networks found that pro-war views were overwhelmingly more frequent.[19] In such an environment, it would not be surprising that the media would downplay the lack of evidence of links between Iraq and al Qaeda, the fact that WMD were not being found, and that world public opinion was critical of the war. Furthermore, the fact shown in the present study that the audiences of the various networks have varied so widely in the prevalence of misperceptions lends credence to the idea that media outlets had the capacity to play a more critical role, but to varying degrees chose not to.

Reluctant to challenge the administration, the media can simply become a means of transmission for the administration, rather than a critical filter. For example, when President Bush made the assertion that WMD had been found, the 31 May 2003 edition of the *Washington Post* ran a front page headline saying, "Bush: 'We Found' Banned Weapons."[20]

There is also striking evidence that the readiness to challenge the administration is a variable that corresponds to levels of misperception among viewers. The aforementioned study of the frequency of commentary critical of the war found that the two networks notably least likely to present critical commentary were Fox and CBS—the same two networks that in the present study had view-

---

[17] David Folkenflik, "Fox News defends its patriotic coverage: Channel's objectivity is questioned," *Baltimore Sun*, 2 April 2003.

[18] Dan Rather, during the 4 April 2003 *Larry King Show*. Quoted in Steve Rendell and Tara Broughel, "Amplifying Officials, Squelching Dissent: FAIR study finds democracy poorly served by war coverage," *Extra!* (May/June 2003), Fairness and Accuracy in Reporting, available at www.fair.org/extra/0305/warstudy.html.

[19] Steve Rendell and Tara Broughel, "Amplifying Officials, Squelching Dissent."

[20] Allen, "Bush: 'We Found' Banned Weapons," 31 May 2001.

ers most likely to have misperceptions. This is clarified by statistics from Rendell and Broughel's content analysis of network coverage: "The percentage of U.S. sources that were officials varied from network to network, ranging from 75 percent at CBS to 60 percent at NBC. . . . Fox's Special Report with Brit Hume had fewer U.S. officials than CBS (70 percent) and more U.S. anti-war guests (3 percent) than PBS or CBS. Eighty-one percent of Fox's sources were pro-war, however, the highest of any network. CBS was close on the Murdoch network's heels with 77 percent. NBC featured the lowest proportion of pro-war voices with 65 percent."[21]

Another contributing factor may also have been a dynamic in reporting that is not unique to the Iraq war: the absence of something does not constitute a compelling story, while even the prospect of the presence of something does. Thus, shortly after the end of the war, numerous headlines trumpeted even faint prospects that evidence of WMD were about to be found. However, when these prospects failed to materialize, this did not constitute a compelling story and, thus, reporting on it was given a far less prominent position. The cumulative effect of repeatedly hearing the expectation that weapons were about to be found, while hearing little or no disconfirmation, could well contribute to the impression that at least one of these leads was indeed fruitful.

Other more subtle dynamics may also have been at work. The fact that world public opinion was so opposed to the United States going to war with Iraq may have been obscured by giving such high visibility to the U.S. conflict with France in the Security Council. The key story became one of French obstructionism, eclipsing the fact that polls from around the world, as well as the distribution of positions in the UN Security Council, showed widespread opposition to U.S. policy.[22]

One could well argue that this plethora of exogenous factors obviates the need for any explanations based on endogenous factors. Indeed, the fact that no particular misperception studied was found in a clear majority of the public and the fact that 40 percent had none of the key misperceptions buttress confidence in the capacity of the public to sort through misleading stimuli. At the same time, a majority had at least one major misperception, raising the question of why so many people have been susceptible.

The seemingly obvious explanation—that the problem is that people just do not pay enough attention to the news—does not hold up. As discussed,

---

[21] See footnote 19. Forthcoming studies by Susan Moeller are likely to offer a much more comprehensive view of these dynamics than is available at the time of writing. A report on media coverage of WMD under the aegis of the Center for International and Strategic Studies at the University of Maryland is in preparation for release in early 2004. See also Susan Moeller, "A Moral Imagination: The Media's Response to the War on Terrorism" in Stuart Allen and Barbie Zelizer, eds., *Reporting War* (London: Routledge, forthcoming). On the issue of embedded reporters, see a content analysis by the Project for Excellence in Journalism, "Embedded Reporters: What Are Americans Getting?" at www.journalism.org/resources/research/reports/war/embed/default.asp.

[22] See footnote 6.

higher levels of attention to news did not reduce the likelihood of misperception, and in the case of those who primarily got their news from Fox News, misperceptions increased with greater attention. Furthermore, the presence of misperceptions was not just noise found randomly throughout an inattentive public—the presence of misperceptions formed strong patterns highly related to respondents' primary source of news.

Perhaps the most promising explanation is that the misperceptions have performed an essential psychological function in mitigating doubts about the validity of the war. Polls have shown that Americans are quite resistant to the idea of using military force except in self-defense or as part of a multilateral operation with UN approval.[23] Even if a country is developing nuclear weapons, there is not a consensus in the public that the United States would have the right to use military force to prevent it, though a very strong majority agrees that the UN Security Council would have this prerogative.[24]

Thus, to legitimate the war without UN approval, the President had to make the case that the war would be an act of self-defense. The war against the Taliban had been overwhelmingly approved as legitimate because the Taliban had provided support to al Qaeda and, thus, was a party to the September 11 attack on the United States. Americans showed substantial receptivity to the administration's assertion that Iraq also had links to al Qaeda and that the possibility that Iraq was developing WMD that could be passed to al Qaeda, creating a substantial threat to the United States. But the public also appeared to recognize that the evidence was circumstantial—and this was not a president who commanded so much respect in foreign policy realms that they could simply take his word for it.

The public felt the need for UN approval as an alternate normative basis for war. Early polls showed that a very strong majority was ready to act with UN approval, but less than a third were ready to act unilaterally, and even days before the war a majority was still saying that the United States needed to wait for UN approval.[25] But even months before the war, a clear majority of the pub-

---

[23] Evidence from the 1990s is reviewed in Steven Kull and I.M. Destler, *Misreading the Public: The Myth of a New Isolationism* (Washington, DC: Brookings Institution Press, 1999), 42–57, 67–80, 94–110. The public's views at the outset of the current Iraq experience are documented and analyzed in the report "Iraq Debate 2002," available at www.americans-world.org.

[24] In January 2003, PIPA/KN asked a series of general questions about whether a right existed "to use military force to prevent a country that does not have nuclear weapons from acquiring them." Only 46 percent thought that, without UN approval, a country had the right to use military force on another country in this situation; virtually the same number (48 percent) thought the United States had this right. Seventy-six percent thought the UN Security Council had the right to authorize military force for this purpose. PIPA/Knowledge Networks Poll, "Americans on Iraq and the UN Inspections I," 27 January 2003, available at www.pipa.org/online_reports.html.

[25] For early polls, see footnote 1. Just days before the war in a CBS News poll conducted 4–5 March, only 36 percent agreed that "Iraq presents such a clear danger to American interests that the United States needs to act now," while 59 percent agreed that "The US needs to wait for approval of the United Nations before taking any action against Iraq."

lic said that if the President were to decide to go to war without UN approval they would support him,[26] and when the time came they did. This was a standard rally-round-the-president effect, no doubt intensified by a felt imperative to close ranks in the post-September 11 environment.[27]

Such rally effects, though, are fairly superficial. Even during and after the war, when asked whether they really approve of the decision to go to war as distinguished from just supporting Bush "because he is the president," only about half or less have said they think that going to war was the best thing, while another 15 to 22 percent have said that their approval of the war was just a way to support the president.[28]

Americans had expected that once the United States went into Iraq, they would find evidence that Iraq was linked to al Qaeda and was developing WMD, thus vindicating the decision to go to war as an act of self-defense. Therefore, it is not surprising that many have been receptive when the administration has strongly implied or even asserted that the United States has found evidence that Iraq was working closely with al Qaeda and was developing WMD, and when media outlets—some more than others—have allowed themselves to be passive transmitters of such messages.

CONCLUSION

From the perspective of democratic process, the findings of this study are cause for concern. They suggest that if the public is opposed to taking military action

[26] In December 2002, January 2003, and February, PIPA/KN presented respondents the following scenario: "Imagine that President Bush moves that the UN approve an invasion of Iraq to overthrow Saddam Hussein, but most of the other members of the UN Security Council want to continue to use threats and diplomatic pressure to get Iraq to comply, and the motion does not pass. President Bush then decides that the US will undertake an invasion of Iraq, even if the US has to do so on its own. Just based on this information, what do you think your attitude would be about this decision?" Respondents were offered the option of agreeing with the President's choice, disagreeing, or choosing "I would not agree with this decision, but I would still support the President." In all cases only a minority of 33 to 43 percent said they would agree, but another 25 to 27 percent said they would support but not agree, thus creating a majority ready to support the President should he decide to proceed.

[27] On the rally effect, see Richard A. Brody, "Crisis, War and Public Opinion: The Media and Public Support for the President" in W. Lance Bennett and David L. Paletz, *Taken by Storm: The Media, Public Opinion, and U.S. Foreign Policy in the Gulf War* (Chicago: University of Chicago Press, 1994); R.A. Brody and C.R. Shapiro, "A Reconsideration of the Rally Phenomenon in Public Opinion" in S. Long, ed., *Political Behavior Annual*, vol. 2 (Boulder, CO: Westview Press, 1989); and John E. Mueller, *War, Presidents and Public Opinion* (New York: Wiley, 1973): 208–213.

[28] Seven times in March and April 2003, Pew Research Center for the People and the Press asked, "Do you think the US made the right decision or the wrong decision in using military force against Iraq?" Those who said it was the right decision were asked whether they supported going to war because they think it was "the best thing for the US to do" or whether they were not sure if it was the best thing to do but they "support Bush's decision, because he is the president." During the war, 69 to 74 percent said the United States made the right decision, of which 48 to 54 percent thought it was the best thing to do, while 15 to 22 percent were unsure of this but supported the President. Each month from May through September, PIPA/KN repeated this question. Over this period, 45 to 53 percent thought that the war was the best thing to do, and 14 to 18 percent were unsure but supported the President.

without UN approval and the President is determined to do so, he has remarkable capacities to move the public to support his decision. This in itself is not worrisome—to the degree it is the product of persuasion, based on the merits of an argument. What is worrisome is that it appears that the President has the capacity to lead members of the public to assume false beliefs in support of his position. In the case of the Iraq war, this dynamic appears to have played a critical role: among those who did not hold the key false beliefs, only a small minority supported the decision to go to war. In a regression analysis, the presence of misperceptions was the most powerful factor predicting support for the war, with intention to vote for the President close behind. This does not prove that the misperceptions alone caused support for the war. It is more likely that it is one key factor that interacted with the desire to rally around the President and the troops. However, it does appear that it would have been significantly more difficult for the President to elicit and maintain support for the decision to go to war if the public had not held such misperceptions.

The President's influence is not limitless. He does not appear to be capable of getting the public to go against their more deeply held value orientations. If he did, then it would not be necessary for the public to develop false beliefs. But he is capable of prompting the public to support him by developing the false beliefs necessary to justify the administration's policies in a way that is consistent with the public's deeper value orientations.

It also appears that the media cannot necessarily be counted on to play the critical role of doggedly challenging the administration. The fact that viewers of some media outlets had far lower levels of misperceptions than did others (even when controlling for political attitudes) suggests that not all were making the maximal effort to counter the potential for misperception.

To some extent, this period may be regarded as unique. We are still living in the aftermath of September 11. With the persisting sense of threat, the public may be more prone to try to accommodate the President, and the media may be more reluctant to challenge the President or to impart news that calls into question the validity of his decisions. And yet, it is also at times of threat that the most critical decisions are likely to be made.

It is likely that with time, public misperceptions will tend to erode. For example, after media coverage of David Kay's interim progress report on the activities of the Iraq Survey Group, the belief that WMD have been found dropped to 15 percent, although the belief that evidence of links to al Qaeda has been found did not drop. At the same time, there was a significant rise in the percentage that said they thought that the President at least stretched the truth when he made the case for war based on Iraq having a WMD program.[29] However, when the mechanisms for informing the public are in some way compromised, the process of the public gradually catching on is a slow one. In the meantime, the administration, by giving incorrect information, can gain sup-

---

[29] See Steven Kull, "Americans Reevaluate Going to War with Iraq," PIPA/Knowledge Networks Poll, 13 November 2003, available at www.pipa.org.

port for policies that might not be consistent with the preferences held by the majority of Americans.

APPENDIX

Methodology

The poll was fielded by Knowledge Networks—a polling, social science, and market research firm in Menlo Park, California—with a randomly selected sample of its large-scale nationwide research panel. This panel is itself randomly selected from the national population of households having telephones and subsequently provided internet access for the completion of surveys (and, thus, is not limited to those who already have internet access). The distribution of the sample in the web-enabled panel closely tracks the distribution of United States Census counts for the U.S. population on such variables as age, race, Hispanic ethnicity, geographical region, employment status, income, and education. The panel is recruited using stratified random digit-dial (RDD) telephone sampling. RDD provides a non-zero probability of selection for every U.S. household having a telephone. Households that agree to participate in the panel are provided with free Web access and an Internet appliance that uses a telephone line to connect to the Internet and uses the television as a monitor. In return, panel members participate in surveys three to four times a month. Survey responses are confidential, and identifying information is never revealed without respondent approval. When a survey is fielded to a panel member, he or she receives an e-mail indicating that the survey is available for completion. Surveys are self-administered. For more information about the methodology, please go to www.knowledgenetworks.com/ganp.

Do Detainees Have Constitutional Rights?: Excerpts from *Hamdi v. Rumsfeld*

SUPREME COURT OF THE UNITED STATES

INTRODUCTORY NOTE: The fractious Supreme Court ruling in the case of *Hamdi v. Rumsfeld* was the judiciary's attempt to grapple with legal quandaries that resulted from the war on terror. The Bush administration introduced the concept of "enemy combatants," and detainees, labeled as such by the government, slipped through the legal cracks of the American justice system. They were neither prisoners of war subject to the rights dictated by the Geneva Conventions, as stated by the administration, nor were they considered criminals to be brought to justice through existing legal channels in domestic criminal courts. *Hamdi v. Rumsfeld* is a landmark case, setting a precedent for the rights of American citizens in an era when threats to U.S. security come increasingly in the form of individuals within terrorist organizations.

Yaser Hamdi was an American citizen who was picked up on the Taliban side of the battlefield in Afghanistan, and yet, despite his American citizenship, he was detained for more than two years without formal charges having been brought against him or access to legal counsel. The question confronting the Supreme Court was, essentially, in the war on terror can the government detain an American citizen on American soil for unspecified reasons for an unlimited period of time without the detainee being afforded the opportunity to contest his or her imprisonment.

The Court was deeply divided over this issue, issuing four separate opinions advocating different judgments and rationales. A majority on the Court was reached only because two judges, Justice Ruth Bader Ginsburg and Justice David H. Souter, chose to align themselves with the opinion that most closely resembled their own, despite being uncomfortable with the absence of certain rights for detainees, which they articulated in a separate opinion written by Justice Souter. They chose this compromise in order to reach a majority consensus so that a ruling favoring Hamdi could be issued. In the end, the Court's ruling, expressed by Justice Sandra Day O'Connor, offered detainees of American citizenship very limited protection from potential abuse. Detain-

KATHLEEN DOHERTY is a research associate at the Academy of Political Science. She has edited the Supreme Court opinions to reflect the most vital elements of each opinion and composed an introductory note to precede the excerpted opinions.

ees do not have the right to a trial by jury, but only to a hearing in front of an "impartial adjudicator," where they may contest the basis for their status as an enemy combatant.

Two members of the Court, Justice Antonin Scalia and Justice John Paul Stevens, strongly disagreed with this logic and thought it a gross intrusion on a citizen's rights. They instead advocated that each citizen deserved the right to a trial. And if the detainee is in fact a dangerous individual, he/she should be charged with a crime or, absent sufficient evidence, released. In contrast, Justice Clarence Thomas found that the executive branch must be granted wide latitude in its prosecution of the war on terror in order to most ably protect U.S. national security. He further argued that the judiciary lacked the appropriate expertise to rule on matters relating to national security, such as the prosecution or detention of an "enemy combatant."

As a result of this ruling, an American citizen is guaranteed only an opportunity to refute the status assigned to them by the government. In the case of Hamdi, however, such an opportunity proved sufficient to secure his release from detention four months following the Court's ruling.

Excerpts from the four opinions issued are included in the pages that follow to display the most vital components of each opinion's rationale and judgment.

KATHLEEN DOHERTY

SUPREME COURT OF THE UNITED STATES

No. 03–6696

YASER ESAM HAMDI AND ESAM FOUAD HAMDI, AS NEXT FRIEND OF YASER ESAM HAMDI, PETITION-ERS *v.* DONALD H. RUMSFELD, SECRETARY OF DEFENSE, ET AL.

ON WRIT OF CERTIORARI TO THE UNITED STATES COURT OF APPEALS FOR THE FOURTH CIRCUIT

[June 28, 2004]

JUSTICE O'CONNOR announced the judgment of the Court and delivered an opinion, in which THE CHIEF JUSTICE, JUSTICE KENNEDY, and JUSTICE BREYER join.

At this difficult time in our Nation's history, we are called upon to consider the legality of the Government's detention of a United States citizen on United States soil as an "enemy combatant" and to address the process that is constitutionally owed to one who seeks to challenge his classification as such. The United States Court of Appeals for the Fourth Circuit held that petitioner's detention was legally authorized and that he was entitled to no further opportunity to challenge his enemy-combatant label. We now vacate and remand. We hold that although Congress authorized the detention of combatants in the narrow circumstances alleged here, due process demands that a citizen held in the United States as an enemy combatant be given a meaningful opportunity to contest the factual basis for that detention before a neutral decisionmaker.

. . .

Striking the proper constitutional balance here is of great importance to the Nation during this period of ongoing combat. But it is equally vital that our calculus not give short shrift to the values that this country holds dear or to the privilege that is American citizenship. It is during our most challenging and uncertain moments that our Nation's commitment to due process is most severely tested; and it is in those times that we must preserve our commitment at home to the principles for which we fight abroad. . . .

With due recognition of these competing concerns, we believe that neither the process proposed by the Government nor the process apparently envisioned by the District Court below strikes the proper constitutional balance when a United States citizen is detained in the United States as an enemy combatant. . . .

We therefore hold that a citizen-detainee seeking to challenge his classification as an enemy combatant must receive notice of the factual basis for his classification and a fair opportunity to rebut the Government's factual assertions before a neutral decisionmaker. . . . These essential constitutional promises may not be eroded.

At the same time, the exigencies of the circumstances may demand that, aside from these core elements, enemy combatant proceedings may be tailored to alleviate their uncommon potential to burden the Executive at a time of ongoing military conflict. Hearsay, for example, may need to be accepted as the most reliable available evidence from the Government in such a proceeding. Likewise, the Constitution would not be offended by a presumption in favor of the Government's evidence, so long as that presumption remained a rebuttable one and fair opportunity for rebuttal were provided. Thus, once the Government puts forth credible evidence that the habeas petitioner meets the enemy-combatant criteria, the onus could shift to the petitioner to rebut that evidence with more persuasive evidence that he falls outside the criteria. A burden-shifting scheme of this sort would meet the goal of ensuring that the errant tourist, embedded journalist, or local aid worker has a chance to prove military error while giving due regard to the Executive once it has put forth meaningful support for its conclusion that the detainee is in fact an enemy combatant. . . .

We think it unlikely that this basic process will have the dire impact on the central functions of warmaking that the Government forecasts. The parties agree that initial captures on the battlefield need not receive the process we have discussed here; that process is due only when the determination is made to *continue* to hold those who have been seized. The Government has made clear in its briefing that documentation regarding battlefield detainees already is kept in the ordinary course of military affairs. . . . Any factfinding imposition created by requiring a knowledgeable affiant to summarize these records to an independent tribunal is a minimal one. Likewise, arguments that military officers ought not have to wage war under the threat of litigation lose much of their steam when factual disputes at enemy-combatant hearings are limited to the alleged combatant's acts. This focus meddles little, if at all, in the strategy or conduct of war, inquiring only into the appropriateness of continuing to detain an individual claimed to have taken up arms against the United States. While we accord the greatest respect and consideration to the judgments of military authorities in matters relating to the actual prosecution of a war, and recognize that the scope of that discretion necessarily is wide, it does not infringe on the core role of the military for the courts to exercise their own time-honored and constitutionally mandated roles of reviewing and resolving claims like those presented here. . . .

In sum, while the full protections that accompany challenges to detentions in other settings may prove unworkable and inappropriate in the enemy-combatant setting, the threats to military operations posed by a basic system of independent review are not so weighty as to trump a citizen's core rights to challenge meaningfully the Government's case and to be heard by an impartial adjudicator.

. . .

In so holding, we necessarily reject the Government's assertion that separation of powers principles mandate a heavily circumscribed role for the courts in such circumstances. Indeed, the position that the courts must forgo any examination of the individual case and focus exclusively on the legality of the broader detention scheme cannot be mandated by any reasonable view of separation of powers, as this approach serves only to *condense* power into a single branch of government. We have long since made clear that a state of war is not a blank check for the President when it comes to the rights of the Nation's citizens. . . . Likewise, we have made clear that, unless Congress acts to suspend it, the Great Writ of habeas corpus allows the Judicial Branch to play a necessary role in maintaining this delicate balance of governance, serving as an important judicial check on the Executive's discretion in the realm of detentions. . . . Thus, while we do not question that our due process assessment must pay keen attention to the particular burdens faced by the Executive in the context of military action, it would turn our system of checks and balances on its head to suggest that a citizen could not make his way to court with a challenge to the factual basis for his detention by his government, simply because the Executive opposes making available such a challenge. Absent suspension of the writ by Congress, a citizen detained as an enemy combatant is entitled to this process.

Because we conclude that due process demands some system for a citizen detainee to refute his classification, the proposed "some evidence" standard is inadequate. Any process in which the Executive's factual assertions go wholly unchallenged or are simply presumed correct without any opportunity for the alleged combatant to demonstrate otherwise falls constitutionally short. As the Government itself has recognized, we have utilized the "some evidence" standard in the past as a standard of review, not as a standard of proof. . . . That is, it primarily has been employed by courts in examining an administrative record developed after an adversarial proceeding—one with process at least of the sort that we today hold is constitutionally mandated in the citizen enemy-combatant setting. . . . This standard therefore is ill suited to the situation in which a habeas petitioner has received no prior proceedings before any tribunal and had no prior opportunity to rebut the Executive's factual assertions before a neutral decisionmaker.

Today we are faced only with such a case. Aside from unspecified "screening" processes . . . and military interrogations in which the Government suggests Hamdi could have contested his classification, . . . Hamdi has received no process. An interrogation by one's captor, however effective an intelligence-gathering tool, hardly constitutes a constitutionally adequate factfinding before a neutral decisionmaker. . . .

There remains the possibility that the standards we have articulated could be met by an appropriately authorized and properly constituted military tribunal. Indeed, it is notable that military regulations already provide for such process in related instances, dictating that tribunals be made available to determine the status of enemy detainees who assert prisoner-of-war status under the Geneva Convention. . . . In the absence of such process, however, a court that receives a petition for a writ of habeas corpus from an alleged enemy combatant must itself ensure that the minimum requirements of due process are achieved. Both courts below recognized as much, focusing their energies on the question of whether Hamdi was due an opportunity to rebut the Government's case against him. The Government, too, proceeded on this assumption, presenting its affidavit and then seeking that it be evaluated under a deferential standard of review based on burdens that it alleged would accompany any greater process. As we have discussed, a habeas court in a case such as this may accept affidavit evidence like that contained in the Mobbs Declaration,[1] so long as it also permits the alleged combatant to present his own factual case to rebut the Government's return. We anticipate that a District Court would proceed with the caution that we have indicated is necessary in this setting, engaging in a factfinding process that is both prudent and incremental. We have no reason to doubt that courts faced with these sensitive matters will pay proper heed both to the matters of national security that might arise in an individual case and to the constitutional limitations safeguarding essential liberties remain vibrant even in times of security concerns. . . .

The judgment of the United States Court of Appeals for the Fourth Circuit is vacated, and the case is remanded for further proceedings.

JUSTICE SOUTER, with whom JUSTICE GINSBURG joins, concurring in part, dissenting in part, and concurring in the judgment.

According to Yaser Hamdi's petition for writ of habeas corpus, brought on his behalf by his father, the Government of the United States is detaining him, an American citizen on American soil, with the explanation that he was seized on the field of battle in Afghanistan, having been on the enemy side. It is undisputed that the Government has not charged him with espionage, treason, or any other crime under domestic law. It is likewise undisputed that for one year and nine months, on the basis of an Executive designation of Hamdi as an "enemy combatant," the Government denied him the right to send or receive any communication beyond the prison where he was held and, in particular, denied him access to counsel to represent him. The Government asserts a right to hold

---

[1] Editor's note: The Mobbs Declaration was the response by the government to the United States Supreme Court of Appeals for the Fourth Circuit's inquiry into the status of Hamdi, an attempt to determine if he was truly an enemy combatant. The government provided a response written by Michael Mobbs, a special advisor to the Undersecretary of Defense for Policy. The Mobbs Declaration is the sole piece of evidence put forward by the government to justify the reason as to why Hamdi has been labeled an enemy combatant. In the document, Mobbs states that Hamdi was given enemy-combatant status "based upon his interviews and in light of his association with the Taliban." The Mobbs Declaration is explained on page 5 of the decision in Justice O'Connor's summary of the case.

Hamdi under these conditions indefinitely, that is, until the Government determines that the United States is no longer threatened by terrorism exemplified in the attacks of September 11, 2001.

In these proceedings on Hamdi's petition, he seeks to challenge the facts claimed by the Government as the basis for holding him as an enemy combatant. And in this Court he presses the distinct argument that the Government's claim, even if true, would not implicate any authority for holding him that would satisfy . . . [the] Non-Detention Act, which bars imprisonment or detention of a citizen "except pursuant to an Act of Congress."

The Government responds that Hamdi's incommunicado imprisonment as an enemy combatant seized on the field of battle falls within the President's power as Commander in Chief under the laws and usages of war, and is in any event authorized by two statutes. Accordingly, the Government contends that Hamdi has no basis for any challenge by petition for habeas except to his own status as an enemy combatant; and even that challenge may go no further than to enquire whether "some evidence" supports Hamdi's designation . . . ; if there is "some evidence," Hamdi should remain locked up at the discretion of the Executive. At the argument of this case, in fact, the Government went further and suggested that as long as a prisoner could challenge his enemy combatant designation when responding to interrogation during incommunicado detention he was accorded sufficient process to support his designation as an enemy combatant. . . . Since on either view judicial enquiry so limited would be virtually worthless as a way to contest detention, the Government's concession of jurisdiction to hear Hamdi's habeas claim is more theoretical than practical, leaving the assertion of Executive authority close to unconditional.

The plurality rejects any such limit on the exercise of habeas jurisdiction and so far I agree with its opinion. The plurality does, however, accept the Government's position that if Hamdi's designation as an enemy combatant is correct, his detention (at least as to some period) is authorized by an Act of Congress as required. . .by the Authorization for Use of Military Force. . . . Here, I disagree and respectfully dissent. The Government has failed to demonstrate that the Force Resolution authorizes the detention complained of here even on the facts the Government claims. If the Government raises nothing further than the record now shows, the Non-Detention Act entitles Hamdi to be released.

. . .

The threshold issue is how broadly or narrowly to read the Non-Detention Act, the tone of which is severe: "No citizen shall be imprisoned or otherwise detained by the United States except pursuant to an Act of Congress." Should the severity of the Act be relieved when the Government's stated factual justification for incommunicado detention is a war on terrorism, so that the Government may be said to act "pursuant" to congressional terms that fall short of explicit authority to imprison individuals? With one possible though important qualification, . . . the answer has to be no. For a number of reasons, the prohibition within . . . [the Non-Detention Act] has to be read broadly to accord the statute a long reach and to impose a burden of justification on the Government. . . .

Finally, even if history had spared us the cautionary example of the internments in World War II, . . . there would be a compelling reason to read . . . [the Non-Detention Act] to demand manifest authority to detain before detention is authorized. The defining character of American constitutional government is its constant tension between security and liberty, serving both by partial helpings of each. In a government of separated powers, deciding finally on what is a reasonable degree of guaranteed liberty whether in peace or war (or some condition in between) is not well entrusted to the Executive Branch of Government, whose particular responsibility is to maintain security. For reasons of inescapable human nature, the branch of the Government asked to counter a serious threat is not the branch on which to rest the Nation's entire reliance in striking the balance between the will to win and the cost in liberty on the way to victory; the responsibility for security will naturally amplify the claim that security legitimately raises. A reasonable balance is more likely to be reached on the judgment of a different branch, just as Madison said in remarking that "the constant aim is to divide and arrange the several offices in such a manner as that each may be a check on the other—that the private interest of every individual may be sentinel over the public rights." The Federalist No. 51. . . . Hence the need for an assessment by Congress before citizens are subject to lockup, and likewise the need for a clearly expressed congressional resolution of the competing claims.

. . .

Next, there is the Government's claim, accepted by the Court, that the terms of the Force Resolution are adequate to authorize detention of an enemy combatant under the circumstances described, a claim the Government fails to support sufficiently to satisfy . . . . [the Non-Detention Act] as read to require a clear statement of authority to detain. Since the Force Resolution was adopted one week after the attacks of September 11, 2001, it naturally speaks with some generality, but its focus is clear, and that is on the use of military power. It is fairly read to authorize the use of armies and weapons, whether against other armies or individual terrorists. But, . . . it never so much as uses the word detention, and there is no reason to think Congress might have perceived any need to augment Executive power to deal with dangerous citizens within the United States, given the well-stocked statutory arsenal of defined criminal offenses covering the gamut of actions that a citizen sympathetic to terrorists might commit.

. . .

. . . [T]here is one argument for treating the Force Resolution as sufficiently clear to authorize detention of a citizen consistently with . . . [the Anti-Detention Act]. Assuming the argument to be sound, however, the Government is in no position to claim its advantage.

Because the Force Resolution authorizes the use of military force in acts of war by the United States, the argument goes, it is reasonably clear that the military and its Commander in Chief are authorized to deal with enemy belligerents according to the treaties and customs known collectively as the laws of war. . . . Accordingly, the United States may detain captured enemies. . . . [T]he Government here repeatedly argues that Hamdi's detention amounts to nothing more than customary detention of a captive taken on the field of battle: if the usages of war are fairly authorized by the Force Resolution, Hamdi's detention is authorized for purposes of . . . [the Anti-Detention Act].

There is no need, however, to address the merits of such an argument in all possible circumstances. For now it is enough to recognize that the Government's stated legal position in its campaign against the Taliban (among whom Hamdi was allegedly captured) is apparently at odds with its claim here to be acting in accordance with customary law of war and hence to be within the terms of the Force Resolution in its detention of Hamdi. In a statement of its legal position cited in its brief, the Government says that "the Geneva Convention applies to the Taliban detainees." . . . Hamdi presumably is such a detainee, since according to the Government's own account, he was taken bearing arms on the Taliban side of a field of battle in Afghanistan. He would therefore seem to qualify for treatment as a prisoner of war under the Third Geneva Convention, to which the United States is a party. . . .

By holding him incommunicado, however, the Government obviously has not been treating him as a prisoner of war, and in fact the Government claims that no Taliban detainee is entitled to prisoner of war status. . . . This treatment appears to be a violation of the Geneva Convention provision that even in cases of doubt, captives are entitled to be treated as prisoners of war "until such time as their status has been determined by a competent tribunal." . . . The Government answers that the President's determination that Taliban detainees do not qualify as prisoners of war is conclusive as to Hamdi's status and removes any doubt that would trigger application of the Convention's tribunal requirement. . . .

Whether, or to what degree, the Government is in fact violating the Geneva Convention and is thus acting outside the customary usages of war are not matters I can resolve at this point. What I can say, though, is that the Government has not made out its claim that in detaining Hamdi in the manner described, it is acting in accord with the laws of war authorized to be applied against citizens by the Force Resolution. I conclude accordingly that the Government has failed to support the position that the Force Resolution authorizes the described detention of Hamdi for purposes of . . . [the Anti-Detention Act].

. . .

Because I find Hamdi's detention forbidden by . . . [the Anti-Detention Act] and unauthorized by the Force Resolution, I would not reach any questions of what process he may be due in litigating disputed issues in a proceeding under the habeas statute or prior to the habeas enquiry itself. For me, it suffices that the Government has failed to justify holding him in the absence of a further Act of Congress, criminal charges, a showing that the detention conforms to the laws of war, or a demonstration that . . . [the Anti-Detention Act] is unconstitutional. I would therefore vacate the judgment of the Court of Appeals and remand for proceedings consistent with this view.

Since this disposition does not command a majority of the Court, however, the need to give practical effect to the conclusions of eight members of the Court rejecting the Government's position calls for me to join with the plurality in ordering remand on terms closest to those I would impose. . . .

It should go without saying that in joining with the plurality to produce a judgment, I do not adopt the plurality's resolution of constitutional issues that I would not reach. It is not that I could disagree with the plurality's determinations (given the plurality's view of the Force Resolution) that someone in Hamdi's position is entitled at a minimum to notice of the Government's claimed factual basis for holding him, and to a fair chance to rebut it before a neutral decision maker, . . . nor, of course, could I disagree with the plurality's affirmation of Hamdi's right to counsel . . . . On the other hand, I do not mean to imply agreement that the Government could claim an evidentiary presumption casting the burden of rebuttal on Hamdi, . . . or that an opportunity to litigate before a military tribunal might obviate or truncate enquiry by a court on habeas. . . .

Subject to these qualifications, I join with the plurality in a judgment of the Court vacating the Fourth Circuit's judgment and remanding the case.

JUSTICE SCALIA, with whom JUSTICE STEVENS joins, dissenting.

Petitioner, a presumed American citizen, has been imprisoned without charge or hearing in the Norfolk and Charleston Naval Brigs for more than two years, on the allegation that he is an enemy combatant who bore arms against his country for the Taliban. His father claims to the contrary, that he is an inexperienced aid worker caught in the wrong place at the wrong time. This case brings into conflict the competing demands of national security and our citizens' constitutional right to personal liberty. Although I share the Court's evident unease as it seeks to reconcile the two, I do not agree with its resolution.

Where the Government accuses a citizen of waging war against it, our constitutional tradition has been to prosecute him in federal court for treason or some other crime. Where the exigencies of war prevent that, the Constitution's Suspension Clause . . . allows Congress to relax the usual protections temporarily. Absent suspension, however, the Executive's assertion of military exigency has not been thought sufficient to permit detention without charge. No one contends that the congressional Authorization for Use of Military Force, on which the Government relies to justify its actions here, is an implementation of the Suspension Clause.

. . .

The proposition that the Executive lacks indefinite wartime detention authority over citizens is consistent with the Founders' general mistrust of military power permanently at the Executive's disposal. In the Founders' view, the "blessings of liberty" were threatened by "those military establishments which must gradually poison its very fountain." The Federalist No. 45, . . . (J. Madison). No fewer than 10 issues of the Federalist were devoted in whole or part to allaying fears of oppression from the proposed Constitution's authorization of standing armies in peacetime. Many safeguards in the Constitution reflect these concerns. Congress's authority "to raise and support Armies" was hedged with the proviso that "no Appropriation of Money to that Use shall be for a longer Term than two Years." U.S. Const., Art. 1. . . . Except for the actual command of military forces, all authorization for their maintenance and all explicit authorization for their use is placed in the control of Congress under Article I, rather than the President under Article II. As Hamilton explained, the President's military authority would be "much inferior" to that of the British King:

> "It would amount to nothing more than the supreme command and direction of the military and naval forces, as first general and admiral of the confederacy: while that of the British king extends to the *declaring* of war, and to the *raising and regulating* of fleets and armies; all which, by the constitution under consideration, would appertain to the legislature." The Federalist No. 69.

A view of the Constitution that gives the Executive authority to use military force rather than the force of law against citizens on American soil flies in the face of the mistrust that engendered these provisions.

. . .

It follows from what I have said that Hamdi is entitled to a habeas decree requiring his release unless (1) criminal proceedings are promptly brought, or (2) Congress has suspended the writ of habeas corpus. A suspension of the writ could, of course, lay down conditions for continued detention, similar to those that today's opinion prescribes under the Due Process Clause. . . . But there is a world of difference between the people's representatives' determining the need for that suspension (and prescribing the conditions for it), and this Court's doing so.

The plurality finds justification for Hamdi's imprisonment in the Authorization for Use of Military Force, 115 Stat. 224, which provides:

> "That the President is authorized to use all necessary and appropriate force against those nations, organizations, or persons he determines planned, authorized, committed, or aided the terrorist attacks that occurred on September 11, 2001, or harbored such organizations or persons, in order to prevent any future acts of international terrorism against the United States by such nations, organizations or persons."

This is not remotely a congressional suspension of the writ, and no one claims that it is. Contrary to the plurality's view, I do not think this statute even authorizes detention of a citizen with the clarity necessary to satisfy the interpretive canon that statutes should be construed so as to avoid grave constitutional concerns . . . or with the clarity necessary to overcome the statutory prescription that "[n]o citizen shall be imprisoned or otherwise detained by the United States except pursuant to an Act of Congress.". . . But even if it did, I would not permit it to overcome Hamdi's entitlement to habeas corpus relief. The Suspension Clause of the Constitution, which carefully circumscribes the conditions under which the writ can be withheld, would be a sham if it could be evaded by congressional prescription of requirements *other than the common-law requirement of committal for criminal prosecution* that render the writ, though available, unavailing. If the Suspension Clause does not guarantee the citizen that he will either be tried or released, unless the conditions for suspending the writ exist and the grave action of suspending the writ has been taken; if it merely guarantees the citizen that he will not be detained unless Congress by ordinary legislation says he can be detained; it guarantees him very little indeed.

It should not be thought, however, that the plurality's evisceration of the Suspension Clause augments, principally, the power of Congress. As usual, the major effect of its constitutional improvisation is to increase the power of the Court. Having found a congressional authorization for the detention of citizens where none clearly exists; and having discarded the categorical procedural protection of the Suspension Clause; the plurality then proceeds, under the guise of the Due Process Clause, to prescribe what procedural due process *it* thinks appropriate. It "weigh[s] the private interest . . . against the Government's asserted interest" . . . and—just as though writing a new Constitution—comes up with an unheard-of system in which the citizen rather than the Government bears the burden of proof, testimony is by hearsay rather than live witnesses, and the presiding officer may well be a "neutral" military officer rather than judge and jury. . . .

It is not the habeas court's function to make illegal detention legal by supplying a process that the Government could have provided, but chose not to. If Hamdi is being imprisoned in violation of the Constitution (because without due process of law), then his habeas petition should be granted; the Executive may then hand him over to the criminal authorities, whose detention for the purpose of prosecution will be lawful, or else must release him.

There is a certain harmony of approach in the plurality's making up for Congress's failure to invoke the Suspension Clause and its making up for the Executive's failure to apply what it says are needed procedures—an approach that reflects what might be called a Mr. Fix-it Mentality. The plurality seems to view it as its mission to Make Everything Come Out Right, rather than merely to decree the consequences, as far as individual rights are concerned, of the other two branches' actions and omissions. Has the Legislature failed to suspend the writ in the current dire emergency? Well, we will remedy that failure by prescribing the reasonable conditions that a suspension should have included. And has the Executive failed to live up to those reasonable conditions? Well, we will ourselves make that failure good, so that this dangerous fellow (if he is dangerous) need not be set free. The problem with this approach is not only that it steps out of the courts' modest and limited role in a democratic society; but that by repeatedly doing what it thinks the political branches ought to do it encourages their lassitude and saps the vitality of government by the people.

· · ·

The Founders well understood the difficult tradeoff between safety and freedom. "Safety from external danger," Hamilton declared,

> "is the most powerful director of national conduct. Even the ardent love of liberty will, after a time, give way to its dictates. The violent destruction of life and property incident to war; the continual effort and alarm attendant on a state of continual danger, will compel nations the most attached to liberty, to resort for repose and security to institutions which have a tendency to destroy their civil and political rights. To be more safe, they, at length, become willing to run the risk of being less free." The Federalist No. 8.

The Founders warned us about the risk, and equipped us with a Constitution designed to deal with it.

Many think it not only inevitable but entirely proper that liberty give way to security in times of national crisis — that, at the extremes of military exigency, *inter arma silent leges*. Whatever the general merits of the view that war silences law or modulates its voice, that view has no place in the interpretation and application of a Constitution designed precisely to confront war and, in a manner that accords with democratic principles, to accommodate it. Because the Court has proceeded to meet the current emergency in a manner the Constitution does not envision, I respectfully dissent.

JUSTICE THOMAS, dissenting.

The Executive Branch, acting pursuant to the powers vested in the President by the Constitution and with explicit congressional approval, has determined that Yaser Hamdi is an enemy combatant and should be detained. This detention falls squarely within the Federal Government's war powers, and we lack the expertise and capacity to second-guess that decision. As such, petitioners' habeas challenge should fail, and there is no reason to remand the case. The plurality reaches a contrary conclusion by failing adequately to consider basic principles of the constitutional structure as it relates to national security and foreign affairs. . . I do not think that the Federal Government's war powers can be balanced away by this Court. Arguably, Congress could provide for additional procedural protections, but until it does, we have no right to insist upon them. But even if I were to agree with the general approach the plurality takes, I could not accept the particulars. The plurality utterly fails to account for the Government's compelling interests and for our own institutional inability to weigh competing concerns correctly. I respectfully dissent.

. . .

"It is 'obvious and unarguable' that no governmental interest is more compelling than the security of the Nation." *Haig* v. *Agee*, 453 U.S. 280, 307 (1981) (quoting *Aptheker v. Secretary of State*, 378 U.S. 500, 509 (1964)). The national security, after all, is the primary responsibility and purpose of the Federal Government. . . . But because the Founders understood that they could not foresee the myriad potential threats to national security that might later arise, they chose to create a Federal Government that necessarily possesses sufficient power to handle any threat to the security of the Nation. The power to protect the Nation

> "ought to exist without limitation . . . *[b]ecause it is impossible to foresee or define the extent and variety of national exigencies, or the correspondent extent & variety of the means which may be necessary to satisfy them.* The circumstances that endanger the safety of nations are infinite; and for this reason no constitutional shackles can wisely be imposed on the power to which the care of it is committed."

See also The Federalist Nos. 34 and 41.

The Founders intended that the President have primary responsibility—along with the necessary power—to protect the national security and to conduct the Nation's foreign relations. They did so principally because the structural advantages of a unitary Executive are essential in these domains. "Energy in the executive is a leading character in the definition of good government. It is essential to the protection of the community against foreign attacks." The Federalist No. 70, . . . (A. Hamilton). The principle "ingredien[t]" for "energy in the executive" is "unity.". . . This is because "[d]ecision, activity, secrecy, and dispatch will generally characterise the proceeding of one man, in a much more eminent degree, than the proceedings of any greater number." *Ibid.*

These structural advantages are most important in the national-security and foreign-affairs contexts. "Of all the cares or concerns of government, the direction of war most peculiarly demands those qualities which distinguish the exercise of power by a single hand." The Federalist No. 74, . . . (A. Hamilton). Also for these reasons, John Marshall explained that "[t]he President is the sole organ of the nation in its external relations, and its sole representative with foreign nations.". . . To this end, the Constitution vests in the President "[t]he executive Power," Art. II, . . . provides that he "shall be Commander in Chief of the" armed forces . . . and places in him the power to recognize foreign governments. . . .

This Court has long recognized these features and has accordingly held that the President has *constitutional* authority to protect the national security and that this authority carries with it broad discretion.

· · ·

Congress, to be sure, has a substantial and essential role in both foreign affairs and national security. But it is crucial to recognize that *judicial* interference in these domains destroys the purpose of vesting primary responsibility in a unitary Executive. I cannot improve on Justice Jackson's words, speaking for the Court:

> "The President, both as Commander-in-Chief and as the Nation's organ for foreign affairs, has available intelligence services whose reports are not and ought not to be published to the world. It would be intolerable that courts, without the relevant information, should review and perhaps nullify actions of the Executive taken on information properly held secret. Nor can courts sit *in camera* in order to be taken into executive confidences. But even if courts could require full disclosure, the very nature of executive decisions as to foreign policy is political, not judicial. Such decisions are wholly confided by our Constitution to the political departments of the government, Executive and Legislative. They are delicate, complex, and involve large elements of prophecy. They are and should be undertaken only by those directly responsible to the people whose welfare they advance or imperil. They are decisions of a kind for which the Judiciary has neither aptitude, facilities nor responsibility and which has long been held to belong in the domain of political power not subject to judicial intrusion or inquiry."

Several points, made forcefully by Justice Jackson, are worth emphasizing. First, with respect to certain decisions relating to national security and foreign affairs, the courts simply lack the relevant information and expertise to second-guess determinations made by the President based on information properly withheld. Second, even if the courts could compel the Executive to produce the necessary information, such decisions are simply not amenable to judicial determination because "[t]hey are delicate, complex, and involve large elements of prophecy." . . . Third, the Court in *Chicago & Southern Air Lines* and elsewhere has correctly recognized the primacy of the political branches in the foreign-affairs and national security contexts.

· · ·

I acknowledge that the question whether Hamdi's executive detention is lawful is a question properly resolved by the Judicial Branch, though the question comes to the Court with the strongest presumptions in favor of the Government. The plurality agrees that Hamdi's detention is lawful if he is an enemy combatant. But the question whether Hamdi is actually an enemy combatant is "of a kind for which the Judiciary has neither aptitude, facilities nor responsibility and which has long been held to belong in the domain of political power not subject to judicial intrusion or inquiry." *Chicago & Southern Air Lines,* 333

U.S., at 111. That is, although it is appropriate for the Court to determine the judicial question whether the President has the asserted authority, . . . we lack the information and expertise to question whether Hamdi is actually an enemy combatant, a question the resolution of which is committed to other branches.

. . .

. . . At issue here is the far more significant interest of the security of the Nation. The Government seeks to further that interest by detaining an enemy soldier not only to prevent him from rejoining the ongoing fight. Rather, as the Government explains, detention can serve to gather critical intelligence regarding the intentions and capabilities of our adversaries, a function that the Government avers has become all the more important in the war on terrorism. . . .

Additional process, the Government explains, will destroy the intelligence gathering function. . . . It also does seem quite likely that, under the process envisioned by the plurality, various military officials will have to take time to litigate this matter. And though the plurality does not say so, a meaningful ability to challenge the Government's factual allegations will probably require the Government to divulge highly classified information to the purported enemy combatant, who might then upon release return to the fight armed with our most closely held secrets.

. . .

I realize that many military operations are, in some sense, necessary. But many, if not most, are merely expedient, and I see no principled distinction between the military operation the plurality condemns today (the holding of an enemy combatant based on the process given Hamdi) from a variety of other military operations. In truth, I doubt that there is any sensible, bright-line distinction. It could be argued that bombings and missile strikes are an inherent part of war, and as long as our forces do not violate the laws of war, it is of no constitutional moment that civilians might be killed. But this does not serve to distinguish this case because it is also consistent with the laws of war to detain enemy combatants exactly as the Government has detained Hamdi. This, in fact, bolsters my argument . . . to the extent that the laws of war show that the power to detain is part of a sovereign's war powers.

Undeniably, Hamdi has been deprived of a serious interest, one actually protected by the Due Process Clause. Against this, however, is the Government's overriding interest in protecting the Nation. If a deprivation of liberty can be justified by the need to protect a town, the protection of a Nation, *a fortiori*, justifies it.

. . .

For these reasons, I would affirm the judgment of the Court of Appeals.

Part IV:
Voting, Elections, and Partisanship

Polarized Politics and the 2004 Congressional and Presidential Elections

GARY C. JACOBSON

The 2004 elections left the Republican Party in its strongest position since Herbert Hoover was elected president seventy-six years ago. George W. Bush won reelection by a modest but unambiguous margin—Bush won the popular vote, but by the narrowest percentage of any reelected president in history—(50.7 percent to John Kerry's 48.3 percent of the popular vote), while the Republicans solidified their congressional majorities by adding three House seats and four Senate seats. The election was not, however, a ringing electoral endorsement of the administration's or the Republican Congress's performance, nor did it represent any global shift in public sentiment to the Republican side. Rather, it was the product of two salient features of present-day American politics: the substantial structural advantage Republicans now enjoy in the struggle for control of Congress, and the extraordinarily polarized public reactions to the Bush administration, sentiments that found their fullest expression in the presidential contest but also spilled over into congressional races. Although strengthening the Republican grip on power, the outcome did not break the national stalemate reflected in election results and public opinion polls over the past decade, and it is likely to intensify rather than diminish the level of partisan conflict among leaders and ordinary Americans alike during the second Bush administration.

Table 1 summarizes the congressional results. The election brought little change to the House. Only seven of the 402 incumbents who sought reelection were defeated, and four of the seven were victims of a Republican gerrymander in Texas (discussed below), not swings in voter sentiment. The party already in control held onto twenty-seven of the thirty-four open seats (those vacated by

GARY C. JACOBSON is professor of political science at the University of California, San Diego. He is the author of *Money in Congressional Elections*, *The Politics of Congressional Elections*, and *The Electoral Origins of Divided Government*, and coauthor of *Strategy and Choice in Congressional Elections*. His current research focuses on partisan polarization in American politics.

TABLE 1

Membership Changes in the House and Senate in the 2004 Elections

	Republicans	Democrats	Independents
House of Representatives			
At the time of the 2004 election	229	205	1
Elected in 2004	232	202	1
Incumbents reelected	208	186	1
Incumbents defeated by challengers	2	3	
Incumbents defeated by incumbents		2	
Open seats retained	17	12	
Open seats lost	2	3	
New open seats	1		
Senate			
At the time of the 2004 election	51	48	1
After the 2004 election	55	44	1
Incumbents reelected	11	13	
Incumbents defeated		1	
Open seats retained	2		
Open seats lost	2	5	

Source: Compiled by author.

the incumbent), and two of the three that were lost by Democrats were also a legacy of the Texas redistricting, as was the Republican pickup of the state's new open seat. Without the Texas remap, only eight House seats would have changed party hands, an all-time low. The Senate elections saw considerably more action. Only one of the twenty-six incumbents seeking reelection lost, but he was the Democrats' minority leader, Tom Daschle of South Dakota. Of the eight open seats, seven changed party control, and it was here that the Republicans enjoyed their greatest success.

THE HOUSE

The fierce battle for the White House remained in doubt until election day, but there was no similar contest for control of the House. Despite data showing Democrats with a lead among voters in both party identification and the generic House vote in polls taken during the months leading up to the election,[1] continued Republican control of the House was never in doubt. The reason is simple: Republican voters are distributed more efficiently across House districts than are Democratic voters, giving the Republicans a major structural advantage in

---

[1] Generic polls ask whether, if the election were held today, the respondent would vote for the Republican or Democratic candidate, without mentioning the candidates' names. In the sixteen CBS News/*New York Times* polls taken between January 2004 and the election, the Democrats' share of party identifiers averaged 53 percent; in thirty generic House polls taken between 1 August and the election, an average of 51.4 percent said they would vote for the Democrat. See http://www.pollingreport.com, accessed 6 November 2004.

the battle for House seats. Without a strong national tide in their favor—and no national partisan tide ran in 2004—Democrats currently have no hope of winning control of the House.

The Republicans' structural advantage is evident in the distribution of the major-party vote for president in 2000. Short-term political forces were evenly balanced that year, and party line voting was the highest it had been in decades, so both the national and district-level presidential vote reflected the electorate's underlying partisan balance with unusual accuracy.[2] The Democrat, Al Gore, won the national popular vote by about 540,000 of the 105 million votes cast. Yet the distribution of these votes across current House districts yields 240 in which Bush won more votes than Gore but only 195 in which Gore outpolled Bush.

Part of the reason for this Republican advantage is demographic: Democrats win a disproportionate share of minority and other urban voters, who tend to be concentrated in districts with lopsided Democratic majorities.[3] But it is also the effect of partisan gerrymanders brought off by the Republicans in states where they controlled the redistricting process after the 2000 census (Figure 1).[4] Although Gore had received nearly 47 percent of the vote in states where Republicans were in charge of redrawing the district lines, Republican gerrymanders reduced the proportion of Gore-majority seats by twelve, from 39 percent of the total in 2000 to 30 percent in 2004. Democrats made small gains by this measure where they controlled the process, but these were offset by pro-Republican changes in states where neither party had full control. The Republican gerrymanders achieved their purpose (Figure 2). Republicans added fifteen seats between 2000 and 2004 in states they redistricted, while losing only six elsewhere.[5]

Indeed, had it not been for the extraordinary second redistricting of Texas in 2003, Republicans would have lost House seats in 2004. At the behest of House majority leader Tom DeLay, the Republican majority that won control of Texas's government in the 2002 election drew a new House district map designed to eliminate as many as seven incumbent Democrats.[6] One (Ralph T.

[2] Gary C. Jacobson, "A House and Senate Divided: The Clinton Legacy and the Congressional Elections of 2000," *Political Science Quarterly* 116 (Spring, 2001): 5–27.

[3] For example, according to the CBS News/*New York Times* poll of 20–25 August 2004, Democratic identifiers outnumbered Republicans nearly five to one in New York City. See "New York City and the Republican Convention" at http://www.cbsnews.com/htdocs/CBSNews_polls/nyc.pdf, 29 August 2004, accessed 6 November 2004.

[4] The most important of these states were Florida, Michigan, Ohio, Pennsylvania, and, after 2002, Texas.

[5] In 2004, in Republican-controlled states, Republicans won 90 percent of the Bush-majority districts, whereas Democrats won 85 percent of the Gore-majority districts; the figures for the other states are 84 percent and 88 percent, respectively.

[6] Not without resistance; Democrats in the state legislature twice tried to thwart the remap by fleeing the state en masse (once to Oklahoma, once to New Mexico) to prevent action by denying legislative quorums while avoiding arrest under a Texas statute aimed at preventing just this tactic. DeLay sought help from federal agencies to track the missing Democrats, a move that earned him a formal admonishment from the House Ethics Committee. It took five months and two special legislative sessions before the Democrats capitulated.

FIGURE 1
The Effects of Redistricting Control on District Partisanship, 2000–2004
(Measured by the Presidential Vote)

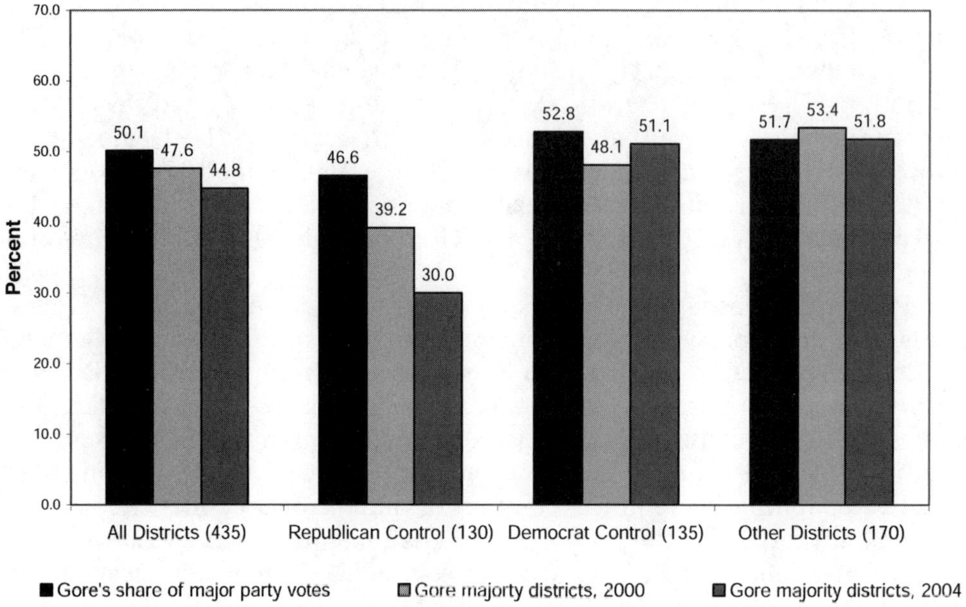

- Gore's share of major party votes
- Gore majorty districts, 2000
- Gore majority districts, 2004

Source: Compiled by author.

Hall) thereupon defected to the Republican Party, another retired, and four were defeated in the general election.[7] Only one targeted Democrat (Chet Edwards) managed to survive. The remap raised the Republicans' share of the Texas delegation from fifteen to twenty-one seats, the gain more than offsetting the party's net loss of three seats elsewhere.

Aside from partisan gerrymandering, redistricting after the 2000 census reduced the overall number of competitive House seats by strengthening about three-quarters of most of the most marginal incumbents.[8] Partly as a result, only four of the 382 incumbents seeking reelection in 2002 were defeated by challengers. (Four more lost to other incumbents in face-offs forced by redistricting.) The 2002 election also extended the long-term decline in the number of seats with a mismatch between the party of the incumbent representative and the partisan leanings of the district as measured by its presidential vote.[9] Thus, approaching the elections of 2004, with no clear partisan tide in sight, neither party

[7] In addition, two incumbent Texas Democrats lost primary contests to other Democrats who went on to win the general election.

[8] Gary C. Jacobson, "Terror, Terrain, and Turnout: Explaining the 2002 Midterm Election," *Political Science Quarterly* 118 (Spring 2003): 10–11

[9] Ibid., p. 12.

FIGURE 2

Control of Redistricting and Change in the Distribution of House Seats,
2000–2004

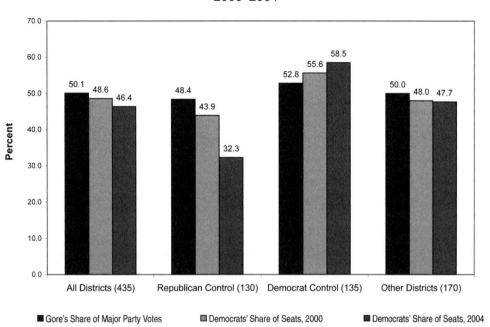

Source: Compiled by author.

saw much opportunity to take many seats from the other, and the consequence was the lowest level of competition for House seats ever observed. *Congressional Quarterly* classified only thirty-seven contests as "no clear favorite" or merely "leaning" to one party, the smallest number of competitive races in the three decades the publication has been handicapping House contests.[10]

Congressional Quarterly's analysts base their risk ratings on a district-by-district analysis of the candidates, the campaigns, and campaign finances. They found that few districts were in play because the ingredients of a competitive race were missing in so many places, reflecting not only the scarcity of seats where local partisanship or missteps by the incumbent gave the out-party hope, but also the absence of a national surge toward either party. Conditions traditionally thought to influence national electoral tides, namely, the state of the econ-

---

[10] *Congressional Quarterly* classifies seats as safe Republican, Republican favored, leaning Republican, no clear favorite, leaning Democratic, Democrat favored, or safe Democratic. These classifications are usually quite accurate; in 2004, all of the seats classified as safe or favored went to the party so designated; only three of the thirty classified as leaning to a party were won by the other party. The 1980–2002 average for the middle three categories was sixty-nine. For 2004, the data are from http://www.nytimes.com/packages/html/politics/2004_ELECTIONGUIDE_GRAPHIC/index_HOUSECQ. html; for earlier years, they are from the October election previews in the *CQ Weekly Report.*

FIGURE 3
Approval of George W. Bush's Job Performance, 2001–2004

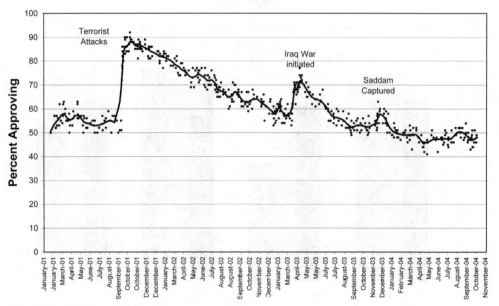

Note: The solid line is estimated by Lowess smoothing.
Source: National polls taken by ten media polling organizations (see footnote 11 for a list).

omy and the public's evaluation of the president's performance, were effectively neutral once the new post-September 11 consideration, terrorism, was added to the mix. The economy's performance during the entire first Bush administration was mediocre by historical standards, but growth was solid in the year leading up to the election and the economy's earlier weakness could be blamed, in part, on the damage done to markets by the attacks of September 11. Real per capita income grew by 2.4 percent during 2004, close to the average of 2.7 for postwar presidential election years. The net loss of jobs since Bush took office in 2001 gave Democrats something to talk about, but the modest improvements during 2004 took the edge off the issue.

President Bush's job approval ratings also fell into a politically neutral range. Although declining from the record high Bush enjoyed during the immediate post-September 11 rally, they generally remained above 50 percent until February 2004 and stayed close to this mark through the election (Figure 3). The relatively low performance ratings Americans gave the president on the economy (an average of 43 percent approving, August through October) were evidently offset by notably higher performance ratings on his handling of terrorism (56 percent approving), keeping the president's overall job approval at a level that offered neither party's congressional candidates a discernable ad-

FIGURE 4
Partisanship and Approval of G.W. Bush's Performance

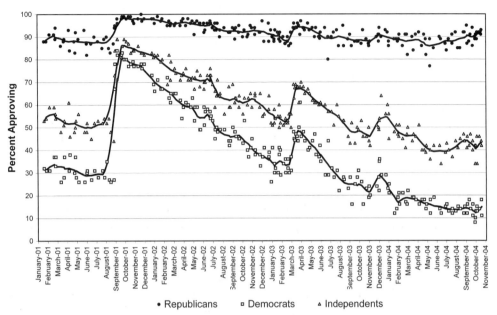

Note: The solid lines are estimated by Lowess smoothing.
Source: CBS News/*New York Times* and Gallup polls.

vantage, even after Bush's handling of the Iraq War had become a net liability (only 44 percent approving during this period).[11]

More important, the *composition* of Bush's overall approval ratings promised neither party's congressional candidates any help. Bush enjoyed overwhelming support from Republicans, achieving the highest job approval ratings within his own party of any president in the more than fifty years pollsters have been asking the question. But his approval rating among Democratic identifiers fell steeply after the post-September 11 rally, and by the beginning of 2004, had dipped below 20 percent (Figure 4). It fell further during the campaign, reaching the lowest point the Gallup poll ever recorded among the rival party's identifiers—8 percent in one October 2004 poll. Ironically, the candidate who had pledged in his 2000 acceptance speech campaign to be "a uniter, not a divider" had become the most polarizing president on record. Before Bush and going back to Eisenhower, the partisan difference in approval ratings had never exceeded 70 percentage points in any Gallup poll. In the twelve Gallup polls

[11] Based on twenty surveys taken between 1 August and 30 October 2004 by the CBS News/*New York Times* Gallup, ABC News/*Washington Post*, *Los Angeles Times*, and Pew Research Center for the People & the Press polls. Figure 3 includes data from these organizations plus the NBC News/*Wall Street Journal*, *Newsweek*, Marist, and Bloomberg polls; all sample adults 18 years and older.

taken during the three months leading up to the election, the gap never fell below 70 points, averaging 79 and peaking at 83 (94–11). Evaluations of Bush's performance in different policy domains were also highly polarized along party lines during this period, on average splitting 82–13 on his handling of the economy, 82–20 on Iraq, and 90–27 on terrorism. These partisan differences were echoed in voters' responses to virtually all of the polling questions regarding which party would handle various policy issues better, as well as about the state of the economy and the overall direction of the country.[12]

In such a highly polarized atmosphere, neither party could anticipate attracting many partisan defectors on election day, so the vast majority of House districts were ceded to the dominant party. Only the most vulnerable House incumbents—very few in number—attracted formidable challenges. And in a departure from past elections, even open House seat contests were relatively quiet in 2004. Only eleven of the thirty-five were classified as competitive by *Congressional Quarterly*. (In 2000 and 2002, by comparison, more than half of the open seats were rated competitive.) One reason is that only nine of these seats were in the "wrong" party's hands according to the district's 2000 presidential vote; in twenty-one open districts, the 2000 presidential vote for the candidate of the party currently holding the seat exceeded 55 percent.

In the end, five of the seven open seats that switched party control in 2004 went to the party with the 2000 presidential majority, as did the new open seat in Texas, the two Texas seats where incumbents faced off, and four of the five other seats where challengers were successful. Thus, although the House elections produced relatively little change, they extended the long-term trend toward increasing the district-level consistency in House and presidential voting that is documented in Figure 5.

Finally, it is worth noting that the net results of the House elections were almost exactly what standard statistical models of the effects of national forces on aggregate election outcomes would predict. For example, an equation estimating inter-election seat swings as a function of presidential approval, real income change, and the quality of each party's challengers predicts a three-seat gain for Democrats, just what they would have achieved had it not been for the Texas redistricting (which was, of course, not factored into the model).[13]

THE SENATE

The same trend toward greater consistency in voting for president and U.S. representative appeared in the 2004 Senate elections, resulting in a four-seat addi-

---

[12] See, for example, the CBS News/*New York Times* poll of 11–12 July 2004, at http://www.cbsnews.com/sections/opinion/polls, accessed 20 July 2004.

[13] The model may be found in Gary C. Jacobson, *The Politics of Congressional Elections*, 6th ed. (New York: Longman, 2004), 176. The prediction is based on the parameters estimated in the second equation in Table 6-6 multiplied by the values of the independent variables for 2004: presidential approval at 48 percent in the final Gallup poll before the election, annual change in real income per capita at 2.4 percent, and the proportion of experienced Republican and Democratic challengers at 14.7 percent and 14.6 percent, respectively.

FIGURE 5
Split House and Presidential Election Results, 1952–2004

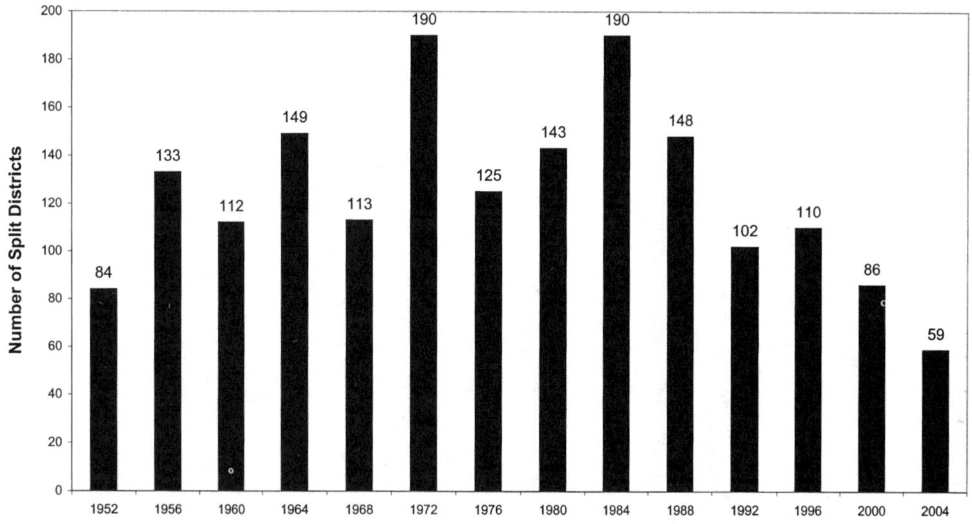

Source: Compiled by author.

tion to the Republicans' Senate majority. Although Democrats had entertained some hope of adding the two seats they needed to become the majority party, their chances were slim. In order to reach fifty-one, they would have had to win every seat where *Congressional Quarterly* gave them an edge and all of the seats rated tossups. Instead, Republicans won five of the six tossup races and another classified as leaning Democratic (Tom Daschle's seat). The Democrats' main problem was again structural: the more-efficient distribution of Republican voters. Although Gore had won the national vote in 2000, Bush carried thirty of the fifty states, including twenty-two of the thirty-four states with Senate contests in 2004. Democrats had to defend ten seats in states Bush had won, including five left open by retirements, all in the South, where support for Democrats has been eroding for several decades. Meanwhile, Republicans were defending only three seats in states won by Gore.

The opportunities offered by the Senate seats up for election in 2004 attracted a much higher proportion of serious aspirants than did the House contests. Six of the eight open seats produced heated, often lavishly-financed contests between first-tier candidates, as did the Republican challenge to minority leader Daschle. The principal contenders included eight current or former members of the House, three statewide officeholders, two former cabinet secretaries, and the heir to the Coors name and beer fortune. In the end, Republicans won all five of the open southern Democratic seats, plus Daschle's. Democrats picked up two open Republican seats with Barak Obama's victory in Illinois over Alan Keyes and Ken Salazar's over Peter Coors in Colorado. Seven of the

FIGURE 6
States Won by Same Party in Senate and Presidential Elections, 1952–2004

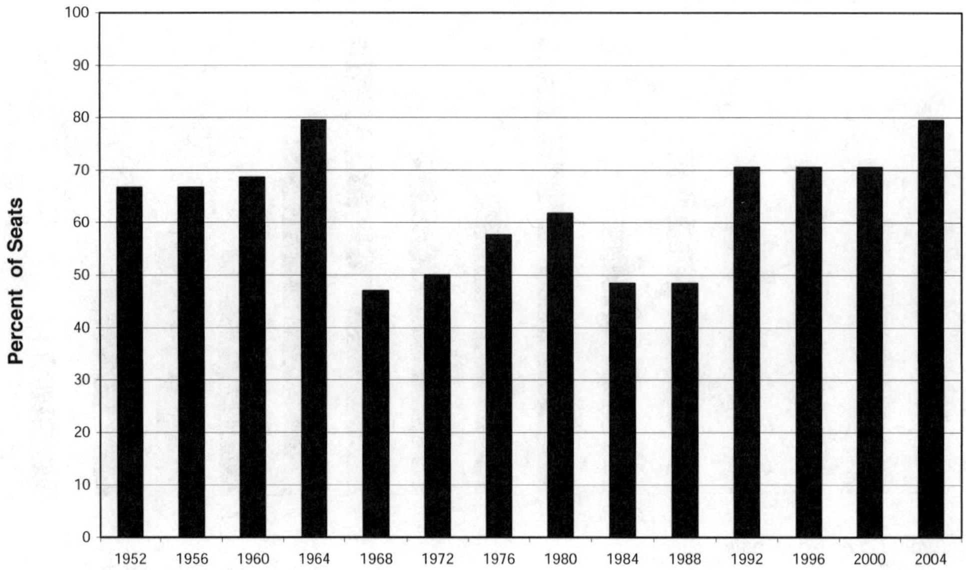

Source: Compiled by author.

eight Senate seats that changed party hands in 2004 went to the party that won the state in the 2000 and 2004 presidential elections; Salazar's victory was the lone exception.

More generally, twenty-seven of the thirty-four Senate contests were won by the party whose presidential candidate won the state's electoral votes, tying 1964 for the highest level of congruence in president–Senate election results in the past half century (Figure 6). When the 2004 winners are added to the continuing Senate membership, fully 75 percent of Senators now represent states where their party's candidate won the most recent presidential election, the highest proportion in at least fifty years (Figure 7).

In both House and Senate elections, then, the trend toward increasing partisan consistency in election results continued in 2004. There is little doubt that the national campaigns and the conditions that had shaped them had a good deal to do with this outcome. With the exceptions of "leave no child behind" and the prescription drug benefit bill, Bush spent his first term catering to his party's base among the corporate and small business sectors, social conservatives, and hard-line foreign-policy nationalists and was rewarded with overwhelming support from Republican identifiers. His approach alienated ordinary Democrats, who objected to the administration's policies on taxes, the environment, regulation, stem cell research, and, most important, the war in Iraq. Partisan differences were reinforced by the Bush campaign's primary focus on mobilizing core Republican supporters, especially religious conservatives, without much effort to reach out to moderates and Democrats.

FIGURE 7

*Senate Seats Held by the Party Winning the State in the Most Recent
Presidential Election*

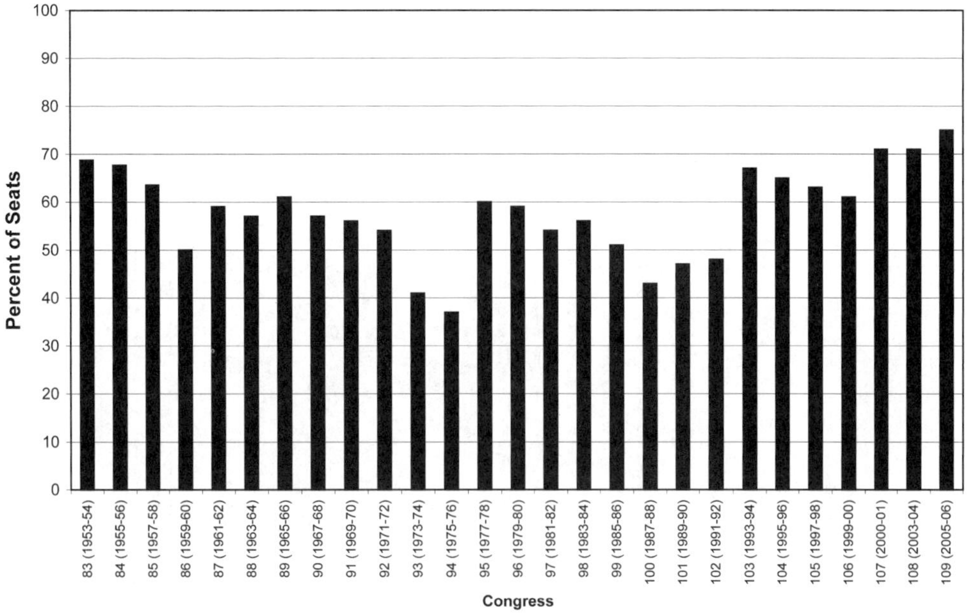

Source: Compiled by author.

It was a successful strategy. Both presidential campaigns invested heavily
in getting supporters to the polls, contributing (along with the strong feelings
aroused by the candidates in 2004) to an increase of more than 17 million voters
over 2000, raising the turnout rate from 55 percent to 60 percent of the eligible
electorate.[14] But the Bush campaign outdid the Kerry campaign on this score,
giving Bush his victory. According to the 2004 American National Election
Study (NES), presidential turnout among Democratic identifiers was 1.9 percentage points higher than in 2000 and 2.6 points higher than their 1972–2000
average; among Republican identifiers, it was 4.8 points higher than in 2000 and
5.0 points higher than their 1972–2000 average.[15] The higher Republican turnout almost completely offset the Democrats' advantage in party identification,
leaving an electorate composed of 47.4 percent Democrats and 46.4 percent
Republicans (leaners treated as partisans). This augmented electorate dis-
played the highest level of partisan loyalty among presidential voters reported

[14] Michael McDonald, "Voter Turnout," accessed at http://www.gmu.edu/voter_turnout.htm, 4
February 2005.

[15] NES respondents always overstate their participation, but this does not prevent valid cross-elec-
tion comparisons. The 2004 data are from the American National Election Study (VERSION 20050418,
Apr 18, 2005), accessed at http://www.umich.edu/~nes/studyres/download/nesdatacenter.htm, 18 April
2005. Earlier data are from the NES 1948–2002 Cumulative Data File available at the same site.

FIGURE 8
Partisans Voting for the Other Party's Candidates in House and
Senate Elections, 1952–2004

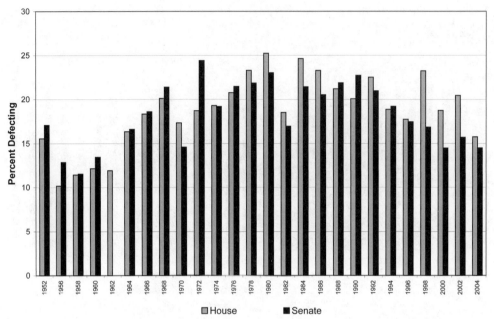

Source: National Election Studies 1948–2002 cumulative data file and 2004 early release file.
Note: Senate vote question was not asked in 1962.

in the half century of NES surveys, 89.8 percent. Republicans were slightly more loyal than Democrats, 90.6 percent compared to 89.0 percent, another small contribution to Bush's success.

In such circumstances, it is no surprise to find that increased turnout in House and Senate elections favored Republicans and that congressional voters were also unusually loyal to their parties. In the previous five NES studies conducted in presidential election years (1984–2000), turnout of Republican identifiers averaged 5.2 percentage points higher than that of Democratic identifiers in House elections, and 6.3 points higher in Senate elections; in 2004, the Republican turnout advantage was 8.7 points in the former and 9.6 points in the latter. NES respondents' partisan defection rates in 2004 were the lowest since 1962 in House races and tied with 2000 for the lowest since 1960 in Senate races, elections prior to the sharp rise in the incumbency advantage of the mid-1960s (Figure 8).[16] Ticket splitting—voting for different parties in the presidential and House or Senate races—was also at its lowest level since the early 1960s.

The NES data also underline how important the enthusiasm for Bush among ordinary Republicans was to both his and his congressional allies' victo-

---

[16] Jacobson, The Politics of Congressional Elections, 26–28.

ries. Notice in Figure 4 that the performance ratings of the president offered by self-identified independents were relatively low, considerably closer to those of Democrats than to those of Republicans. Bush's weakness among independents was also evident in the NES survey, where 58 percent (defined as either pure independents or as pure independents plus independents who said they leaned toward a party) reported voting for Kerry.[17] Only once before, in 1960, did the loser receive a majority of votes from independents in an NES survey. Majorities of independents also favored Democratic Senate and House candidates in 2004. The high turnout and solid support of Republican identifiers for Republican candidates, then, was essential to offset the equally solid opposition among the Democrats who did vote and the Republicans' relatively weak showing among independents.

High turnout and high party loyalty, combined with the Republicans' structural advantage in House elections and the mix of Senate seats up in 2004, served to strengthen the Republican grip on Congress despite the absence of any pro-Republican trend in voter opinion. The aggregate vote totals indicate that Democrats actually ran stronger in House races than they had in 2002. Their mean vote was higher (51.1 percent compared to 49.9 percent); in districts with major-party competitors in both 2002 and 2004, the Democrats' share of votes increased an average of 1.4 percentage points, with nearly two-thirds of the Democrats improving on their party's 2002 performance. As noted, only the Texas gerrymander saved Republicans from a net loss of House seats. Yet any election that, like 2004, is characterized by high levels of party polarization and loyalty simply reinforces the Democrats' structural disadvantage in the distribution of voters, leaving them virtually no chance of making significant gains.

The highly polarized electorate was most damaging, however, to Democrats' Senate hopes. As noted above, eight of the nine Senate seats that changed party hands conformed to the red state–blue state presidential division. Most devastating to Democrats was the loss of all five of the open seats they were defending in the South. Figure 9 shows why they were shut out. For many years, a substantial proportion of Southerners who preferred Republican presidential candidates had nonetheless been willing to vote for Democrats for Senate; between 1960 and 1992, an average of 40 percent did so. After the Republican takeover of the Senate in 1994, that average fell to 15 percent; in 2004, it was down to 8 percent, and if the analysis is confined to open seats, a mere 4 percent.[18] Consequently, the five Democrats defending open Senate seats in the South ran only slightly ahead of Kerry (3 percentage points on average), doom-

[17] Both the Gallup poll and the national exit poll also showed Kerry winning among independents, although by smaller margins (4 points and 1 point, respectively). See Jeffrey M. Jones, "How American Voted," Gallup News Service, 5 November 2004; and "Results from the Times National and California Exit poll," *Los Angeles Times Poll Alert*, Study #513, 3 November 2004.

[18] The same trend shown in Figure 10 is evident in Southern voting for U.S. Representatives, although it is not so pronounced and was lowest in 1996, not 2004.

FIGURE 9
Ticket Splitting by Republican Presidential Voters in the Southern Senate
Elections, 1952–2004

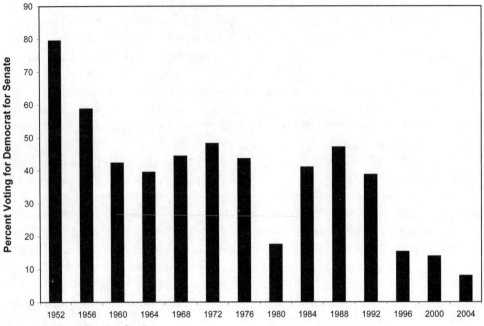

Source: National Election Studies.

ing their candidacies in states where Bush was very popular and won handily.[19] Tom Daschle's narrow defeat by John Thune in South Dakota (49.4 percent to 50.6 percent) was also probably a consequence of tightening party lines. Daschle had run 92,000 votes ahead of Bill Clinton in 1992 but outpolled Kerry by only 44,000 in 2004, not enough in a state that Bush won with 61 percent of the major-party vote.

In sum, the Bush administration's strategy of serving the party's base while in office and putting most of its energies into mobilizing core supporters during the campaign was at least as productive for congressional Republicans as it was for the president. A partisan standoff with both sides highly motivated and loyal to their parties guarantees, at present, Republican control of Congress.

CAMPAIGN MONEY IN 2004

The 2004 elections were the first conducted under the Bipartisan Campaign Reform Act (BCRA), which, among other things, doubled the individual contribution limit to $2,000 per candidate per campaign, closed the "soft money"

[19] According to the 2004 NES survey, Bush's approval rating was 63.9 percent in these five states, compared to 49.4 percent elsewhere.

loophole in party fundraising and spending, and imposed restrictions on advocacy groups that had been spending unlimited and unreported sums on independent campaigns under the guise of "voter education" or "issue advocacy." BCRA was not without effect—the share of campaign contributions from individuals increased, parties shifted from spending soft money to spending hard money on independent campaigns, and 527 groups took up some of the space formerly occupied by advocacy groups funded by unions and corporations[20]—but the flow of campaign funds was determined much less by BCRA than by the fundamental strategic considerations that always shape congressional campaign finance.

Money of all sorts—contributions to candidates' campaigns, independent party spending, 527 and other independent campaigns—was heavily concentrated in the small number of competitive House races and in the ten or so hottest Senate contests. With one possible exception, every House or Senate candidate with a plausible chance of winning was amply funded.[21] In a few Senate contests, spending reached astonishing levels. Daschle and Thune between them spent a total of more than $34 million in South Dakota, a state with fewer than 502,000 registered voters, amounting to a record $67 per eligible voter. In Alaska, the candidates spent $11 million to reach an electorate of fewer than 480,000 (nearly $23 per voter). Independent spending by parties and organizations was also heaviest in these and the other competitive races, combining with the candidates' efforts to produce a level of saturation campaigning difficult to imagine without living in a targeted state or district. The election results suggest that the product of all of this extravagance was a standoff: neither party enjoyed a financial advantage, so outcomes were largely determined by the underlying partisan disposition of the electorate. Given the Republicans' structural advantage in the distribution of partisans, such a standoff could only be to their candidates' benefit.

THE 109TH CONGRESS

The results of the 2004 elections are unlikely to mitigate the intensely partisan atmosphere in which they took place. Indeed, the turnover of congressional seats points in the opposite direction. All six of the Senate Democrats replaced by Republicans were more moderate than their party's average, with mean DW

[20] Gary C. Jacobson, "The First Congressional Campaign After BCRA," in *One Election Later: 2004 Politics After the Bipartisan Campaign Reform Act* (Lanham, MD: Rowman & Littlefield, forthcoming).

[21] In Kentucky, Democratic challenger Daniel Mongiardo was given little chance until the incumbent, Republican Jim Bunning, began behaving erratically during the campaign. Some late money flowed into Mongiardo's campaign and he eventually received help from his party, but the $3 million he spent was still 30 percent lower in real terms than Bunning's 1998 opponent had spent. Mongiardo won 49.3 percent of the vote. This is the only Senate or House race in 2004 in which a timely infusion of money might have altered the outcome; Ibid.

Nominate scores for the 108th Congress (2003–2004) of −.220, compared to −.409 for the other Senate Democrats (the difference is significant at $p <$ 0.01).[22] Six of the newly elected Republican senators, including four of the five who replaced southern Democrats, had served in the House. Four of the six had more-conservative DW Nominate scores than their party's average in that body. Moreover, the two retiring Republican senators whose seats were won by Democrats (Peter Fitzgerald of Illinois and Ben Nighthorse Campbell of Colorado) were both to the left of their party's mean (.235 and .248, respectively, compared to the party average of .393). Thus in the Senate, both parties lost moderates and, at least on the Republican side, gained more extreme ideologues.

Changes brought about by the House elections had a similar thrust, although the effect is smaller because a much smaller proportion of House seats changed party hands. All five of the Texas Democrats who were pushed out by redistricting and replaced by Republicans had been more moderate than average for their party; if we include Hall, the party-switcher, the average DW Nominate score for the six departing Democrats is −.179 compared to −.409 for all other House Democrats (the difference is significant at $p < 0.001$). The net ideological effect of the other six party turnovers in the House is, however, likely to be neutral.

More broadly, the electoral coalitions served by the congressional parties in each house continue to diverge ideologically. As Figure 10 shows, the consistency between ideological self-placement and congressional voting reached a peak in 2004. A substantial majority of voters (about 61 percent) now place themselves on the seven-point NES liberal–conservative scale and to the right or left of its center point. Among these voters, 82 percent voted appropriately (liberals for Democrats, conservatives for Republicans) in House elections and 84 percent in Senate elections, the highest levels yet in the NES time series. Consequently, the congressional parties in the 109th Congress will be representing the most ideologically divergent electoral coalitions since NES began measuring respondents' ideologies in 1972. Figure 11 displays the growing ideological gap between the parties' respective electoral coalitions in both chambers (defined by the NES respondents who voted for their successful candidates). Whereas thirty years ago, the mean self-placements of the voters responsible for electing Republicans and Democrats to Congress were only about 0.5 points apart on the scale, the gap has since tripled, to about 1.5 points. Looking at the data another way, back in the early 1970s, the ratio of liberals to conservatives

---

[22] The DW Nominate scale is a measure of ideological location calculated from all the nonunanimous roll call votes cast in all congresses since the 80th (1947–1948). Each member's pattern of roll call votes locates him or her on a liberal–conservative scale ranging from −1.0 (most liberal) to 1.0 (most conservative). See Nolan M. McCarty, Keith T. Poole, and Howard Rosenthal, *Income Redistribution and the Realignment of American Politics* (Washington DC: The AEI Press, 1997); DW Nominate is an updated version of their D-Nominate measure; I am obliged to Keith Poole for providing these data, which may be found at http://voteview.com/dwnl, accessed 4 January 2005.

FIGURE 10

Ideology and Voting in Congressional Elections, 1972–2004

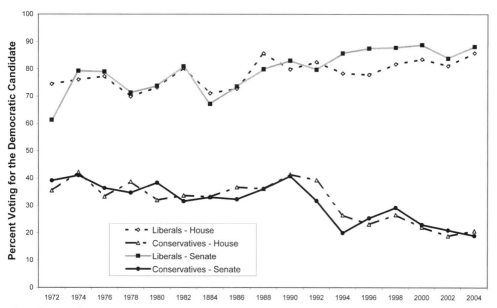

Note: Data are for contested elections only. Liberal, those who place themselves at 1–3 on the NES 7-point liberal–conservative scale; conservative, those who place themselves at 5–7 on the scale.
Source: National Election Studies.

in the Democrats' House and Senate coalitions was about an even 1:1; now, liberals outnumber conservatives by more than 2:1 in both. Conservatives outnumbered liberals among Republican electoral constituencies in the early 1970s by ratios of about 2:1 in both chambers; by 2004, the ratio of conservatives to liberals had grown to more than 7:1 in the House and more than 10:1 in the Senate.

The election, then, reinforced the already sturdy electoral roots of partisan and ideological polarization in national politics. It also left the nation as sharply divided along party lines in their assessments of the winner as they had been before the election. As a result, Bush received the lowest overall approval ratings of any newly reelected president for whom survey data are available, as his sky-high ratings among Republicans were offset by extraordinarily low approval among Democrats (Figure 12). The president's Second Inaugural and State of the Union addresses left these assessments largely unaffected.[23] If anything, the president's declared second-term domestic agenda—partial privatization of Social Security, making the 2001 tax cuts permanent, cutting social programs, pursuing pro-industry tort reform, energy and environmental policies—is even more polarizing than his first. Add to it the president's renomina-

[23] In two Gallup polls taken in February after the State of the Union speech, Bush's approval rating averaged 92.5 percent among Republicans, 17.5 percent among Democrats, and 53 percent overall.

FIGURE 11

Ideological Divergence of Electoral Constituencies of House and Senate Parties, 1972–2004

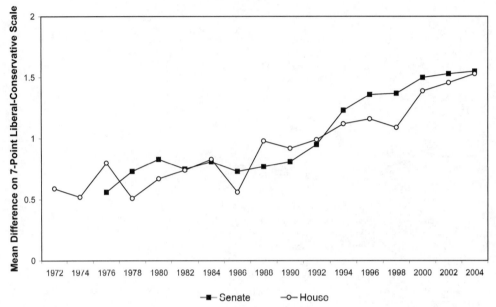

Source: National Election Studies.

tion of conservative judges, the chipping away at abortion rights, and continued pursuit of the neo-conservative vision in foreign policy, and it is difficult to imagine that partisan and ideological conflict will subside any time soon. The enlarged Republican House and Senate majorities should, in theory, make it easier for Bush to prevail in these conflicts. But the hostility of their own supporters to the administration leaves congressional Democrats with little incentive to help Bush in any way and every reason to mount all-out resistance on issues such as Social Security privatization, on which their constituents remain overwhelmingly opposed to his policies.

LOOKING TO 2006

Democrats also have ample reason to consider adopting the obstructionist tactics pioneered by Newt Gingrich and Bob Dole when the Democrats had undivided control of the government—and thus full responsibility for its performance—during the 103rd Congress (1993–1994). Refusing any serious participation in the attempt to reform the health care system or to balance the budget, Republicans put all their energy into making the Clinton administration and its Democratic allies in Congress look bad. The strategy worked, and Republicans have run Congress ever since.[24] Democrats are now in a position where

---

[24] With the exception of the period during the 107th Congress, after James Jeffords's exit from the Republican Party gave Democrats temporary control of the Senate.

FIGURE 12

First Post-election Approval Ratings of Presidents Elected to Second Terms

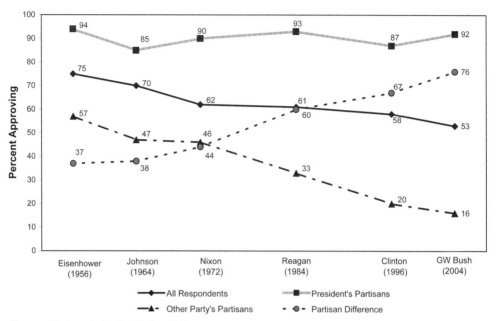

Source: First post-election Gallup Poll.

they have little hope of retaking either chamber without the help of a strong pro-Democratic (or, more probably, anti-Republican) national tide. Such a tide could, in principle, break the Republican hold on the House. Figure 13, which displays the frequency distribution of Republican and Democratic House seats according to the size of Gore's share of the major-party vote in 2000, suggests why. The Democratic seats at the far right of the figure outnumber the Republican seats at the far left, evidence of the larger number of "wasted" Democratic voters in House elections. But the Republican seats just to the left of the 50-50 line outnumber the Democratic seats just to its right, indicating that, at least in theory, more Republican than Democratic House seats would be vulnerable to an unfavorable national swing. Thus, if national conditions—the economy's performance, Bush's standing with the public, unpopular Republican action on the budget or in tinkering with Social Security, deteriorating conditions in Iraq—were to favor the Democrats at the time of the 2006 midterm, they might be able to retake the House, always assuming that the party recruited enough high-quality candidates with the skill and resources to take advantage of the electoral opportunities such conditions would offer.

The configuration of Senate seats that will be on the ballot in 2006 is also more favorable to the Democrats than it was in 2002 or 2004, although not enough to make a Democratic Senate majority more than a long shot, even with favorable national conditions. Sixteen of the thirty-three seats that are up in 2006 are in states won by Gore and Kerry, but only three of them are currently

FIGURE 13
Party Control of House Seats after the 2004 Election

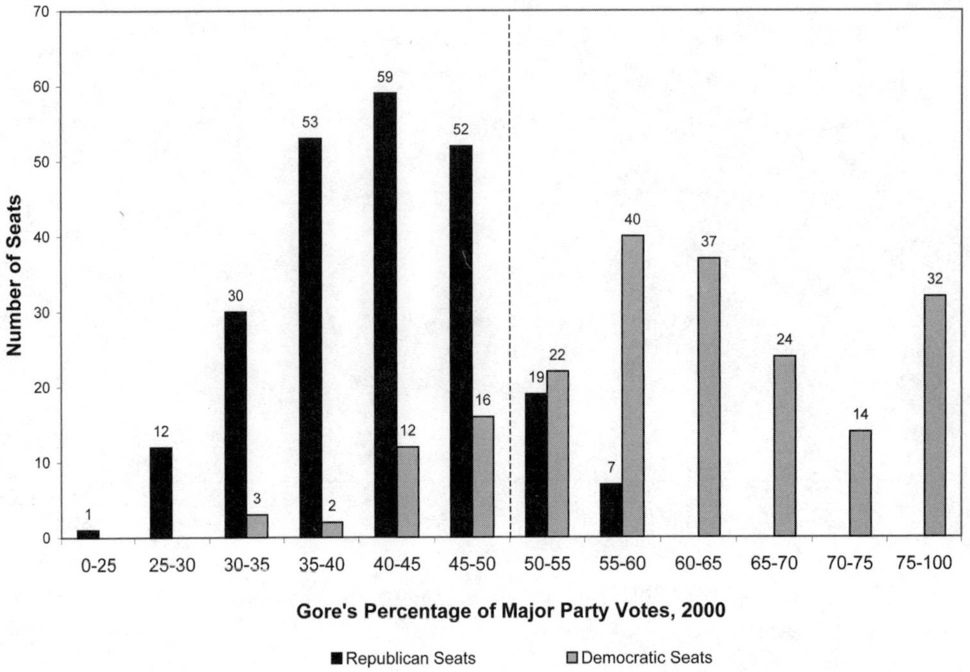

Gore's Percentage of Major Party Votes, 2000

■ Republican Seats   ▢ Democratic Seats

Source: Compiled by author.

held by Republicans, two of whom are popular moderates, Olympia Snowe of Maine and Lincoln Chafee of Rhode Island. Only the third, Rick Santorum of Pennsylvania, a hard-line social conservative in a state that leans Democratic, seems potentially vulnerable. Moreover, five of the seventeen seats Democrats will be defending in 2006 are in states won by Bush in 2004 (Florida, Nebraska, New Mexico, North Dakota, and West Virginia).

In future contests for control of either chamber, a continuation of the current era of relatively high partisan loyalty and sharp partisan polarization would appear to serve congressional Republicans well. As long as voters in an evenly divided electorate stick to their parties, the Republicans' structural advantage will keep the party on top. Republican leaders, then, have little electoral incentive to accommodate congressional Democrats or to avoid actions that might intensify partisan and ideological divisions.

Why Bush Won the Presidential Election of 2004: Incumbency, Ideology, Terrorism, and Turnout

JAMES E. CAMPBELL

More than 122 million Americans voted in the 2004 presidential election, nearly 17 million more than in 2000. This was a 16 percent increase in the total vote, the largest percentage increase in turnout since 1952.[1] Of the more than 121 million who voted for a major-party candidate, 51.2 percent voted for President George W. Bush and 48.8 percent voted for his Democratic rival, Senator John Kerry. President Bush carried thirty-one states and accumulated 286 electoral votes, making him only the sixteenth president in American history to be elected to two terms in the White House—and only the fourth since 1960. Republicans have now won seven of the last ten presidential elections.

Although the 2004 election was not as close as many observers had anticipated in the last weeks of the campaign nor as close as the election of 2000, it nonetheless ranks in the top tier of narrowly decided presidential elections. Of the thirty-five presidential contests since 1868, the 2004 election is one of only nine in which the winning presidential candidate received less than 51.5 percent of the two-party popular vote.[2] President Bush received the narrowest popular

---

[1] The estimated turnout in 2004 as a percentage of the voting age population was 56.2 percent, according to Dave Leip, "Dave Leip's Atlas of U.S. Presidential Elections," accessed at http://uselection atlas.org/, (26 January 2005). This was 60 percent of the voting eligible population according to Michael P. McDonald, "Up, Up, and Away! Voter Participation in the 2004 Presidential Election," *The Forum: A Journal of Applied Research in Contemporary Politics*, (December 2004) Vol. 2: No. 4, Article 4, accessed at http://www.bepress.com/forum/vol2/iss4/art4, 6 January 2005.

[2] James E. Campbell, *The American Campaign: U.S. Presidential Campaigns and the National Vote* (College Station, TX: Texas A&M University Press, 2000), 165. Of the nine "near dead-heat elections," the 2004 election ranked ninth or was not as close as the other eight.

JAMES E. CAMPBELL is professor of political science at the University at Buffalo, SUNY. His research interests are presidential and congressional elections. He has published several books and numerous articles in leading journals. His most recent books are *The American Campaign: U.S. Presidential Campaigns and the National Vote* and *The Presidential Pulse of Congressional Elections*.

vote margin of any of the twenty-two incumbents who won reelection during this period (although seven lost their bids) and fell 2 percentage points short of the average vote for an incumbent. In terms of the electoral vote margin, the 2004 election ranks as the fourth closest since 1868. In the twentieth century, only Woodrow Wilson's 1916 victory over Charles Evans Hughes and Bush's contentious victory in 2000 over Al Gore were decided by smaller electoral vote margins. Each of these three elections turned on the outcome in a single, closely decided state.[3]

What explains the election's outcome? This general question subsumes two interrelated sub-questions. First, why did a majority of American voters decide to reelect President Bush rather than elect Senator John Kerry? Second, why was the election between Bush and Kerry as close as it was? The answers to these questions require an examination of both the fundamental conditions that set the context for the election (the long-term influences on the vote) and the developments of the campaign itself (the short-term influences).

Experience with presidential forecasting models suggests three sets of pre-campaign fundamentals that are important to setting the context for presidential elections.[4] Using an analogy to a card game, the fundamentals are the cards dealt to the candidates. In this game, each side knows what cards the other holds — so although it is possible for either side to misplay its cards (to fritter away its advantages [see, Al Gore]), in general, the candidate dealt the stronger hand wins the game.[5] The three fundamentals are the public's opinion about the candidates at the outset of the campaign, the growth in the election year economy, and incumbency (both personal and the number of terms that a party has occupied the White House). The candidates who have the stronger hand are those who are highly regarded by the public at the outset, in-party candidates running when the election year economy is strong and out-party candidates running when the election year economy is weak, and incumbents who are seeking a second consecutive term in the White House for their party. To varying degrees, all three of these fundamentals favored President Bush in 2004.

The dividing line between the pre-campaign fundamentals and the short-term considerations of the campaign is anything but clear. In the end, all influences on the vote are short-term, but all of these considerations are influenced (either directly or conditionally) by the pre-campaign fundamentals. Voters are

[3] The election-deciding state was California in 1916, Florida in 2000, and Ohio in 2004. Actually a shift in a smaller number of votes in New Mexico, Iowa, and Colorado also could have tipped the electoral vote toward Kerry.

[4] See James E. Campbell, "The Fundamentals in U.S. Presidential Elections: Public Opinion, the Economy, and Incumbency in the 2004 Presidential Election," *Journal of Elections, Public Opinion & Parties* 15 (Issue 1 2005):73–83; Campbell, *The American Campaign*, 13–22.

[5] Lazarsfeld offered a different analogy. He wrote, "The campaign is like the chemical bath which develops a photograph. The chemical influence is necessary to bring out the picture, but only the picture pre-structured on the plate can come out." Paul F. Lazarsfeld, "The Election is Over," *Public Opinion Quarterly* 8 (Autumn 1944): 330. This portrays the campaign as a more-passive, less-influential process than in the card game analogy.

not amnesiacs. They evaluate what they hear in the course of the campaign in light of what they understood coming into it. Although many voters focus on politics only during the campaign, they still bring to the campaign experiences and impressions gathered between campaigns. Most often, these pre-campaign-based judgments and the partisanship they support strongly guide short-term evaluations to the vote. The nearly equal campaign efforts of both sides also limit the net impact of the overall campaign. Although overstating the case somewhat, Paul Lazarsfeld, more than a half century ago, made this point in concluding that "elections are decided by the events occurring in the entire period between two presidential elections and not by the campaign."[6] In the elections since Lazarsfeld wrote, campaigns between the conventions and Election Day have, on average, shifted the vote by only about 3.5 to 4 percentage points, maybe less.[7] In the 2004 election, the shift was even smaller than this. Bush held a slight lead in the preference polls after the conventions, and his share of the vote was within 1 percentage point of that lead. Still, although the net effects of the 2004 campaign were small, there were significant (albeit largely offsetting) effects. Most notably, Senator Kerry received a boost from the three presidential debates and President Bush benefitted from the large increase in turnout. The key to understanding the 2004 election, however, rests with the political context of the election, the fundamentals. The first and most important of these is the public's predisposition toward the candidates.

PRE-CAMPAIGN PUBLIC OPINION

At the outset of the general election campaign, in the period surrounding the national conventions in July until the first week of September, public opinion about the reelection of President Bush was divided but tilted slightly in his favor. Table 1 displays the vote and the two best indicators of the public's pre-campaign predisposition about the election: the approval rating of the president in July and the in-party share of preferences among registered voters at Labor Day for the fifteen elections from 1948 to 2004.[8] Both opinion measures

[6] Lazarsfeld, "The Election is Over," 330.
[7] James E. Campbell, "When Have Presidential Campaigns Decided Election Outcomes?" *American Politics Research* 29 (September 2001): 437–460.
[8] Both sets of poll numbers are from The Gallup Organization and the national popular vote is calculated from data in *Congressional Quarterly's Guide to U.S. Elections, Fourth Edition, Volume 1* (Washington, DC: CQ Press, 2001), 675–688; Leip, "Dave Leip's Atlas." The approval numbers from 1948 to 2000 have been gathered from various Gallup poll releases over the years. The 2004 number is from the 8–11 July poll by Gallup, "Presidential Ratings–Job Approval," accessed on the website of The Gallup Organization at http://www.gallup.com/ (28 November 2004). The preference or trial-heat numbers for elections from 1948 to 1992 were obtained from Gallup. The 1996 and 2000 numbers were calculated from "General Election Tracking Polls" accessed at the Gallup Poll website at http://www.gallup.com/, 28 November 2004. The 2004 number is from Gallup, "Trial Heat–Bush vs. Kerry (Registered Voters)," http://www.gallup.com/election2004/numbers/heats/default.asp, 5 November 2004. The preference poll numbers are of registered (not "likely") voters.

TABLE 1

Pre-Campaign Public Opinion and the In-Party Vote, 1948–2004

	Presidential Approval in July			Labor Day Preference for In-Party Candidate	
Year	Approval Rating (%)	In-Party Vote (Two-Party %)	Year	In-Party % in Poll at Labor Day	In-Party Vote (Two-Party %)
1964	74	61.3	1964	69.2	61.3
1956	69	57.8	1972	62.9	61.8
2000	59	50.3	1996	60.8	54.7
1996	57	54.7	1984	60.2	59.2
1972	56	61.8	1956	55.9	57.8
1984	52	59.2	1988	54.4	53.9
1988	51	53.9	2000	52.1	50.3
1960	49	49.9	1960	50.5	49.9
2004	47	51.2	2004	50.5	51.2
1976	45	49.0	1980	48.7	44.7
1968	40	49.6	1948	45.6	52.3
1948	39	52.3	1952	42.1	44.6
1952	32	44.6	1992	41.9	46.5
1992	31	46.5	1968	41.9	49.6
1980	21	44.7	1976	40.0	49.0
In-Party	Below 46%	Above 46%		Below 50%	Above 50%
Won	1	8		1	8
Lost	5	1		5	1
Correlation with vote	.82			.86	

Note: Win and loss refer to achieving a majority of the popular two-party vote. The poll data are from Gallup surveys. The Labor Day preference polls are the two-party division of registered voters. Based on the bivariate linear regression, the estimated tipping point for 50 percent of the two-party vote is 40.5 percent of July approval and 47.3 percent of the Labor Day preference poll.

are strong precursors of the vote several months later, having correlations with the vote of .82 and .86. The table orders the fifteen elections from 1948 to 2004 by each indicator from the most- to least-positive for the in-party candidate, along with the corresponding election results. The gap in each listing marks where public opinion appears to cross over from indicating a popular vote win to a loss. The cut-point for July approval is set at 46 percent (although a linear regression suggests an even lower threshold) and the cut-point for the Labor Day preference is set at 50 percent.

As the table shows, by both measures of public opinion, the reelection of President Bush sat at the cusp of the favorable numbers. President Bush's approval rating in July was 47 percent. Seven of the eight in-party candidates who had enjoyed higher approval at this point won their election. Only Richard Nixon in 1960 fell short in his razor-thin loss to John Kennedy. Five of the six in-party candidates whose incumbents had lower approval ratings in July lost their elections. The only survivor was Harry Truman, who, with the help of a booming second quarter economy, reassembled the splintered majority New Deal coalition just in time to fend off Thomas Dewey.

Labor Day preference polls tell the same story: on the eve of the campaign, the public was closely divided, but with a slight tilt toward Bush. Seven of the eight in-party candidates that stood at 50 percent or higher in the polls at Labor Day won their popular votes in November. Nixon in 1960 was again the exception. Of the six in-party candidates who trailed their opponents at Labor Day, again only Truman in 1948 came back to win the popular vote. The regression of the poll against the vote indicated that the critical threshold for an in-party candidate to reach an expected 50 percent of the vote is short of 50 percent in the polls, so Bush's 50.5 percent of support in the polls set his candidacy on the positive side of the line. The pre-campaign tilt toward Bush is also evident in the American National Election Study (NES) data concerning when voters report having decided their vote choice.[9] Those who said that they had decided how they would vote at or before the time of the national conventions reported voting for Bush over Kerry by 52.5 to 47.5 percent.

Why was pre-campaign opinion so divided, but with a slight tilt toward Bush? To a substantial degree, this reflects the defining feature of recent American politics: the evenly divided and party-polarized electorate.[10] By party polarization, I mean an intensely felt affection for one political party (and its candidates and policy positions) accompanied by an intensely felt disaffection for the opposite party (and its candidates and policy positions). Although there is some debate over how divided the public is over policy issues, there is little question that the electorate is much more sharply divided into partisan camps than it has been since at least the 1960s.

There is a good deal of evidence of party polarization in recent surveys. For example, an October Gallup poll found that 71 percent of Republicans strongly approved and 68 percent of Democrats strongly disapproved of President Bush's job performance. According to Gallup's Jeffrey Jones, "Prior to Bush, no president had seen 60% of both parties with strong opposing views of his performance."[11] This polarization was by no means limited to views of President Bush, although NES data indicate that 84 percent of voting Democrats said that Bush had made them feel angry and 91 percent of voting Republicans said that he had made them feel proud. Since 1952, the NES has asked potential voters whether there were important differences in what the Republicans and

[9] The American National Election Study (NES) 2004 data are the advance release, accessed at www.umich.edu/~nes/, 13 February 2005. I have weighted the data to the actual vote division to improve the accuracy of the data.

[10] See Morris P. Fiorina, Samuel J. Abrams, and Jeremy C. Pope, *Culture War? The Myth of a Polarized America* (New York: Pearson Longman, 2005).

[11] Jeffrey M. Jones, "Views of Bush Reach New Heights of Polarization," accessed on the website of The Gallup Organization at http://www.gallup.com/, 21 October 2004. See also Jeffrey M. Jones, "Bush Ratings Show Historical Levels of Polarization," accessed at the website of The Gallup Organization at http://www.gallup.com/, 4 June 2004. Current partisan differences in rating Presidents Reagan and Clinton are quite large as well. See Jeffrey M. Jones, "Roosevelt, Kennedy Most Positively Rated Recent Presidents," accessed at the website of The Gallup Organization at http://www.gallup.com/, 6 November 2004.

Democrats stood for. In the typical election up until 1980, just barely half said they saw important party differences. This increased to about 62 percent in elections from 1984 to 2000. The number soared in 2004. More than 80 percent (and 86 percent of voters) said that they perceived important differences between what the parties stood for.[12] In the end, about 83 percent of voters in the NES (85 percent of Bush voters and 81 percent of Kerry voters) said that their candidate preference was strong.

There are several explanations for this party polarization. The first is the realignment that began in the late 1950s and culminated in the Republican majority in the U.S. House of Representatives in 1994.[13] As Edward Carmines and James Stimson demonstrated some time ago, the collapse of the racial issue into the traditional government activism issue set in motion a domino effect, mobilizing and pulling African American voters into the Democratic Party and, over time, moving conservative white Southerners into the Republican Party.[14] The Democratic Party became more homogeneously liberal, and the Republican Party became more homogeneously conservative. What Everett Carll Ladd referred to as the "post-industrial party system" is most clearly evident in the evolution of our political geography, with Northeastern states becoming solidly Democratic and the "Solid South" solidly Republican.[15] This realignment set the parties near parity (similar to the party system in place from 1876 to 1896), adding further fuel to polarization. According to 2004 NES data, about 48 percent of voters identified themselves as Democrats and about 47 percent as Republicans.[16] Moreover, partisanship is resurgent.[17] Nearly 40 percent of voters indicated that they strongly identified themselves with the Democratic or Re-

[12] This comports with the findings of an ideological sorting out in the realignment. See Alan I. Abramowitz and Kyle L. Saunders, "Ideological Realignment in the U.S. Electorate," *Journal of Politics* 60 (August 1998): 634–652. See also Marc J. Hetherington, "Resurgent Mass Partisanship: The Role of Elite Polarization," *American Political Science Review* 95 (September 2001): 619–631. NES data for 2004 even report wide partisan divisions over perspectives on the nation. While 41 percent of voting Republicans agreed with the statement that there were "some things about America today that make me feel ashamed of America," 74 percent of voting Democrats agreed with the statement. Sixty-five percent of voting Republicans, but only 35 percent of voting Democrats, said that it made them feel "extremely good" to see the American flag flying.

[13] See Everett Carll Ladd, "The 1994 Congressional Elections: The Postindustrial Realignment Continues," *Political Science Quarterly* 110 (Spring 1995): 1–23.

[14] Edward G. Carmines and James A. Stimson, *Issue Evolution: Race and the Transformation of American Politics* (Princeton, NJ: Princeton University Press, 1989).

[15] Everett Carll Ladd, "1996 Vote: The 'No Majority' Realignment Continues," *Political Science Quarterly* 112 (Spring 1997): 2.

[16] This parity is consistent with both the Edison-Mitofsky and *The Los Angeles Times* exit polls. Leaners in the NES data are counted as partisans and the data have been weighted to the actual vote division. Both the exit polls and NES indicate that the electorate was more Republican in 2004 than in 2000.

[17] See Larry M. Bartels, "Partisanship and Voting Behavior, 1952–1996," *American Journal of Political Science* 44 (April 2000): 35–50; Hetherington, "Resurgent Mass Partisanship," 619–631; Campbell, *The American Campaign*, 216.

publican Parties (about as many strong partisans as in the 1950s and more than in any election since 1964) and about 90 percent of party identifiers voted for their respective party's presidential candidate.[18]

Adding to the long-term reasons for polarization in 2004 are two potent reasons particular to 2004. First, memories of the disputed 2000 election were still vivid. Adherents of both parties thought that the other side had attempted to steal the election. The everyday rhetoric of political discussions after 2000 became intemperate and harsh. Nearly 70 percent of Democratic voters in the 2004 NES survey said that they still felt strongly that the outcome of the 2000 election had been unfair. The war in Iraq further fueled polarization. As the war continued and casualties mounted, conflicting views about the war overshadowed the short-lived bipartisanship following al Qaeda's attacks on September 11, 2001 and the international efforts to hunt down terrorists. Some thought that the war was unnecessary, ill-conceived, based on inaccurate claims or lies, motivated by oil, poorly executed, too expensive in lives and resources, and ultimately counterproductive. Others thought that the war was necessary, in light of our international intelligence about the threat at the time (intelligence that initially received bipartisan support, including from Senator Kerry), fought to the best of our capabilities and with the best of intentions—that it would at least eliminate a brutal regime and might ultimately contain or reduce hostilities and terrorism exported from a perennially troubled region of the world. Reactions to Michael Moore's highly controversial film, *Fahrenheit 911*, exemplified just how bitter the political divisions had become.

Opinions regarding the war on terror and the war in Iraq (issues that Democrats separated, but Republicans regarded as part and parcel of the same issue) help to explain both the tilt of public opinion in Bush's favor as well as the closeness of the vote. Opinion about the war on terror consistently favored President Bush's reelection. A Gallup poll in late August (23–25) found Bush to be favored over Kerry in handling terrorism by a margin of 54 to 37 percent. The exit polls similarly found that Bush was more trusted to handle terrorism by a margin of 58 to 40 percent. NES data indicate that voters approved of Bush's handling of the war on terror by a margin of 55 to 45 percent. When asked which party would do a better job in handling the war on terror, voters favored the Republicans over the Democrats by a margin of 45 to 27 percent (with 27 percent saying that they thought both parties would handle it about equally well). The war on terror, along with the fact that Bush's general political perspectives were viewed by more voters as being more ideologically acceptable than Kerry's, were decided advantages for President Bush before and throughout the campaign.[19]

[18] This is from NES data. The exact figures are that 89 percent of Democrats voted for Kerry and 92 percent of Republicans voted for Bush.

[19] Gallup, "Political Ideology," accessed on the website of The Gallup Organization at http://www.gallup.com/, 4 November 2004.

Opinion on the war in Iraq was more evenly divided. Gallup in late August found that Bush was favored in handling "the situation in Iraq" by a margin of 49 to 43 percent.[20] Similarly, the exit polls showed that Bush's decision to go to war in Iraq was supported by a margin among voters of 51 to 45 percent. On the other hand, only 44 percent of voters in the NES approved of Bush's handling of the war, and 59 percent said that they thought the war was not worth the cost.[21] This division of the public over Iraq and the slight lead that Kerry had over Bush on a number of domestic issues (the economy, healthcare, social security, the environment) of lesser salience in 2004 partially offset the advantages that Bush held on the terrorism issue and on his more conservative political perspective—but only partially.

Beyond the issues of the war on terror and the war in Iraq, the nominating conventions may have also contributed to Bush's slight lead entering the fall campaign. Conventions provide candidates an opportunity to reunite their party after intra-party conflicts over nominations and to set forth their message for why the larger audience of the general electorate should vote for them. As a consequence of the party holding the national "floor" for a week during its convention, the candidate typically emerges with an increased amount of support in the polls, a convention "bump." Candidates received positive convention bumps in eighteen of the twenty national conventions between 1964 and 2000.[22] Only Lyndon Johnson, who was already sky-high in the polls in 1964, and George McGovern, who had a divisive convention in 1972, failed to receive convention bumps. The Democrats had even received a bump from their disastrous 1968 convention in Chicago. Typically, a candidate has received a bump of about 6 or 7 percentage points, and the out-party has averaged closer to a nine-point bump. Although the Republican convention in 2004 only bumped Bush's preferences up by about one point (according to registered voters in Gallup, and three or four points in other polls), Senator Kerry actually appeared to get no bump or to have lost ground during the Democratic convention. Although some polls showed a very slight bump for Kerry, the polls in general indicated a slight lead for Kerry before the conventions and a slight lead for Bush after them.[23]

[20] Gallup, "Importance and Candidate Performance," accessed on the website of The Gallup Organization at http://www.gallup.com/, 4 November 2004.

[21] See CNN, "Election Results: Exit Polls." accessed at http://www.cnn.com/ELECTION/2004/pages/results/states/US/P/00/epolls.0.html, 25 November 2004. This is the Edison-Mitofsky exit poll. Subsequent mentions of the exit poll are to this reference.

[22] Campbell, *The American Campaign*, 145–151.

[23] Although there is concern about relying on a single polling organization, James Stimson's pooled data on the preference polls corroborate the Gallup picture in this regard. See http://www.unc.edu/~jstimson/, accessed 14 November 2004. According to Stimson's pooled data, Kerry dropped from 51.8 percent in the 25 July pre-convention polls to 50.5 percent in the 30 July post-convention polls. Although the *Washington Post* poll showed a four-point gain for Kerry after the convention, the Pew Research Center and NBC/*Wall Street Journal* polls separately show essentially no change from before to after the Democratic convention, the Zogby poll showed about a one-point decline, the CBS poll showed less than a one-point gain, and the Fox News poll showed about a 1.5-point gain. See, Polling Report.com, "White House 2004: General Election," www.pollingreport.com/wh04gen.htm, 6 November 2004. With this variance, a real increase in Kerry's poll standing after the convention was possible, but

Why did Senator Kerry receive either no bump or a very slight one from the Democratic convention? Party polarization may have limited poll movement.[24] According to NES data, 56 percent of voters indicated that they had decided whom they would vote for before the national conventions. In the fourteen elections for which data are available, only in the 1956 election rematch between Dwight Eisenhower and Adlai Stevenson had this many voters decided this early how they would vote.[25] Most Democrats were already strongly united behind Kerry before the convention. Once the Howard Dean campaign for the Democratic nomination imploded in Iowa, Democrats flocked to Kerry as the "anybody-but-Bush," unite-the-party candidate. Kerry also had announced his vice presidential selection of nomination rival Senator John Edwards several weeks before the convention and thus may have already received whatever bump he might have received before the convention took place.

Beyond these factors for Kerry's non-bump is the content of the Democratic Convention. The core message of the convention was about Senator Kerry's war record in Vietnam.[26] This was captured in Kerry's salute while reading the opening line of his nomination acceptance speech: "I'm John Kerry, and I'm reporting for duty." Although this message may have been meant to neutralize the foreign policy advantage of a Republican incumbent and dissuade voters from the view that Democrats were soft or irresponsible on foreign policy, it may also been a lost opportunity to present a compelling reason to voters to cast their ballots for Kerry over Bush. Voters may well have walked away from the Democratic Convention thinking that it was terrific that Kerry was a war hero over thirty years ago, but that this was not much of a reason to elect him president. The "Swift-Boat" ads run by veterans opposed to Kerry (particularly his Vietnam War protest activities) and challenges to accounts of his heroism, along with the controversy that surrounded the issue, made the decision to focus the convention on Kerry's Vietnam War record all the more questionable.[27]

The decision to make "Kerry as war hero" the convention's theme may also reflect the difficulty of finding a positive theme that could both energize and unite the party already united (but not fully so) around the negative theme of

---

it is probably also safe to conclude that whatever increase might have occurred was small and probably smaller than the slight bump Bush received from the Republican convention. Both CBS and Zogby data separately indicated a four-point bump for Bush from the GOP convention, and the *Washington Post* poll showed a three-point gain.

[24] The declining coverage of conventions by the broadcast networks and the expansion of cable network entertainment alternatives to the conventions may also have diminished the magnitude of convention bumps.

[25] Campbell, *The American Campaign*, 8.

[26] See Evan Thomas and *Newsweek*'s Special Project Team, "The Inside Story: How Bush Did It," *Newsweek*, 15 November 2004, 80–81.

[27] According to *Newsweek*'s coverage of the campaign, this point had been made later in the campaign to Senator Kerry by former President Clinton. Clinton advised Senator Kerry in early September to "spend less time talking about Vietnam and more time engaging on Iraq." Thomas, "The Inside Story: How Bush Did It," 102.

opposing President Bush—a constraint that is part of the natural advantage of incumbency. The Kerry bandwagon had been set in motion by the desire to get behind someone who could defeat Bush—not by a positive attraction of support to the candidate.[28] In the end, the exit polls showed as much: Bush received nearly 60 percent of the votes of those who said that they were voting *for* their candidate, while Kerry received 70 percent of the votes of those who said that they were voting *against* the opponent.[29] With opposition to Bush as the fuel running the Democratic engine, the positive war hero theme fell flat in attracting further support.

THE PRE-CAMPAIGN ECONOMY

The second fundamental is the state of the economy leading into the election and, particularly, economic growth in the months immediately before the fall campaign. Economic growth is important to voters in a direct and tangible sense, but is also important to establishing the electorate's receptivity to the in-party (on non-economic issues as well as on economic matters). When the economy is doing well, voters look for reasons to continue the in-party's tenure. When it is not, they are more receptive to calls for ending that tenure. The election year economy is a good barometer of the mood that voters are likely to be in during the fall campaign.[30]

Despite much of the rhetoric of the campaign, the economy tilted in favor of President Bush's reelection in 2004. Although Democrats hammered on the lack of job creation and the slow recovery from the recession in the first years of the Bush term, the real economic growth in the last two years of the Bush term and in the election year itself should have been an asset for the Bush campaign.

Table 2 presents a comparison of broad-based objective and subjective economic indicators well before the fall campaign for 2004 and the previous three presidential elections. The table includes the annual growth rate in the gross domestic product for the two years leading into the campaign, the percentage of Gallup poll respondents in the spring of the election year who indicated that they thought the economy was in excellent or good shape, and (more broadly) the percentage of respondents who were satisfied "with the way things are going in the United States." The pattern of the three indicators is consistent across the years. Public satisfaction and recent economic growth were greater in 2000 than in either 1996 or 1992 and greater in 1996 than in 1992, and 2004 looks more like 1996 than either the boom leading into 2000 or the sluggish economy

---

[28] This is not to say that the Bush campaign and the Republican convention were without their share of negativity. Any witness to Democratic Senator Zell Miller's fiery condemnation at the Republican Convention of Senator Kerry's record can attest to this.

[29] CNN, "Election Results: Exit Polls," 25 November 2004.

[30] Campbell, *The American Campaign*, 126–139.

TABLE 2

Economic Conditions Leading into the Presidential Campaigns, 1992–2004

Pre-Campaign Indicators of National Economy	Elections			
	1992	*1996*	*2000*	*2004*
Average economic growth rate in previous two years (GDP through first quarter of the election year, annualized)	0.8%	2.9%	4.2%	3.5%
Rate economic conditions as excellent or good (April or May)	12%	30%	66%	29%
Satisfied with "the way things are going in the United States" (May)	20%	37%	55%	37%

Sources: Gallup, "Economy (U.S.)" and "General Mood of the Country," accessed at http://www.gallup.com, 28 November 2004 and the U.S. Bureau of Economic Analysis, "Table 1.1.6. Real Gross Domestic Product, Chained Dollars," accessed at http://www.bea.gov, 28 November 2004. The economic conditions poll dates are 9–12 April 1992, 9–12 May 1996, 18–21 May 2000, and 2–4 May 2004. The satisfied with the way things are going poll dates are 7–10 May 1992, 9–12 May 1996, 18–21 May 2000, and 7–9 May 2004. The average economic growth rate in the GDP is the annual rate of growth in the "chained" GDP from the first quarter of the second year of the president's term to the first quarter of the fourth year of the term. The computation was half of [(GDP quarter 1 in year 4 − GDP quarter 1 in year 2)/GDP quarter in year 2].

leading into 1992. The circumstances leading into 1992 contributed to the defeat of President George H.W. Bush. The circumstances leading into 1996 contributed to President Bill Clinton's reelection, and it is commonly conceded that the circumstances of 2000 were advantageous for Al Gore. In short, an early reading of the economy before the 2004 election is that it should have been a political asset for President Bush.

The economy during the election year also favored President Bush. Table 3 provides some historical perspective on the election year economy, as measured by growth in the real GDP. Elections from 1948 to 2004 are ordered according to the extent of real GDP growth in the first half of the election year (January to June) and in the second quarter (April to June). The annualized data are from the U.S. Bureau of Economic Analysis.[31] Economic growth in both series is strongly correlated with the November vote (correlations of .51 and .60), but not as strongly associated with the vote as is either indicator of pre-campaign opinion. Each series is broken into three groups: those with growth rates in excess of 4 percent, those with growth between 2.5 and 4 percent, and those with growth rates lower than 2.5 percent. These may be thought

---

[31] U.S. Bureau of Economic Analysis, "Table 1.1.6. Real Gross Domestic Product, Chained Dollars," http://www.bea.gov, 28 November 2004.

TABLE 3

Election-Year Economies and the In-Party Vote, 1948–2004

	First Half Year GDP Growth			Second-Quarter GDP Growth	
Year	GDP Growth (%)	In-Party Vote (Two-Party %)	Year	GDP Growth (%)	In-Party Vote (Two-Party %)
1972	8.4	61.8	1972	9.4	61.8
1968	7.6	49.8	1948	7.1	52.3
1984	7.4	59.2	1984	6.9	59.2
1964	6.9	61.3	1968	6.8	49.6
1948	6.8	52.3	2000	6.3	50.3
1976	6.0	49.0	1988	5.1	53.9
			1964	4.7	61.3
1992	4.0	46.5			
2004	3.9	51.2	1992	3.9	46.5
2000	3.7	50.3	2004	3.3	51.2
1988	3.5	53.9	1956	3.2	57.8
1960	3.4	49.9	1976	3.0	49.0
1996	2.9	54.7	1996	2.8	54.7
1952	2.2	44.6	1952	0.3	44.6
1956	0.6	57.8	1960	−2.0	49.9
1980	−3.4	44.7	1980	−8.1	44.7
In-Party	2.5%−	2.5 to 4%	4%+	2.5%−	2.5 to 4%	4%+
Won	1	4	4	0	3	6
Lost	2	2	2	3	2	1
Correlation with vote		.51			.60	

Note: Win and loss refer to achieving a majority of the popular two-party vote. The gross domestic product (GDP) economic data are annualized and obtained from the Bureau of Economic Analysis. Based on the bivariate linear regression, the estimated tipping point for 50 percent of the two-party vote is 1.60 percent growth in the first half of the year and only .33 percent in the second quarter.

of, respectively, as "great," "pretty good," and "not so good" economic conditions. In-party candidates who have run with growth rates over 4 percent have usually won, and the elections they have lost have been close. Hubert Humphrey, in 1968, and Gerald Ford, in 1976, ran with the economy growing at a rate of 6 percent or stronger in the first half of the election year, but narrowly lost their elections. These booms were not enough to save Humphrey from the splintering of his division-wracked party, nor could they save Ford from the fallout from Watergate and his pardon of President Nixon. At the other end of the spectrum, candidates running with sub-2.5 percent economies have usually lost. The only candidate to survive this pattern was Eisenhower, in 1956, and the economy that year was rebounding by the second quarter.

By either measure, the economy in the months leading up to the campaign was "pretty good." It ranks eighth or ninth of the fifteen election years. This is at or close to the median case in this period, and the median election year economy has generally been strong enough to help elect the in-party candidate. That said, it is interesting to observe the limits to the effects of the election year economy. Although economic growth in the first part of 2004 was stronger than it had been when Bill Clinton was reelected in 1996, it was not quite as strong as it had been in 1992, when the president's father was defeated by Clinton. The elder Bush did not lose because of the election year economy. The damage had been done earlier and is reflected in the economic numbers in Table 2 and the poll numbers in Table 1.

The limits of economic effects also could be observed in the issue polls conducted during the campaign. Despite objective economic indicators tilting a bit in President Bush's favor, the economy as an issue worked to Senator Kerry's advantage. In five separate polls conducted in October by Gallup, respondents favored Kerry over Bush in dealing with the economy by an average margin of 51 to 44 percent.[32] Eight polls by ABC News conducted in October also indicated that Kerry held, on average, a 48 to 46 percent advantage over Bush regarding who likely voters thought would do a better job of handling the economy.[33] *The Los Angeles Times* exit poll found that nearly half of Kerry voters said that the economy was the most important problem, whereas fewer than one in five Bush voters had the economy at the top of their concerns.[34] The exit polls indicated that Kerry received 80 percent of the votes of those who thought that the economy (and jobs) was the most important issue in the election.[35] Finally, although Bush had a general job approval rating of 52 percent of reported voters in the NES, only 44 percent of them indicated that they approved of his handling of the economy.

Why did the economy as an issue favor Kerry when the broad-based economic measures indicated that it should have helped Bush? The answer may be that the Bush campaign decided early on that the strongest message for the president's reelection concerned his leadership in the war against terrorism. Nearly half of the issue content of his speeches concerned terrorism or Iraq.[36] With Bush staying on the antiterrorism message, Kerry was allowed to frame the economic issue as a jobs loss issue, the terms most favorable to Kerry. Once Kerry (aided by media reports emphasizing negative news about the economy) framed the economic issue as a jobs loss issue, President Bush was on the defensive.[37] According to data reported by Paul Abramson, John Aldrich, and David

[32] Gallup, "Importance and Candidate Performance," accessed on the website of The Gallup Organization at http://www.gallup.com/, 4 November 2004.

[33] ABC News. "Poll: Campaign '04 Closes With a One-Point Race," Campaign Tracking #26, accessed at http://abcnews.go.com/Politics/Vote2004/, 31 October 2004.

[34] PollingReport.com. "Exit Poll: Los Angeles Times exit poll," accessed at http://www.pollingreport.com/2004.htm#Exit, 26 November 2004.

[35] One-fifth of all voters, according to the exit poll, rated the economy as their top concern. There is also some evidence that the economy did not favor Kerry. The exit polls indicated that more voters said that they trusted Bush to handle the economy (49 percent) than Kerry (45 percent). Nevertheless, the bulk of the evidence suggests that the economy as an issue cut in Kerry's favor.

[36] Paul R. Abramson, John H. Aldrich, and David W. Rohde, "The 2004 Presidential Election: The Emergence of a Permanent Majority?" *Political Science Quarterly* 20 (Spring 2005): 33–57.

[37] Thomas M. Holbrook, "Good News for Bush? Economic News, Personal Finances, and the 2004 Presidential Election," *PS: Political Science and Politics* 37 (October 2004): 759–761.

Rohde, the economy was the subject of less than 30 percent of the issue content of Bush's campaign speeches, but nearly 40 percent that of Kerry's campaign speeches.[38] So despite respectable (albeit not glowing) economic numbers, the economy as an issue was owned by Kerry in this election. As an issue, the economy was expendable to the Bush campaign because it could be largely neutralized and ultimately trumped by the terrorism issue.

INCUMBENCY AND THE PARTY TERM

The third fundamental is incumbency, both personal and party term.[39] The advantages of personal presidential incumbency, from the risk aversion of voters to agenda-setting to the "Rose Garden" strategy to greater intraparty unity are well established. As the failed campaigns of Presidents Gerald Ford, Jimmy Carter, and George H.W. Bush demonstrate, these advantages are no guarantee of reelection. Nevertheless, incumbency is a substantial asset. Since 1868, there have been seventeen elected incumbents who sought reelection, and eleven (65 percent) were successful. Four of the five incumbents who reached the office by succession and then stood for election during this period were successful. Only Gerald Ford fell short and then only barely so. Presidents as candidates are rarely trounced at the polls.[40] Even President Carter, who ran with a foreign policy debacle, a terrible economy, and a divided party, garnered about 45 percent of the vote. Incumbents simply seeking a second term for their party in the White House are especially advantaged.[41] Whether it is their greater party unity or the ability to be viewed simultaneously as both an experienced Washington insider offering stability and a political newcomer/outsider pushing for change, incumbents seeking a second party term historically have an enviable track record.

Table 4 presents the track record on incumbency and party terms for the thirty-five presidential elections from 1868 to 2004. The elections are grouped into those in which the in-party candidate was not an incumbent, those in which the in-party candidate was an incumbent and was seeking to extend his party's tenure in the presidency beyond a second term, and those in which the in-party candidate was an incumbent seeking a second presidential term for his party. Both the win-loss records and the median votes tell the same story. Non-incumbent in-party candidates and incumbents seeking more than a second term for their party are at neither a competitive advantage or disadvantage. Their me-

[38] Abramson, Aldrich, and Rohde, "The 2004 Presidential Election," 40, 45.

[39] Campbell, *The American Campaign*, 101–125.

[40] Of the twenty-two incumbents who sought reelection between 1868 and 2004, only two (Taft and Hoover) lost in landslides. Nine nonincumbents during this period lost in landslides.

[41] See, Alan I. Abramowitz, "Bill and Al's Excellent Adventure: Forecasting the 1996 Presidential Election," and Helmut Norpoth, "Of Time and Candidates: A Forecast for 1996," both in James E. Campbell and James C. Garand, eds., *Before the Vote: Forecasting American National Elections* (Thousand Oaks, CA: Sage, 2000), 47–81.

TABLE 4

Incumbency, the Party Term and the Vote, 1868–2004

	In-Party Nonincumbents	Incumbents Seeking beyond a Second Party Term	Incumbents Seeking a Second Party Term
Median vote (%)	49.9	52.3	54.7
Won	6	5	11
Lost	7	4	2

Note: N = 35. Win and loss refer to achieving a majority of the popular two-party vote. A regression analysis indicates that seeking more than a second term for a party costs the candidate 5.1 percent of the two-party vote ($p < .02$, one-tailed). The expected vote of seeking a second term is 55.0 percent and the expected vote of seeking more than a second term is 49.9 percent. Since 1948, the median vote percentages are 49.9 (N = 5) for nonincumbents, 48.9 (N = 3) for incumbents seeking more than a second party term, and 57.8 (N = 7) for incumbents seeking a second party term.

dian votes and win-loss records are nearly fifty-fifty. Incumbents seeking a second term for their party, however, have a considerable advantage. Of the thirteen cases that fit this description since 1868, the incumbent won on all but two occasions.[42] Their median two-party vote is nearly 55 percent. The median vote for these incumbents since 1948 is a remarkable 57.8 percent. Eisenhower in 1956, Johnson in 1964, Nixon in 1972, and Ronald Reagan in 1984 were all second party term incumbents who won in landslides or near-landslides. Clinton, in 1996, won with a fairly safe margin. Carter, in 1980, is the outlier.

As an incumbent seeking a second party term for the Republicans, President Bush enjoyed a considerable advantage—but why didn't he receive the large vote majority of most previous second party term presidents? One reason is polarization. With the nation as polarized as it was, Democrats were more united than an out-party would normally be opposing a first party term president. Many Democrats loathed President Bush. Perhaps the most tangible evidence of this is the speed with which Democrats abandoned nomination front-runner Howard Dean for Senator Kerry (but some bumper stickers could also be produced as evidence). Which Democrat received the nomination was not as important to these voters as nominating someone who could defeat President Bush. Poll after poll following the Iowa caucus indicated that Kerry was the runaway choice of those Democrats deciding how to vote in the primaries and caucuses based on the candidate's ability to win in November.[43] Normally, a party out of the White House for just four years would still be engaged in internal struggles for control of the party.[44] They might even think that the election

[42] The two incumbents seeking a second party term who lost were Benjamin Harrison, who lost to Grover Cleveland in 1892, and Jimmy Carter, who lost to Ronald Reagan in 1980.

[43] Gallup, "Seen as Best Candidate to Beat Bush, Kerry Poised for N.H. Victory," accessed at the website of The Gallup Organization at http://www.gallup.com/, 26 January 2004.

[44] Elsewhere, I have presented evidence of greater early internal party unity for incumbents, especially those seeking a second party term. See James E. Campbell, "Nomination Politics, Party Unity, and Presidential Elections" in James P. Pfiffner and Roger H. Davidson, eds., *Understanding the Presi-*

of the opposition had been a fluke, a one-termer, who could be easily beaten in the next contest. This is not so clearly the case with polarized politics.

A second reason for the close election of a second party term incumbent was the war in Iraq. Although the president received high marks from voters for his decisiveness and strength of leadership, the war in Iraq (both concern about it and opposition to it) made the election closer than it might have been otherwise. Although voters in various pre-election polls and the exit polls favored Bush over Kerry on the war against terrorism, they were more evenly divided about Iraq. In the October Gallup polls, Bush was favored over Kerry on the war against terrorism by an average margin of 56 to 40 percent.[45] Among exit poll respondents who said that terrorism was the most important issue, Bush won 86 percent of the votes. Regarding the war in Iraq, on the other hand, Bush's lead over Kerry in the October Gallup polls was a more narrow 51 to 46 percent margin. In the exit polls, among the 52 percent who thought that "things were going badly for the U.S. in Iraq," Kerry received 82 percent of the votes. Kerry might have done even better on this issue if his position on it had been less nuanced and more stable. As it stood, Kerry won the votes almost by default of those of various stripes who were dissatisfied with Bush's Iraq policy and simply favored an "anybody-but-Bush" Democrat.

CAMPAIGN EFFECTS: THE DEBATES AND TURNOUT

Although the campaign left the race pretty much where it had begun, it had its definite ups and downs for the candidates.[46] The Kerry campaign experienced the upside with the three presidential debates. This was negated, in large part, by the tremendous surge in turnout that defied the conventional wisdom that high-turnout elections help the Democrats. The huge increase in turnout, on balance, and quite to the contrary of conventional wisdom, boosted the Republican vote.

Throughout September, President Bush held a small but steady lead in the polls over Senator Kerry. This all changed with the three presidential debates. As Table 5 demonstrates, at the end of September, Bush led Kerry by 54 to 46 percent among registered voters in the Gallup poll.[47] About two weeks later, a few days after the third debate, the Bush lead over Kerry had been reduced to

---

dency, Third Edition, 2004 Election Season Update (New York: Pearson Longman 2005), 71–84. Although there were early outward signs of Democratic Party unity behind Kerry in 2004, NES data indicate that Republicans outnumbered Democrats among early-deciding voters and that although early-deciding Democrats were united (94 percent voting for Kerry), early-deciding Republicans were even more so (97 percent voting for Bush).

[45] Gallup, "Importance and Candidate Performance," 4 November 2004.

[46] The largest systematic effect of campaigns is the result of intense and balanced competition (Campbell, *The American Campaign*). This makes presidential elections closer than they appeared at the outset. Because the 2004 race was close from the beginning, the effect of competition was slight, but still helps to explain the narrowness of the Bush majority.

[47] Gallup, "Trial Heat," 5 November 2004.

TABLE 5

The Campaign Effects of the 2004 Presidential Debates

	Who Did the Better Job in the Debate?		Was Your Opinion of the Candidate More Favorable After Debate?		Candidate Preference	
	Bush	*Kerry*	*Bush*	*Kerry*	*Bush*	*Kerry*
First debate (30 September)	37	53	21	46	54.1	45.9
Second debate (6–8 October)	45	47	31	38	52.1	47.9
Third debate (11–13 October)	39	52	27	42	48.9	51.9
Post-debates (14–16 October)					51.3	48.7
Net change (from pre- to post-debates)					−2.8 Bush	

Note: The data are from Gallup polls conducted on the indicated dates. The numbers are percentages. The "better job" question was: "Regardless of which candidate you happen to support, who do you think did the better job in the debate?" The "more favorable" question was: "How has your opinion of [candidate] been affected by the debate? Is your opinion of [candidate]—More favorable, Less favorable, or Has it not changed much?"

51 to 49 percent. *Time* polls had Bush slipping from 52.2 percent of two-party support before the debates to a tie with Kerry after the debates, and *The Los Angeles Times* polls had nearly identical numbers.[48] A compilation of polls of registered voters in the four days before the first debate had Bush with a 53 to 47 percent lead over Kerry. A similar compilation of polls in the four days after the debate had Bush leading Kerry by 51.8 to 48.2 percent, a decline of 1.2 points.[49]

In each of the three debates, Gallup respondents were much more likely to say that their views of Kerry had become more favorable than their views of Bush.[50] The biggest difference was in the first debate, in which respondents were more than twice as likely to have been impressed by Kerry than Bush. Although much of this effect was probably ephemeral, some of this effect may have survived to the election. Kerry had established his credibility with many voters. Kerry lagged behind Bush before the debates, but the race was tight in the weeks that followed. Although their effects are more difficult to track, the fact that Democratic-oriented "527" groups in the campaign were outspending Republican-oriented groups by almost four to one ($321 million to $84 million) probably also helped to tighten the race.[51]

The debates and the campaign surrounding them rejuvenated the Kerry campaign, but the second major campaign effect largely offset this and also

[48] PollingReport.com, "White House 2004," 14 November 2004.

[49] Ibid.

[50] Gallup, "Kerry Wins Debate," 1 October 2004, "Standoff in Second Debate," 9 October 2004, and "Kerry Wins Third Debate," 18 October 2004, accessed on the website of The Gallup Organization at http://www.gallup.com/.

[51] Steve Weissman and Ruth Hassan, "BCRA and 527 Groups" in Michael J. Malbin, ed., *The Election after Reform: Money, Politics and the Bipartisan Campaign Reform Act* (Lanham, MD: Rowman and Littlefield, forthcoming).

took many by surprise. Most of the final polls and projections in the final day or two before Election Day expected a closer popular vote than the final count reflected. Thirteen of sixteen final polls and projections expected Bush to receive a smaller vote than he actually received.[52] The median projection was about three-quarters of a point lower than Bush's actual vote share. Part of this shortfall can be traced to the pollsters' reliance on the "incumbency rule," that those undecided in the last days of the campaign split heavily against the incumbent. This rule, however, does not seem applicable to presidential contests, because both candidates are so well known. Very late deciders are more likely to split evenly, with a tilt toward their party's candidate.[53]

Final polls and projections may also have underestimated the Bush vote because they did not anticipate Republicans receiving a boost from the election's unusually high turnout. The belief that Democrats routinely benefit from high turnout has managed to survive evidence to the contrary. The conventional wisdom that Democrats are helped by high turnout is based on the well-established relationships between sociodemographic factors, partisanship, and turnout. However, what is most important about nonvoters is not that they are sociodemographically similar to voting Democrats, but that they are politically distinct from either voting Democrats or voting Republicans. For instance, NES data indicate that among nonvoters with a preference in 2004, Bush was preferred to Kerry (51.2 percent to 47.6 percent). Moreover, there are not simply two kinds of potential voters (voters and nonvoters) but at least three (voters, nonvoters who might conceivably vote, and those who could not be dragged to the polls), and the usual nonvoters who could be mobilized may not look as much like would-be Democrats as the hard-core nonvoters.

Although both Bush and Kerry added voters to their parties' columns compared to the 2000 election, the increase in turnout in 2004, on balance, helped Bush and hurt Kerry. Table 6 presents the evidence. Because there is some debate about how turnout is best measured, I calculated two different measures of turnout change in the states from the 2000 election to 2004. The first is the difference in the traditional turnout rates (the number of voters divided by the voting age population in each year). The second is the increase in the number voting in a state as a percentage of those who had voted in 2000. The growth in turnout, measured in these two different ways, is explained by the closeness of the election in the state and the percentage of the state vote cast for President Bush. By both measures of turnout change, turnout increased more if the state

[52] PollingReport.com, "White House 2004," 14 November 2004.

[53] James E. Campbell, "Presidential Election Campaigns and Partisanship" in Jeffrey E. Cohen, Richard Fleisher, and Paul Kantor, eds., *American Political Parties: Decline or Resurgence?* (Washington, DC: CQ Press, 2001), 11–29. The exit poll and NES data are at odds over who was favored by very-late-deciding voters. The exit poll indicates that the 11 percent of voters deciding in the last week to Election Day divided about 54 to 46 percent in favor of Kerry. The NES data indicate that those deciding in the last week or on Election Day (codes 9 and 10 of the time-of-decision question) split about 58 to 42 percent in favor of Bush.

TABLE 6

Explaining Turnout Change in the States from 2000 to 2004

	Dependent Variable: State Turnout Change from 2000 to 2004	
Independent variables	Change in Turnout Rates (1.)	Change in Total Turnout as a % of Prior Turnout (2.)
Bush vote percentage in 2004 (two-party vote)	.34* (6.29)	.46* (3.99)
Closeness of the vote (negative of absolute vote margin)	.43* (5.24)	.81* (4.57)
Constant	−11.64	−2.62
Adjusted R^2	.45	.30
Standard error	2.44	5.21

Note: $N = 50$. *$p < 0.01$. In equation 1, the dependent variable is the state's turnout rate in 2004 as a percentage of its voting age population minus the same rate in 2000. In equation 2, the dependent variable is the difference between the total vote in the state in 2004 and 2000 as a percentage of the state's total vote in 2000. Closeness of the vote in the state is the negative of the absolute difference between the Bush two-party vote and 50 percent. The correlation between the two turnout change measures is .51. Because the District of Columbia was identified as an influence point in an initial analysis and is also an obvious outlier in its vote, it is excluded from the analysis.

was a battleground, closely fought state. Turnout also increased more in states in which Bush won a larger share of the vote.[54] President Bush carried each of the top nine states to register the largest turnout increases by the proportional measure and twelve of the top fifteen to see the greatest gains by the traditional voting-age population measure.

Why did President Bush benefit from high turnout? Contrary to speculation in the aftermath of the election, the gay marriage referenda on the ballots in eleven states apparently had nothing to do with this. After considering the Bush appeal in a state and the closeness of the presidential contest in the state, whether a state had a gay marriage referendum on the ballot made no difference to turnout change. The carefully coordinated Republican GOTV effort may have boosted turnout to President Bush's advantage; but perhaps more importantly, high turnout may have favored the president because marginal voters were more likely to be energized by the positive messages of voting for Bush than the negative messages for voting against him.[55] Whatever the cause,

[54] One might expect that the Bush vote share would be the dependent variable, affected by turnout levels. However, the Bush vote share here is regarded as a surrogate for the effort and appeal of Bush in a state, a condition potentially affecting turnout. The analysis indicates that with the closeness of states held constant, those in which Bush exerted a greater appeal were likely to experience greater gains in turnout than those in which Kerry exerted a greater appeal.

[55] See Jonathan Tilove, "Cutting-edge Mobilization May Have Won the Day for Bush," Newhouse News Service, accessed at http://www.newhousenews.com/archive/tilove112604.html, 25 November 2004. On the other hand, there were more potential voters in the NES reporting that they were contacted by the Democrats than by the Republicans and a larger portion of those contacted by the Democrats reported that they turned out to vote.

Republicans were mobilized. The percentage of voters identifying themselves as Republicans (leaners included) increased by 2.1 percentage points over 2000, whereas the percentage identifying themselves as Democrats (including leaners) and Independents dropped by .4 and 1.7 percentage points, respectively. Moreover, for the first time in the over fifty-year history of the NES, strong Republicans comprised more than one-fifth of all voters and (also for the first time in at least fifty years) they outnumbered strong Democrats. Among voters, 21 percent identified themselves as strong Republicans and 19 percent identified themselves as strong Democrats. The 2004 election took the conventional wisdom that high turnout helps Democrats, shook it by its heels, and stood it on its head.

THE MORAL OF THE STORY

The fundamentals in the 2004 election established a setting somewhat favorable to the reelection of President Bush, and the net effect of the campaign did not alter this much. The public was predisposed, if only slightly, toward President Bush's reelection. The economy was favorable, again, if only slightly. And the fact that the president was seeking a second term for the Republicans after the eight years of the Clinton presidency also favored his reelection. Partially offsetting these Bush advantages were the divisions over the war in Iraq and the vehemence with which Democrats wanted Bush out of office. These conditions made the election a close one.

In the end, with considerations of how polarization and the Iraq war made the election tighter, the election turned out not much different than one would have expected if one looked at the match-up from a longer perspective: an election between a sitting conservative Republican president from the south against a northern liberal Senator. Figure 1 tells the story. It plots an index of ideological acceptability over three Gallup polls conducted in early August, early September (the kickoff of the general election campaign), and mid-October.[56] The index is the percentage of respondents who thought that the political views of the candidates were just about right or maybe not far enough removed from the other party. Was Senator Kerry too liberal for voters or was President Bush too conservative? The answer about what voters thought is clear: more thought that Senator Kerry was too liberal than thought that President Bush was too conservative.[57] In the August Gallup poll, half of the respondents thought that

[56] Gallup, "Political Ideology," accessed at the website of The Gallup Organization at http://www. gallup.com/, 4 November 2004.

[57] About 12 to 14 percent found Bush to be too liberal for their tastes. Only 8 or 9 percent found Kerry to be too conservative. A proximity index using self-placement and perceptions of the candidates' ideologies in NES data (both adjusted so that the "slight" liberal and conservative positions were coded as liberals and conservatives, much as leaners are coded as partisans in the party identification scale) finds Bush to be the more ideologically proximate candidate to 47.4 percent of voters, while Kerry was closer to 39.6 percent and the candidates were equally close to 13.2 percent.

FIGURE 1
*Acceptability of President Bush's and Senator Kerry's
Political Ideologies*

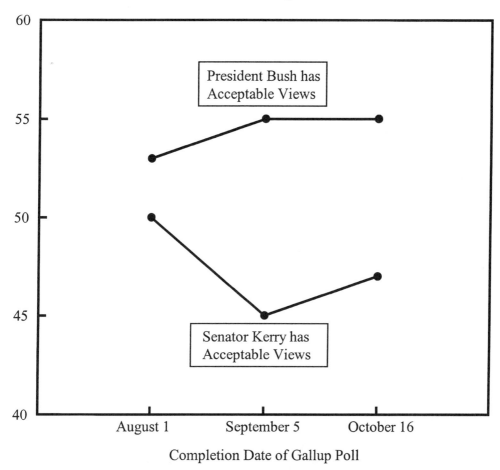

Completion Date of Gallup Poll

Note: Acceptability Ideology Index. The data are from Gallup Polls. Acceptable ideology is calculated with reference to each candidate's ideological position. For President Bush, it is the percentage of respondents who said that his political views were "about right" or "too liberal." For Senator Kerry, it is the percentage of respondents who said that his views were "about right" or "too conservative."

Kerry's political views were about right or even too conservative, but 44 per-cent thought that they were too liberal. In the same poll, 53 percent thought President Bush's views were about right or even too liberal and 41 percent thought that they were too conservative. In the September and October polls, more respondents found Senator Kerry's views to be unacceptably liberal than found them to be acceptably mainstream or conservative. In contrast, in each of the surveys, between 53 and 55 percent found President Bush's views to be acceptable and only 40 or 41 percent thought them too conservative. The ideo-logical acceptability gap ranged from three points to ten points, but at all times favored President Bush. In short, the results of 2004 would appear to once again confirm the conventional wisdom that Northern Democratic liberals (Hubert Humphrey, George McGovern, Walter Mondale, Michael Dukakis, and now John Kerry) are too far out of sync with the views of America's median voter to be elected president.

Although there is no doubt that voters mean different things when they respond to the liberal and conservative labels, there is also no doubt that there is meaning there. In five September and October Gallup polls, respondents consistently named President Bush more often as the candidate who "shares your values." Although the margins were slightly smaller than on the ideology question (+2 to +5 Bush), the gap was consistent. The exit polls also indicated that while Kerry received 85 percent of the liberal vote, Bush received 84 percent of the conservative vote. The difference is that conservatives greatly outnumber liberals. In both the exit polls and the NES (for reported voters) the ratio was eight conservatives for every five liberals.

In the aftermath of the 2004 vote, analysts expressed surprise at responses to "the most important issue" question: more voters mentioned "moral values" as the most important issue than mentioned terrorism, or Iraq, or the economy. In the exit poll, 22 percent mentioned "moral values" as their greatest concern, and Bush received four out of five of these votes. Some interpreted this as an outpouring of the evangelical vote. Undoubtedly this was a portion of the vote. Bush won 78 percent of the votes of those who said that they were evangelicals or born-again. The surge in turnout is more accurately interpreted as a broader phenomenon of a mobilized conservative base rallying to the side of a conservative president conducting a war and under siege—from the harsh attacks of the opposing party and allied critics (both at home and overseas). Together with a share of moderates, they constituted the reelection majority. However, although he received 91 percent of the votes of exit poll respondents who said that "religious faith" was the most important quality in a candidate, only 8 percent of respondents named this quality as most important. Although incumbency played a role in Bush's reelection, there was more substance to it than that alone would suggest. A slim majority of voters, but at any rate a majority, preferred the perspective on leadership that President Bush brought to the presidency to that offered by Senator Kerry.

For Democrats, the 2004 election brought bad and perhaps worse news. President Bush, a president for whom many Democrats had developed a visceral distaste, was reelected with a popular vote majority. This was the bad news for Democrats. The potentially worse news for them is that the election was close. The fact that Senator Kerry came as close to defeating President Bush as he did may convince Democrats that there is no compelling reason to moderate their perspectives to bring them more into line with the median American voter. Some in the party continue to believe that the problem is not with excesses in the party's liberal philosophy, but with its candidates, tactics, public relations, or even with Republican shenanigans at the polls.

This may well be whistling past the political graveyard. The election was close because of party polarization, and that looks to be here to stay, but also because some of the fundamentals were less tilted in the Republicans' favor than they might have been and, in several respects, this particular campaign developed favorably for Democrats. Beyond party polarization, the election was close because pre-campaign public support for Bush was dampened by divisions over the war in Iraq. Developments during the campaign also kept the election close—the strategic considerations that allowed Senator Kerry to benefit from the economic issue, Kerry's stronger performance in the debates, the Democrats' money advantage from the 527 groups, the mobilization of Democrats partially offsetting the Republican turnout surge, and the anemic showing by Ralph Nader. These conditions helped Democrats in 2004, but may not be factors in future contests. Moreover, even with these campaign developments favorable to the Democrats, Republicans won the election with a popular vote majority while adding to their majorities in both the House and the Senate. The silver linings to the 2004 clouds hovering over Democrats is that their candidate in 2008 will not face President Bush, that it is unknown whether the Republicans can replicate their turnout surge of 2004, and that the Republicans will be seeking a third consecutive party term—at least initially placing the parties on a more level playing field.*

* This article is a greatly expanded and revised version of an article that appeared in the electronic journal *The Forum*.

Part V:
WHY ELECTIONS ARE NOT ENOUGH

Complications of American Democracy:
Elections Are Not Enough

DEMETRIOS JAMES CARALEY

An elective despotism was not the government we fought for.
— Thomas Jefferson

The American democracy is a very complicated one. The Framers thought that three major features were critical to the working of our democratic institutions: free elections, separation of powers and checks and balances, and government limited by constitutional guarantees, especially those in the Bill of Rights. The aims of this essay are to remind the reader of how those complications were justified by the Framers, to raise implicitly the realization that exporting democracy to other lands is not just a matter of having one set of free elections, and to comment explicitly on whether some traditional characteristics of American democracy have come under serious threat. A pessimistic reading of developments would argue that we are already on the way to government by an elective tyranny of the majority that violates checks and balances and the rights of the minority. The more pessimistic reading is that this tyranny of the majority is even trying to impose the doctrines of religious conservativism on officials and on the public in direct violation of the First Amendment and of the constitutional provision barring religious tests for holding public office. And feeding that pessimism is the absence in 2005 of any major political or public leader with the courage and self-interest, as John F. Kennedy had in 1960, to take on this religious right head-on and say, as Kennedy did during his campaign, "I [do not] look with favor upon those who would work to subvert Article VI of the Constitution by requiring a religious test—even by indirection—for it. If they disagree with that safeguard they should be out openly working to repeal it."[1]

[1] Remarks of Senator John F. Kennedy on church and state delivered to the Greater Houston Ministerial Association, Houston, Texas; www.jfklibrary.org/j091260.htm. I have incorporated virtually the entire speech into an appendix because of its topicality and the forcefulness of its arguments.

DEMETRIOS JAMES CARALEY is Research Professor of Political Science at Barnard College, Professor of International and Public Affairs at Columbia University, and Editor of *Political Science Quarterly*. He has published extensively on different aspects of American politics, national security policy, and democratic political theory.

FUNCTIONS OF ELECTIONS

Elections have always been deemed important. According to the Founding Fathers—who did not claim to be democrats—elections were the main guarantee against oppressive government. In the Declaration of Independence, the Founders argued as a "self-evident" "truth" that governments derived "their just powers from the consent of the governed." Even before the Revolutionary War, colonists had argued that the lack of opportunity to vote for representatives to Parliament made its laws illegitimate when applied to them. Moreover, the colonists had over a century of experience with elections; they had been voting for at least one house of the normally two-house colonial legislatures and thus had the experience of being voted in and out of office.

In the Constitution of 1787, the Founders provided for the direct election of the members of the House of Representatives by those eligible in each state to vote for the lower house of the state legislature, a large franchise for the time, although it excluded women and people of color. The Founders made members of the Senate appointive by their state legislatures, which contained representatives elected directly by the people. In the clumsy electoral vote system for choosing the president, the Founders did not make the president a popularly elective official.[2] But they also did not give the appointment of the president to Congress. If they had, the chances of Congress agreeing later to a constitutional amendment to provide for the almost direct election of the president that developed would have been zero.

The Founders deliberately left open for each state to decide how its presidential electors were to be selected. As early as Thomas Jefferson's election in 1800, the electors did not act as sets of elites who, as the Founders intended, used independent judgment to cast their ballots for the person the electors felt best fit to become president. By 1800, the electors had become slates of party rubber stamps, who promised, if elected, to cast their electoral votes for one or the other party's informal nominee—John Adams for the Federalists and Thomas Jefferson for the Jeffersonian-Republicans. By Andrew Jackson's presidency, almost all state legislatures mandated that electors be chosen by essentially universal white, male suffrage.

Today we take the choosing of rulers in elections for granted, but this was not the case in 1787. The most "election-based" government of the time was that of the British. And while Britain had restricted its king to reigning rather than ruling and was governed by a cabinet and Parliament, the right to vote for members of Parliament was extended to only about one-fifth of the adult male population.

The Founders insisted that this was not enough and that it was "essential" that the right to vote be extended to:

---

[2] Hamilton had argued with his typical modesty that with respect to "the mode of selection of the Chief Magistrate, . . . I affirm that if the manner of it not be perfect, it is at least excellent." *The Federalist Papers, No. 68.*

the great body of the society, not . . . an inconsiderable proportion, or a favored class of it; otherwise a handful of tyrannical nobles, exercising their oppressions by a delegation of their powers, might aspire to the rank of republicans, and claim for their government the honorable title of republic.[3]

The Founders were proud that in the House of Representatives they provided the strongest restraint to would-be oppressive rulers—frequent elections occurring every two years.[4] As Alexander Hamilton asked in *The Federalist, No. 35*:

> Is it not natural that a man who is a candidate for the favor of the people, and who is dependent on the suffrages of his fellow-citizens for the continuation of his public honors, should take care to inform himself of their dispositions and inclinations . . . ? This dependence [creates] strong chords of sympathy between the Representative and the constituent.[5]

The Founders never stated that they were building a "democracy." To them, a "democracy" meant "direct democracy," "a society consisting of a small number of citizens who assemble and administer the government in person," and where there would be "nothing to check the inducements to sacrifice the weaker party or an obnoxious individual."[6] The Founders saw democracy, through the reading of Plato and Thucydides, as equivalent to a tyranny of the majority or even mob rule. They feared such a government would expropriate the rights and property of the minority of the better off and oppress unpopular individuals, as, for example, the Athenian democracy had done in executing Socrates.

The Founders preferred what they called a "republic," because in a republic "the scheme of representation takes place," and the government is delegated "to a small number of citizens." This small number would be able "to refine and enlarge the public views" and their wisdom could "best discern the true interest of their country."[7] Since it was taken for granted that the legislative bodies would function by majority rule, they had set up the framework for the representative democracy that continues to exist.

There was, however, one built-in constitutional exception to representative majority rule, and that was in the Senate, where senators representing states with great disparities in population were granted equal voting power. Members of the constitutional convention from states with small populations would not accept a constitution that allowed a small number of states with the largest populations to be able to prevail in a single legislative body, as the original Virginia Plan proposed. In 1790, the largest states, Virginia, Pennsylvania, and North

---

[3] *The Federalist Papers, No. 39* (Madison). Madison had also experienced what he considered tyranny of the majority in the Virginia state government.

[4] *The Federalist Papers, No. 37* (Madison).

[5] *The Federalist Papers, No. 35* (Hamilton).

[6] *The Federalist Papers, No. 10* (Madison).

[7] *The Federalist Papers, No. 10* (Madison).

Carolina, had populations of 691,737, 434,373, and 393,751, respectively, while the smallest states, Delaware, Rhode Island, and Georgia had populations of only 59,056, 68,825, and 82,548.[8] Because the House of Representatives did reflect population, the granting of equal voting power in the Senate was "the price of union."[9] This disparity still exists today, where two senators each represent the populous states of California, Texas, and New York, with populations of 35,893,799, 22,490,022, and 19,227,088, and two senators each represent the least populous states, Wyoming, Vermont, and North Dakota, with populations of only 506,529, 621,394, and 634,366.[10] As the price of union, the equal voting provision for the Senate was so important that the Constitution provides that it cannot even be changed by constitutional amendment unless the states being affected adversely each consent to it.[11] The electoral vote system for electing the president, which grants electoral votes to states equal to their number of representatives in the House plus their two senators, also dampens the majority rule principle, since the vote of voters from the small states counts somewhat more than that of voters from the larger states.

Do Elections Serve Any Purpose?

Because our top officials are chosen in free elections—because, as in the literal translation of democracy from the Greek, the *demos* or "people" *kratein* or "hold power"—what we have in our national government certainly is a democracy. But it is a democracy of a special kind and most emphatically not a direct, majority-rule democracy. The chief role of voters in federal elections is not to decide policy in a kind of continuing referendum, but to elect officials who make policy. And the top official elected—the president—may be chosen as the result of his party affiliation and personality characteristics, such as his likability and warmth relative to his opponent's, rather than on the basis of his policy stances and, indeed, even despite policy stances that the voters dislike.

By choosing a president, voters also do have a major, albeit unpredictable, impact on policy. Given the president's Article II powers of appointment,[12] the election of one candidate instead of the other means the appointment of one rather than another set of high-level presidential appointees (some needing but almost always receiving senatorial confirmation): departmental cabinet and subcabinet heads; White House staff members, including a chief of staff and the national security adviser; a council of economic advisers; ambassadors; federal reserve board members and the chairman; and especially District Court, Court

---

[8] Bureau of the Census, Table 16, *Population: 1790 to 1990*, United States Summary: Population and Housing Counts, 1993.

[9] See Herbert Agar, *The Price of Union* (Boston: Houghton-Mifflin, 1966).

[10] Bureau of the Census, *United States, Regions, States and Puerto Rico Population Estimates and Population Change*, Press Release, 22 December 2004.

[11] U.S. Const. art. I, sec. 3.

[12] U.S. Const. art. II, sec. 2.

of Appeals, and Supreme Court judges with lifetime terms. The substantial discretion that top executive branch officials and members of the judiciary have in making executive and judicial decisions allows changes in policy even without the president and voting majorities in Congress acting through legislation.

Elections, finally, do serve another important policy function, even though it is neither much discussed nor much appreciated. Some policy departures are not made or even attempted because of the anticipated reaction of the voters in the next election. If there were no elections, even imperfectly conducted as they are, the preferences of the citizenry could be largely disregarded because the public would lose its chief sanction. As A. D. Lindsay once put it, the voters know if the "shoes pinch" and if they didn't have the power to remove those who make bad shoes, the incumbent shoemakers could stay in power forever with the claim that the shoes pinch not because the shoes were badly made but because the voters have crooked feet.[13]

Today, as a result of constitutional provisions and the 15th, 17th, 19th, and 26th Amendments, plus the Voting Rights Act of 1965, presidential electors, senators, and representatives are directly chosen by the people in all states and the suffrage for all offices has essentially been extended to every citizen over the age of eighteen, regardless of race or gender. There is, however, the antidemocratic proviso in the election of the president that formally persists: After the 2000 presidential election, the electoral vote majority hinged on how the popular vote would come out after recounts in Florida. The Supreme Court took jurisdiction in the case of *Bush v. Gore*,[14] and stopped the recounts. The Court reminded us that there is no constitutional right for voters to choose electors, and under provisions of Article II, the state legislatures are empowered to decide whether the electors can be chosen by methods other than the voters, including by the legislatures themselves.[15] According to the majority of the Court, this means of appointment could be mandated even after the popular vote has taken place,[16] so that in the leading democracy of the world, its citizens still do not have a constitutional right to vote directly or even indirectly for its president.[17] As the Supreme Court majority opinion in *Bush v. Gore* reminded us:

> The individual citizen has no federal constitutional right to vote for electors for the President of the United States unless and until the state legislature chooses a statewide election as the means to implement its power to appoint members of the Electoral College. . . . When the state legislature vests the right to vote for the President in its people, the right to vote as the legislature has prescribed is fundamental; and one source of its fundamental nature lies in the equal weight accorded to each vote and the equal dignity owed to each voter. The State, of course, after granting

---

[13] A. D. Lindsay, *The Modern Democratic State* (New York: Oxford University Press, 1962).

[14] *Bush v. Gore*, 531 U.S. 98 (2000).

[15] U.S. Const. art. II, sec. 1.

[16] *Bush v. Gore*.

[17] Demetrios James Caraley, "Why Americans Need a Constitutional Right to Vote for Presidential Electors," *Political Science Quarterly*, 116 (Spring 2001): 1–3.

the franchise in the special context of Article II, can take back the power to appoint electors.[18]

SEPARATION OF POWERS AND CHECKS AND BALANCES

Elections were not the only features that were built into American representative democracy by the Founders. The Founding Fathers saw elections as essential protection against oppressive rulers and, at the extreme, against tyranny, but not as sufficient protection. Jefferson wrote in his "Notes on the State of Virginia" that if "all the powers of government, legislative, executive, and judiciary" were given to the legislative body, which Jefferson assumed would be elective:

> it will be no alleviation, that these powers will be exercised by a plurality of hands, and not by a single one. One hundred and seventy-three despots would surely be as oppressive as one. . . . An elective despotism was not the government we fought for.[19]

The Founders felt the same way about an all-powerful chief executive, who they feared would be the equivalent of an elective king.

To prevent this kind of "elective despotism" or "tyranny," they resorted to "auxiliary precautions." In the new national government, they separated constitutionally—as a matter of supreme constitutional law not subject to change by ordinary legislation passed by congressional majorities and signed by the president—they separated governmental powers among the executive, the legislative, and the judiciary. This way they gave "to those who administer each department the necessary constitutional means and personal motives to resist encroachments of the others." As Madison phrased it:

> Ambition must be made to counteract ambition. The interest of the man must be connected with the constitutional rights of the place. It may be a reflection on human nature that such devices should be necessary to control the abuses of government. But what is government itself, but the greatest of all reflections on human nature? If men were angels, no government would be necessary. If angels were to govern men, neither external nor internal controls on government would be necessary. In framing a government which is to be administered by men over men, the great difficulty lies in this: you must first enable the government to control the governed; and in the next place oblige it to control itself. A dependence on the people [that is, elections] is, no doubt, the primary control on the government; but experience has taught mankind the necessity of auxiliary precautions.[20]

The Founders were particularly specific about separating the power to declare war from the power to conduct a war as commander in chief. Alexander

---

[18] *Bush v. Gore.*
[19] Quoted in *The Federalist Papers, No. 51* (Madison).
[20] *The Federalist Papers, No. 51* (Madison).

Hamilton explained in *The Federalist, No. 69*, the clear distinction between the presidential position of commander in chief and the congressional power to declare war:

> The President is to be commander-in-chief of the army and navy of the United States. . . . In this respect his authority would be nominally the same with that of the king of Great Britain, but in substance much inferior to it. It would amount to nothing more than the supreme command and direction of the military and naval forces, as first general and admiral of the Confederacy; while that of the British king extends to the *DECLARING* of war and to the *RAISING* and *REGULATING* of fleets and armies, all [of] which, by the Constitution under consideration, would appertain to the legislature.[21]

The Framers thus specifically insisted that the president as commander in chief, a single person, would not possess the power to make war, because that was akin to the monarchical power of a king, and that was not the form of government for which they had fought.

CONSTITUTIONALLY LIMITED GOVERNMENT AND JUDICIAL REVIEW

Over and above trying to protect the people against oppression and tyranny by means of elections and separation of powers, the Founders also bequeathed to us a government that as a whole was constitutionally limited. Certain kinds of individual activity and belief and certain procedures in criminal trials, the Founders believed, were so important that they had to be protected even against voting majorities working through elections and with the support of a particular president and majorities in a particular Congress.

The Constitution written by the Founders contained, as Hamilton put it, "certain specified exceptions to the legislative authority; such, for instance, as that it shall pass no bills of attainder, no *ex post facto* laws, and the like."[22] The Founders also mandated in the Constitution, under the powers of Congress, that "The Privilege of the Writ of Habeas Corpus shall not be suspended, unless when in cases of Rebellion or Invasion the public Safety may require it."[23] Further limitations were to be those protective of civil liberties and procedural due process in criminal trials that everyone agreed would be added to the Constitution as soon as the first Congress met and had the opportunity to propose the necessary amendments, and the states had the opportunity to ratify them. These protections now constitute the Bill of Rights.

But these limitations could be preserved, according to the Founders, "no other way than through the medium of courts of justice, whose duty it must be to declare all acts contrary to the manifest tenor of the Constitution void. Without this all the reservations of particular rights or privileges would amount to

---

[21] *The Federalist Papers, No. 69* (Hamilton).
[22] *The Federalist Papers, No. 78* (Hamilton).
[23] U.S. Const. art. I, sec. 9.

nothing."[24] Justice Robert Jackson, speaking for the Supreme Court when it declared unconstitutional in 1943, in the middle of World War II, the requiring of schoolchildren to say the Pledge of Allegiance and salute the flag every morning, probably put it best:

> The very purpose of a Bill of Rights was to withdraw certain subjects from the vicissitudes of political controversy, to place them beyond the reach of majorities and officials and to establish them as legal principles to be applied by the courts. One's right to life, liberty, and property, to free speech, a free press, freedom of worship and assembly, and other fundamental rights may not be submitted to vote; they depend on the outcome of no elections. . . .
>
> If there is any fixed star in our Constitutional constellation, it is that no official, high or petty, can prescribe what shall be orthodox in politics, in nationalism, religion, or other matters of opinion or force citizens to confess by word or act their faith therein. If there are any circumstances that permit an exception, they do not now occur to us.[25]

Constitutional safeguards of free speech, free press, freedom of assembly, and freedom of religion for those who become at odds with majority thinking, and also constitutional procedural due process in criminal trials for individuals accused of crimes, have historically been perceived as not being in the interests of liberals only, or of conservatives only, but in the interests of all. This is because no one can know in advance when he or she will be in the minority in terms of party or ideological viewpoint or be unjustly accused of a crime and, therefore, will need constitutional protections to escape oppression of the weak and innocent by the strong.

But equally important, these constitutional limits on majorities are also essential for maintaining our political system as a democratic government. Constitutional limitations, beyond the reach of majorities to change, ensure that losers in a particular election will be allowed to survive as the "outs." Not only will the losers be allowed just to survive, they will also not be arrested or imprisoned, and they will be allowed to compete for office unhindered by the majority-supported "ins," whom they will be trying to displace in the next election.

The Constitution makes no provision for political parties. According to nineteenth-century journalist Henry Jones Ford, it was the "great unconscious achievement" of Jefferson to take advantage of these "open constitutional channels of political agitation," and create a party as early as 1796.[26] Jefferson and his allies thus channeled and organized the forces of discontent against the Washington-Adams Federalists through elections, so that by the election of 1800, change "became possible without destruction."[27]

An even more crucial element in preserving democracy was the noninterference with Jefferson's election campaign by the Federalists and the acquies-

---

[24] *The Federalist Papers, No. 78* (Hamilton).

[25] *West Virginia Board of Education v. Barnett*, 319 U.S. 624 (1943).

[26] Henry Jones Ford, *The Rise and Growth of American Politics* (New York: Macmillan, 1898), 126.

[27] Ibid.

cent, peaceful, and voluntary leaving of presidential power by John Adams after Jefferson won the 1800 election. This voluntary relinquishing of the presidency and control of Congress in 1801 by the Federalists to the victorious Jeffersonian-Republicans established the precedent that fundamental change in personnel and policies could be accomplished by free elections protected by constitutional guarantees without the violence of a war, revolution, or coup d'etat.

In only one American election, that of 1860, did the losers refuse to accept the election returns peacefully and chose instead to resist them by the use of force. The result was the Civil War and the greatest loss of life of any war in which the United States has participated.

Constitutional limits obviously put a damper on the ability of a newly elected majority to enact its programs if they contain infringements of civil liberties and procedural due process as most recently defined by the Supreme Court by justices with lifetime tenure. This doesn't mean that majorities can be frustrated forever and that here is, finally, the fatal dilemma in our democracy. It does mean that to prevail, those majorities need to be extraordinarily large — two-thirds majorities in the House and Senate to propose constitutional amendments — and must be sustained long enough to secure separate ratification by additional majorities in three-fourths of the states. The Founding Fathers saw the conundrum; Hamilton wrote that he trusted that:

> the friends of the Constitution [will never question] that fundamental principle of republican government, which admits the right of the people to alter or abolish the established Constitution, whenever they find it inconsistent with their happiness. [But] until the people have, by some solemn and authoritative act, annulled or changed the established form, it is binding.[28]

Had Hamilton lived long enough, he would also have explained that sustained majorities that continuously elect presidents with their overall constitutional point of view can count on those presidents appointing enough new justices to the Supreme Court to redefine the views of the Court on the constitutionality of some burning issues, and even sitting justices have been known to change their positions when very much out of sync with the policy positions of the electorate. The voters who oppose constitutional freedom of choice to have an abortion, oppose gay marriage, oppose due process in criminal trials that is highly protective of accused criminals, and who want schoolchildren to be required to recite the Pledge of Allegiance and participate in school prayers have not yet been numerous enough or present long enough to impose their definition of what is constitutionally permissible on the remainder of the population.

The Founding Fathers gladly sacrificed government that could provide speedy, effective, cohesive, and internally consistent policies. They opted for one that had a maximum number of veto points and checks and balances and

---

[28] *The Federalist Papers, No. 78* (Hamilton).

protections against tyranny by particular officials or tyranny by selfish majorities. These veto points and checks and balances have also prevented radical changes in policy from administration to administration and have kept voters and public opinion from becoming polarized at opposite ends of the policy and ideological spectrum.

What in the Equilibrium Is Being Threatened?

The preceding discussion argues that the American democracy is certainly a democracy by virtue of the citizenry electing their rulers in free elections and the citizenry having some influence on policy, albeit indirectly and mostly retrospectively. It is also a constitutional democracy, in that there are limits to what the government has the right to do in restricting civil liberties or abridging constitutional due process guarantees in criminal trials. But, especially in the last decade, a number of these tenets protecting our constitutionally limited, elected democracy have become threatened.

The Perceived Legitimacy of Presidential Elections

The Electoral Vote System of Choosing. The perceived legitimacy of the formal means for choosing the president has eroded since the 2000 presidential election. Although it did not happen in the entire twentieth century, in the 2000 election, George W. Bush became the president despite having had 539,947 fewer popular votes than Albert Gore.[29] Then in the 2004 election, if 59,229 Ohio voters had voted for John Kerry rather than George W. Bush,[30] Kerry would have been elected president despite an approximately 3 million vote deficit recorded by the popular vote. If these close elections continue in the future, and especially if candidates winning only a minority of the voters are elected president due to the electoral vote system, the sense of democratic legitimacy surrounding the presidential electoral system will begin to dissipate. It has also, for example, allowed Russian President Vladimir Putin, when criticized about his regime not being sufficiently democratic, to point out that different nations have different democratic systems, and that in Russia, a candidate not having the most votes could not be elected president. Changing the electoral vote system would, however, require a constitutional amendment, something that senators from the least populous states would almost certainly block.

Winner-Take-All. The legitimacy of presidential elections is also being strained by the state-imposed rule, in all but two of the states, that the winner of the popular vote in a state receives all of the electoral votes allocated to that

[29] David Stout, "The 43rd President: The Final Tally," *New York Times*, 30 December 2000.
[30] Albert Salvato, "Ohio Recount Gives a Smaller Margin to Bush," *New York Times*, 29 December 2004.

state regardless of the margin of victory. The winner-take-all system was from the beginning intended to be anti-democratic by disenfranchising party minorities in a state. It was originated in 1800 by Thomas Jefferson to ensure that all of the electoral votes from Virginia went to Jefferson and none to Adams, because Jefferson knew the electoral vote contest would be close. Once news of Jefferson's move reached Adams's home state of Massachusetts, the legislature there too instituted a winner-take-all rule so as to equally ensure that no electoral votes from Massachusetts would go to Jefferson. The winner-take-all system and polarization between the "red" and "blue" states now results in the de facto disenfranchisement of minority party–inclined voters in non-battleground states. Presidential candidates have directed their appeals to the interests of only a dozen or so battleground states that early polls predict may go in either direction, even though those states are not representative of the nation as a whole. Thus, the candidates ignore the rest of the country, both in the "ground war" and in the "air war." This is because it is of no consequence to a candidate if he/she wins the non-battleground states by 55 percent or 75 percent or loses by 10 percent or 25 percent. It would not require a constitutional amendment to eliminate the winner-take-all proviso and allot electoral votes proportionately to reflect the division of the popular vote. If this were done, the presidential candidates would have to campaign in almost all states and every voter would feel his vote counted.

The Buying of Presidential Elections. The absolutely colossal amount of spending for presidential nominating and general election campaigns gives a feeling of corruption to the entire process. In the 2003–2004 election cycle, George W. Bush raised $260.6 million for his presidential reelection campaign, and his opponent, John Kerry, raised a total of $233.4 million,[31] which clearly demonstrates the astronomical sums of money that come into play in U.S. elections at this point. Congress, in a bipartisan move after long study, did seriously limit spending by individuals and campaigns in 1971 with the Federal Election Campaign Act. But in 1976, in *Buckley v. Valeo*,[32] the Supreme Court ruled with a variety of opinions and rationales that a central part of that measure was unconstitutional. All the justices essentially equated the nonverbal spending of millions or hundreds of millions of dollars to a citizen's First Amendment rights to free speech and free association. When the Framers crafted the Bill of Rights, free speech consisted of actual speaking with a voice that had only lung power to reach an immediate audience; could they come back and speak, it is very doubtful that these realistic politicians would equate freedom of speech with the use of money to buy professionally crafted commercials that can reach hundreds of millions at a time. Indeed, without the spending limitations, the

---

[31] FEC Candidate Summary Reports, Presented by the Federal Elections Commission 2003–2004 Cycle, accessed at http://herndon1.sdrdc.com/cgi-bin/cancomsrs/?_04+P80000235 and http://herndon1.sdrdc.com/cgi-bin/cancomsrs/?_04+P800003335, 14 April 2005.

[32] *Buckley v. Valeo*, 424 U.S. 1 (1976).

value of an average individual's free speech is actually diminished, because it will go nowhere unless the person is a celebrity or has millions of dollars with which to buy and run a television ad. Also, while having now a new Supreme Court membership that might uphold a limit on individual spending, we also have a president and Congress that were elected with even more massive spending than the politicians of the 1970s and, therefore, it is unlikely that they will think that the rules, which allowed for their successful election, should be changed.

Incomplete Media Coverage. A further threatening development in American presidential campaigns is the manner in which the current television, radio, and print media frequently provide incomplete, inaccurate, and differential coverage of facts and analyses to inform the voters in election campaigns. Voters rely on the media to provide them with the accurate information necessary to make informed judgments in elections. It is clear that voters receive a different set of facts on some major events and policy decisions depending on the source from which they get their political news. A report published by the Program on International Policy Attitudes (PIPA) in October 2004 shows the public's differential perception of the facts used to justify going to war in Iraq—a major issue in 2004:

> Views about the decision to go to war are highly correlated with beliefs about prewar Iraq. Among those who say that going to war was the right decision, 73% believe that Iraq had WMD (47%) or a major program for developing them (26%), and 75% believe that Iraq was providing substantial support to al Qaeda. Among those who say it was the wrong decision, only 29% believe that Iraq had WMD (10%) or a major program for developing them (19%), and 33% believe that Iraq was providing substantial support to al Qaeda.[33]

This report links a person's choice to support a policy decision to their understanding or misunderstanding of the facts. In a previous analysis, PIPA discovered a widespread correlation between a person's misperceptions and their chosen media outlet. FOX viewers held the highest percentage of misperceptions, while PBS/NPR viewer/listeners maintained the fewest misperceptions regarding issues such as the presence of weapons of mass destruction in Iraq and a link between Saddam Hussein and al Qaeda.[34] A voter's misperceptions, strongly connected to their media provider, affect the policy decisions they are willing to support, such as the war in Iraq, and thus their willingness to vote or not vote for the candidate responsible for those policy decisions. If a presidential administration chooses to manipulate public opinion and if the media out-

---

[33] Excerpted from a report distributed by PIPA (Program on International Policy Attitudes), School of Public Affairs, University of Maryland, entitled "What's New: Three in Four Say If Iraq Did Not Have WMD or Support al Qaeda, US Should Not Have Gone to War," 28 October 2004.

[34] See Steven Kull, Clay Ramsay, and Evan Lewis, "Misperceptions, the Media, and the Iraq War," *Political Science Quarterly* 118 (Winter 2003–2004): 569–598.

lets serve as cheerleaders for a particular agenda or administration rather than as critical filters and analysts, the efficacy and legitimacy of elections come into doubt. American democracy relies on the transparency and integrity of elected government officials and critical media concerned with informing the public, especially in presenting facts and analyses about complex events that the voters cannot see or access directly for themselves. Without these two factors in place, elections cannot serve their original purpose of holding rulers accountable by knowledgably rewarding or punishing for successes or failures in broad policy areas.

Congressional Abdication of War Powers

Congressional majorities have shown themselves to be largely indifferent to their constitutional prerogatives in war making, most egregiously when they granted President George W. Bush the discretionary authority to initiate and conduct the 2003 war in Iraq. But Congress also implicitly acquiesced to the trespassing on their authority when President Bill Clinton used military force during the conflicts in Bosnia and Kosovo.

In *The Federalist, No. 51*, Madison states that he expected "the private interest of every individual may be a sentinel over the public rights,"[35] and thus the interest of each member of Congress would protect the citizens of the nation from any rush to war or improper executive use of power. The Framers presumed that Congress's desire for sharing power or their ambition to protect their constitutional duties by having the final say in major decisions involving the life and death of American military forces would cause Congress to prevent the executive branch from usurping their prerogatives.

The case made to Congress by the Bush administration for a resolution authorizing the use of force in Iraq has now been shown to have been based on an incorrect or misleading reading of intelligence reports that Iraq had weapons of mass destruction that could be given to terrorists to be used against the United States, that Saddam Hussein was connected with the September 11 attack on the United States, and that the Iraqis so hated their government that they would immediately welcome American forces as liberators. Majorities in both the House and Senate transferred to the president the power to decide both whether and when the United States would go to war in Iraq through a broadly worded joint resolution that authorized him "to use the U.S. military as he deems necessary and appropriate to defend U.S. national security against Iraq and enforce U.N. Security Council resolutions regarding Iraq."[36] Not only did Congress abdicate its constitutional duties in the Iraq Resolution, but it did so in haste, without sufficient debate and deliberation, and against strong arguments to refrain because the case against Iraq had not been proven. The haste

[35] *The Federalist Papers, No. 51* (Madison).
[36] House Joint Resolution 114, Use of Force, 11 October 2002.

244 DEMETRIOS JAMES CARALEY

was the result of the President arguing that the danger from Saddam Hussein was increasing daily and of even the Democratic congressional leadership wanting to get the Iraq vote "out of the way" before the 2002 midterm elections, because they thought they would profit by having economic issues as the central agenda. It would have been inconceivable to our Framers that congressional leaders would have abdicated their constitutional powers to decide on war. The Founders were all ambitious politicians, jealously guarding their constitutional prerogatives, and they expected their successors to be likewise.

Not all members of Congress were willing to roll over. Senator Robert C. Byrd of West Virginia, the Senate's constitutional expert, challenged both the wisdom and constitutionality of the resolution. In an op-ed piece for *The New York Times*, Senator Byrd declared:

> We may not always be able to avoid war, particularly if it is thrust upon us, but Congress must not attempt to give away the authority to determine when war is to be declared. We must not allow any president to unleash the dogs of war at his own discretion and for an unlimited period of time.[37]

Nevertheless, majorities in Congress, including Democratic ones in the Senate, did not heed the warnings. Both Senator John Kerry and Senator John Edwards—the Democratic ticket in 2004—voted for the resolution and later turned against the war, claiming that that they were not given accurate information and intelligence reports. But other prominent Democratic Senators Edward Kennedy, Patrick Leahy, Paul Wellstone, Carl Levin, Barbara Boxer, Bob Graham, the Republican, Lincoln Chafee, and the sole Independent in the Senate, James Jeffords, felt they had enough information to justify their responsibly voting "no."

By launching a war without really convincing majorities in Congress of the case's merits, the President violated at least the spirit of the Constitution. But he also lost the opportunity to engage in an intellectual give-and-take with officials who were separately elected and therefore not beholden to him, from whom he could gain fresh perspectives to balance those generated and debated by his subordinates in the secret recesses of the Office of the Secretary of Defense, The National Security Council, the CIA, and the State Department. It was this failure of past presidents to consult more broadly and to rely instead on executive branch groupthink that played a large part in the 1961 Bay of Pigs fiasco and in the disastrous decisions, starting in 1964, to expand the war in Vietnam.[38] It appears that it was this kind of groupthink that prevented intelligence officers who had a different take on the danger of Iraq from getting their views to the top decision makers in the executive branch and in Congress.[39]

[37] Robert C. Byrd, "Congress Must Resist the Rush to War," *New York Times*, 10 October 2002.

[38] Irving Janis, *Groupthink: Psychological Studies of Policy Decisions and Fiascoes* (Boston: Houghton Mifflin, 1983).

[39] National Commission on Terrorist Attacks upon the United States, *The 9/11 Commission Report: The Final Report of the National Commission on Terrorist Attacks upon the United States* (New York: Norton, 2004).

If the manner in which the United States went to war against Iraq in 2003 becomes accepted as a legitimate precedent, we run this risk: Any president, in what may be a perpetual "war on terrorism," can find misleading and allegedly very confidential intelligence with which to scare Congress into giving him authority to use the military (or even worse, do so on his own, with the claim that it is within his inherent power as commander in chief) to forestall attacks from some alleged terrorist group or rogue nation.[40] Because the United States has an all-volunteer military force, there will be no objections from people concerned about themselves or their children being drafted to serve in the war. Also, funding a war entirely by issuance of debt, instead of by raising taxes to produce the necessary revenues, results in the broad general public not feeling any kind of monetary pinch. The Framers would probably have called this kind of institutional process for waging war an "elective despotism."

Threats to Due Process Guarantees

Another weakening of our traditional constitutional democracy is the direct outcome of some of the broad power given to the executive branch after the September 11 terrorist attacks through the USA Patriot Act and a general deferring to the president, the military, FBI, CIA, and attorney general during wartime. The ability of the government to monitor phone and email communications of anyone at any time and to incarcerate even American citizens on American soil by designating them as enemy combatants is a shift from what has in the past been acceptable in American constitutional democracy. Clearly some of this authority is necessary in order to detect terrorists in the United States, thwart their plans to launch other terrorist attacks, and incapacitate those who might engage in terrorist actions. But holding American citizens indefinitely, without having filed charges against them, without their being given access to a lawyer, and without their being able to apply for a writ of habeas corpus is a major departure from the protections of the Bill of Rights.

In the first case on this issue to come before the Supreme Court, *Hamdi v. Rumsfeld*,[41] the Supreme Court ruled on 28 June 2004 that detainees (in this case the actual detainee was an American citizen being held in a military installation within the United States after being picked up on the battlefield in Afghanistan in the war against the Taliban) had to at least be given the right to challenge the facts on the basis of which they were designated enemy combat-

---

[40] When in the House of Representatives Abraham Lincoln argued during "preventive" war with Mexico: "Allow the President to invade a neighboring nation whenever he shall deem it necessary to repel an invasion . . . and you allow him to make war at pleasure. . . . If today he should choose to say he thinks it necessary to invade Canada to prevent the British from invading us, how could you stop him? You may say to him, 'I see no probability of the British invading us'; but he will say to you, 'Be silent: I see it, if you don't.'" Arthur Schlesinger, Jr., "Eyeless in Iraq," *New York Review of Books*, 23 October 2003, 24.

[41] *Hamdi v. Rumsfeld*, 542 U.S. __ (2004).

ants before an impartial hearing officer.[42] During that hearing, the detainees would not be entitled to all the regular due process guarantees for criminal trials. What turned out to be the majority opinion had the support of only four justices: Chief Justice William H. Rehnquist, Justice Sandra Day O'Connor, Justice Anthony M. Kennedy, and Justice Stephen G. Breyer; in that opinion, written by Justice O'Connor, she spoke in broad protective language about rights for detainees:

> It would turn our system of checks and balances on its head to suggest that a citizen could not make his way to court with a challenge to the factual basis for his detention by his government, simply because the Executive opposes making available such a challenge. . . .

> We have long since made clear that a state of war is not a blank check for the president when it comes to the rights of the nation's citizens.

But Justice O'Connor further observed that:

> We do not question that our due process assessment must pay keen attention to the particular burdens faced by the Executive in the context of military action.[43]

The detainee in question, Yaser Hamdi, had already been detained for more than two years before the case was decided.[44]

Justice David Hackett Souter and Justice Ruth Bader Ginsburg joined in the majority judgment in order to have six votes for a ruling that Hamdi had to be given a hearing, but dissented in part with the majority opinion because it did not stipulate additional protections they thought were owed to the detainees.[45]

Justice Antonin Scalia and Justice John Paul Stevens dissented because they believed the government either needed to charge an American citizen with a crime and prosecute him or needed to release him. Justice Scalia warned:

> Many think it not only inevitable but entirely proper that liberty give way to security in times of national crisis—that, at the extremes of military exigency, *inter arma silent leges.* Whatever the general merits of the view that war silences law or modulates its voice, that view has no place in the interpretation and application of a Constitution designed precisely to confront war and, in a manner that accords with democratic principles, to accommodate it. Because the Court has proceeded to meet the current emergency in a manner the Constitution does not envision, I respectfully dissent.[46]

---

[42] The issue of non-citizens incarcerated at Guantanamo Bay was not raised in this case.

[43] *Hamdi v. Rumsfeld.*

[44] Yaser Hamdi was finally released from U.S. custody in October of 2004 after nearly three years of detention. He was never charged with a crime.

[45] *Hamdi v. Rumsfeld.* Justices Souter and Ginsburg wrote in their own separate opinion that "Since this disposition does not command a majority of the Court, however, the need to give practical effect to the conclusions of eight members of the Court rejecting the Government's position calls for me to join with the plurality in ordering remand on terms closest to those I would impose."

[46] *Hamdi v. Rumsfeld.*

Only a single justice, Clarence Thomas, dissented from the judgment and all the other opinions, arguing that the president, under his constitutional powers as commander in chief, has the right to designate any citizen as an enemy combatant and detain him without hearings or habeas corpus.

If another massive terrorist attack should come again from within the United States and perhaps involve chemical or biological weapons, it will be very difficult to prevent the wholesale detention of persons who have the same ethnic and religious affiliations as those associated with the September 11 terrorists.

Intrusion into Personal Behavior and Religious Beliefs

The attempt to use government to interfere with what has been seen as behavior within a citizen's right of privacy and to impose the religious beliefs of a minority of the electorate who are fundamentalist Protestants and conservative Catholics is an extremely disturbing evolution in American politics. This minority wishes to impose their stance on issues of private behavior and scientific research, such as birth control, when life begins, stem cell research, decriminalizing homosexuality, gay marriage/civil unions, the right to die, comprehensive sex education, the distribution of condoms to countries severely afflicted with AIDS, and the teaching of evolution versus Genesis[47] in public schools.

Many, primarily Republican, politicians placate this vocal minority of Protestant Evangelicals and conservative Roman Catholics because they consider the first a bedrock of their support and the second a way to garner the votes of a group that has traditionally voted Democratic.[48] This minority has also successfully demonized an ineptly led Democratic Party into being seen as a party for limitless abortion, gay marriage, the harvesting of stem cells from live fetuses, and other extreme positions that most Democrats do not, in fact, agree with, including the most recent Democratic president, Bill Clinton, and the Democratic nominees for president in 2000 and 2004, Al Gore and John Kerry.

A great many of the early American settlers emigrated from their various homelands in Europe in order to escape the frequent religious wars and killings between Catholics and Protestants, and even among different Protestant churches, and the persecution in trials for heresy or treason of those who did not share the beliefs of their religious and governmental leaders. The Founding Fathers desired to create a government and society in which a person's religious beliefs would not affect politics or their standing in the political system. That is why they inserted into the Constitution the provision that "No religious Test shall ever be required as a Qualification to any Office or public Trust under the

[47] President Bush still claims that the "jury is still out" on evolution. See Paul Krugman, "An Academic Question," *New York Times*, 5 April 2005.

[48] In the 2004 election, 52 percent of Catholics voted for President Bush and 47 percent voted for Senator Kerry. See James E. Campbell, "Why Bush Won the Presidential Election of 2004: Incumbency, Ideology, Terrorism, and Turnout," *Political Science Quarterly* 120 (Summer 2005): 219–241.

United States"[49] and a bar from making any "law respecting an establishment of religion or prohibiting the free exercise thereof."[50]

While the United States opposes theocracy abroad in Iraq and seeks the overthrow of the Mullahs in Iran, the Republican Party has embraced the ideology of the religious right to a frightening extent at home. In an op-ed for *The New York Times*, former Republican senator and ordained Episcopal priest John Danforth criticized the Republican Party as "a party that has gone so far in adopting a sectarian agenda that it has become the political extension of a religious movement."[51] The congressional role in the Terri Schiavo case further demonstrates the extremes to which pleasing the religious right can drive the congressional leadership and even President Bush. In a congressional session called at night, Congress passed legislation to give jurisdiction to the federal courts of a case that had gone through the entire Florida court system and had been denied certiorari by the Supreme Court, and which allowed the withdrawal of a feeding tube from a forty-one-year-old woman who had been declared by her doctors to be in a persistent vegetative state for the previous seventeen years. In another extreme move, President Bush interrupted his Texas vacation (where he could have signed the legislation anyway) and flew to Washington to sign it in a media moment. The Federal District Court in Florida refused to consider the case anew, as did the Federal Court of Appeals by a 10–2 decision. Only one judge, Judge Stanley F. Birch, Jr., in the appeals court, was brave enough to issue an opinion that stated how wrong this procedure had been. He wrote that the legislation was:

> Demonstrably at odds with our Founding Fathers' blueprint for the governance of a free people. . . . Legislative dictation of how a federal court should exercise its judicial functions invades the province of the judiciary and violates the separation of powers principle.[52]

These warnings were from a self-proclaimed conservative judge who had been appointed by former President George H. W. Bush.

It has come to a point where Democrats are chastised for not discussing their faith more openly and frequently with the public and attacked for purportedly opposing some conservative nominees for the federal courts because they are "against people of faith."[53] What we should abide by is the American tradition as it was expressed by John F. Kennedy in the presidential campaign of 1960 that would make him the first Catholic elected to the presidency:

[49] U.S. Const. art. VI.

[50] U.S. Const. amend. I.

[51] John C. Danforth, "In the Name of Politics," *New York Times*, 30 March 2005.

[52] Abby Goodnough and William Yardley, "Federal Judge Condemns Intervention in Schiavo Case," *The New York Times*, 31 March 2005.

[53] David D. Kirkpatrick, "Frist Set to Use Religious Stage on Judicial Issue," *The New York Times*, 15 April 2005.

I believe in an America that is officially neither Catholic, Protestant nor Jewish, where no public official either requests or accepts instructions on public policy from the Pope, the National Council of Churches or any other ecclesiastical source— *where no religious body seeks to impose its will directly or indirectly upon the general populace or the public acts of its officials*, and where religious liberty is so indivisible that an act against one church is treated as an act against all. . . .

I do not speak for my church on public matters and the church does not speak for me. Whatever issue may come before me as President, if I should be elected—on birth control, divorce, censorship, gambling, or any other subject—I will make my decision in accordance with these views, in accordance with what my conscience tells me to be in the national interest, and without regard to outside religious pressure or dictate. And no power or threat of punishment could cause me to decide otherwise. . . .

Neither do I look with favor upon those who would work to subvert Article VI of the Constitution by requiring a religious test—even by indirection—for it. *If they disagree with that safeguard they should be out openly working to repeal it.*[54]

If the Catholic clergy had been threatening in 1960 to refuse communion to those Catholic officeholders who voted against the Church's preaching on a range of issues, Kennedy would never have been elected, because too many would have doubted that he could put Catholic doctrine aside when making presidential decisions. As it was, he won by only 110,000 votes, because many fundamentalist Protestants were still afraid that, if elected, Kennedy would do the Pope's bidding.[55]

Polarization and the Tyranny of the Majority

Politics in Washington has taken on a particularly nasty air in recent years. There has been a departure from the political parties of the past, which contained significant overlap in policy positions. Civility between elected officials on opposing sides of the aisle has diminished as politicians have come to see their fellow elected officials of the opposing party almost as enemies to be destroyed rather than colleagues to be won over and, if not, then just as opponents to be defeated. And it must be said that the personalities of Bill Clinton and George W. Bush have had an unparalleled capacity to generate strong animosity from party activists and even voters who had opposed their candidacies.

The years since 2002 have resulted in significant changes in the manner in which Congress operates in the House of Representatives, with the majority monopolizing power traditionally shared with the minority party. In the House, legislation traditionally emerged from committee and carried a rule from the Rules Committee to permit a certain amount of time for debate to be shared between the parties and provided for the offering of amendments from the

---

[54] At www.jfklibrary.org/j091260.htm.
[55] White, *The Making of the President*.

floor. This process, by which both parties were permitted input into legislation, has been altered. The Republican majority in the House during the 108th and 109th Congresses has not allowed the Democrats in the minority the opportunity to offer debate or amendments to important Republican-crafted legislation that the majority leadership decides it does not want to be changed in any way. The House Democrats are reduced to simply registering a "no" vote to Republican legislation on final passage. This tyranny of the majority in the House has led to the disempowerment of the minority House members, who represent approximately 47 percent of the seats in the House.

The Republican majority leadership in the House has gone even to the extreme of stating that they will not bring up for debate legislation that has not been approved by the majority of their party's representatives. The result is that a small section of the Republican party can block any legislation they don't like unless amended to their point of view. In late November of 2004, the Bush administration and both parties in the Senate were supporting the new Intelligence Bill recommended by the 9/11 Commission to create an overall Director of National Intelligence, and it passed the Senate by a bipartisan vote of 96 to 2. After the elections, the bill came to the House, where it faced opposition by some conservative Republicans who argued the bill would take away too much control over intelligence from the Defense Department. There were clearly enough votes from the Democrats and a minority of Republicans to pass the bill on the House floor, but Speaker Dennis Hastert refused to allow it to come up. As his spokesman put it, "Mr. Hastert did not want to split his caucus, and did not want the bill to pass with less than a majority of the majority. What good is it to pass something where most of our members don't like it?"[56] After a month of negotiations and the direct involvement of President Bush and Vice President Dick Cheney, several provisions were added, mostly to ensure that the power of the Secretary of Defense over the defense budget for intelligence was still completely intact.[57] But the logic of Speaker Hastert can be seen as instituting a "tyranny of the majority of a majority," which really means a tyranny of a minority of the entire House, which the Framers certainly would have found even more disturbing than the "tyranny of the majority" to which they were so strongly opposed.

Historically, the Senate has been known for its sense of comity, bolstered by its tradition of allowing every senator the opportunity to speak without limit in support of or in opposition to a presidential nomination or a piece of legislation. Even as this is being written (in June of 2005), there is a threat by the Senate majority leader to use an unprecedented parliamentary maneuver to prevent use of the filibuster to block certain judicial nominees whom the Democrats deem unacceptable by a simple majority of fifty votes plus the Vice Presi-

[56] Sheryl Gay Stolberg, "Republican Defiance on Intelligence Bill Is Surprising. Or Is It?" *New York Times*, 22 November 2004.

[57] Philip Shenon, "Senate Approves Intelligence Bill and Sends It to President," *The New York Times*, 9 December 2004; and Philip Shenon, "House Approves Broad Overhaul of Intelligence," *New York Times*, 8 December 2004.

dent's tie-breaking vote as presiding officer of the Senate. A filibuster means that, under the current rules of the Senate, a minority can try to block a nomination or a piece of legislation by extended debate unless there is a minimum of sixty Senators prepared to vote for cloture and end the debate.[58]

A formal or de facto rules change that would allow cloture by simple majority vote, especially on presidential nominations, where the Senate has a constitutional obligation to give advice and to give or withhold consent, would very likely be extended to apply to all voting in the Senate and make that body susceptible to a tyranny of a simple majority. In addition, because of every state having two senators regardless of population, the majority of Republican senators that might change the Senate rules in fact represent fewer people — 144,765,157 to 148,026,027 — than the population represented by the Democrats plus the Independent Jeffords.[59]

During the Clinton administration, Republicans blocked many of President Clinton's judicial nominees,[60] but because the Republicans were in the majority in the Senate, they did not need to filibuster. The majority in the Judiciary Committee simply refused to report the nominations out. The filibuster has been present in the Senate since 1806, and enlightened self interest should dictate keeping it in place as a seldom-used "gun behind the door" so that when the Republicans again become a minority, the Democratic leadership will not be able to ram through certain contentious and extreme judicial nominees or pieces of legislation.

ELECTIONS ARE NOT ENOUGH

Elections are not enough for sustaining American-style democracy because elections are episodic, and therefore between elections, a president has four

---

[58] Formally changing the rules to allow cloture by a simple majority vote would be subject to the existing cloture provisions as it was when the rules were changed to reduce the majority needed for cloture from two-thirds to three-fifths of the Senate, but it did not appear that the Majority Leader had sixty votes available to change the rules to eliminate the filibuster. The Majority Leader's maneuver would actually go around the rules by moving to close debate without a cloture motion but by a simple motion to close debate, having the Vice President rule that such a motion was in order, having the Minority Leader object or raise a point of order, and then having the Majority Leader move to table the objection or point of order, which is a non-debatable killing-motion that can be imposed by a simple majority.

[59] The numbers were reached through data obtained from United States Census Bureau population estimates as of 4 July 2004. To determine how much of the country was represented by Democratic senators versus Republican senators, for Republicans, the population of the state was multiplied by the number of Republican senators from that state and then each number was added together. The same was done for the Democrats. The numbers at that point added up to twice the population of the United States, so the totals for Democrats and Republicans were both divided by two so that they would add up to the population of the United States.

[60] In his second term, Clinton nominated fifty-one candidates for the Court of Appeals, and thirty-five were confirmed. In his first term, Bush nominated fifty-two judges, and thirty-five were confirmed. Jeffrey Toobin, "Blowing Up the Senate: Will Bush's Judicial Nominees Win with the 'Nuclear Option'?" *The New Yorker*, 7 March 2005.

years and senators six years to make and implement policy before they are called to account in an election. As for House members—who Hamilton argued would be especially responsive to the public because they faced election every two years—they are almost all in gerrymandered or redistricted areas that are purposely made safe for the incumbent, and thus reelection is not a practical problem. In 2004, only seven incumbents were defeated, in contrast to the 394 who were reelected. In addition, four of the incumbent defeats were the result of the gerrymandering in Texas at Republican House Majority Leader Tom Delay's direction—the Republican state legislature redrawing of the district lines for a second time after the 2002 census in order to almost ensure the defeat of Democratic congressmen.[61] In the Senate, only a single incumbent, Tom Daschle of South Dakota, the Democratic leader, was defeated. The rest of the changes in the party ratio of the Senate were the result of Republicans winning more open seats than the Democrats.

To use the "shoes pinching" analogy once again, in the course of four years, the feet being forced to wear crooked shoes might become gangrenous and a later change in shoemakers would not be able to restore the foot that might have had to be amputated. Certainly in the twenty-first century, in an age of the spread of weapons of mass destruction and of terrorist attacks, the Internet, global economics, and massive air travel, a great deal of damage—even a great deal of irreversible damage—can be done between elections.[62] The good will generated for Americans throughout the world after September 11 was destroyed by the decision to go ahead with the Iraq war despite almost worldwide opposition to it. Even in domestic policy, the elimination of massive budget deficits that had taken the hard work and courage of three presidents and majorities in twelve congresses to achieve was undone in four years, to produce the largest budget deficits in American history (see Figure 1).[63]

If a president has the support of his own party majorities in both houses of Congress, and if a filibuster can successfully be limited by majority vote, or if the majority party contingent itself reaches sixty, the minority will become impotent in blocking appointments or amending legislation. Then the American democracy will be headed down a dangerous path toward precisely the kind of government that will bring about extremism and abuse of power, becoming, to paraphrase Jefferson, a de facto elective despotism.

[61] See Gary Jacobson, "Polarized Politics and the 2004 Congressional Elections," *Political Science Quarterly* 120 (Summer 2005): 199–218.

[62] Lyndon B. Johnson felt he could not run for president again in 1968, despite his landslide victory in 1964, because of dissatisfaction with his conduct in escalating the Vietnam War and bringing about huge casualties. But that did not bring back the 35,751 lives lost between 1964 and 1968 or ease the civil discord that had spread across the nation and would exist for decades. See numbers of casualties at www.archives.gov/research_room/research_topics/vietnam_war_casualty_lists/statistics.htm.

[63] Presidents Reagan, George H. W. Bush, and Clinton all were forced to raise taxes to create a balanced budget, and finally, by 1998, the government produced a small surplus. See The Budget for Fiscal Year 2005, Historical Tables, Office of Management and Budget, Executive Office of the President of the United States.

FIGURE 1
Federal Surpluses and Deficits in Current Dollars (in millions)

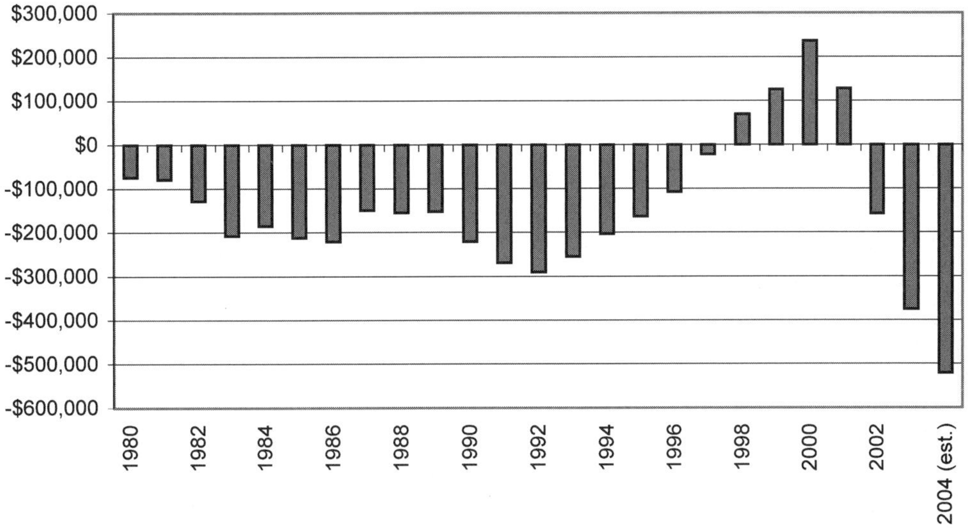

Source: The Budget for Fiscal Year 2005, Historical Tables, Office of Management and Budget, Executive Office of the President of the United States.

The spirit of civility and cooperation must be restored so that not just the party in the White House and bare majorities of the two chambers of Congress can create or change policy. First, the 49 percent of the population that did not vote to reelect President Bush, the population represented by the Democrats who hold 47 percent of the seats in the House of Representatives, the 50.5 percent of the population represented by Democratic senators, are still Americans who pay their taxes, do their work, serve in the military, and are therefore entitled to be represented in the House and the Senate. One way is for the majority leaderships to give the minority some opportunities to have the minority's legitimate points incorporated, or at least voted upon, before the final product. Second, engaging the minority in legislation will also give them some spirit of ownership of a policy and will therefore preclude their criticizing it if it goes poorly or repealing it once they become the majority.

Third, it must be conceded by the majority that it is the Constitution, and not some fringe group, that gives to the Senate the responsibility to advise and consent, or not consent, to presidential nominations for positions in the executive branch, as well as for all of the federal judges in the district courts, the courts of appeal in each circuit, and finally the Supreme Court. All federal judges, of course, have lifetime tenure and will therefore serve for decades beyond the elections that brought into power the president who nominated them and claimed some mandate for appointing judges like them.[64] Recognizing the

[64] See Robert A. Dahl, "The Myth of the Presidential Mandate," *Political Science Quarterly* 105 (Autumn 1990): 355–372.

absolute legitimacy of Senate involvement in the appointing process means that Senate opposition to a relatively few appointees should be reacted to by giving the reasons why the objections are invalid and not by trying to de-legitimize the objections by calling them "just politics." The Constitution simply gives a share of the appointment power to the Senate as well as to the president, and there is absolutely nothing in Madison's diary of the constitutional convention or in *The Federalist Papers* even to suggest that the Senate should just be a rubber stamp. As Hamilton explained:

> It will be the office of the president to *nominate*, and with the advice and consent of the senate to *appoint*. There will of course be no exertion of *choice* on the part of the senate. They may defeat one choice of the executive and oblige him to make another; but they cannot themselves *choose*—they can only ratify or reject the choice, he may have made.[65]

If a single oppressive majority dominates all the levers of power, including by new appointments over a few years of the majority of the members of the Supreme Court, we will have turned our government into an elective despotism, and, as Jefferson wrote, the fact that it will be elective brings no solace.

If a democracy is to remain real and stable, the majority must be humane and farsighted enough to take care of minorities who have serious objections to the majority's point of view and who, because of lack of numbers, do not have the political strength to impose their own policy solutions through their own political power. Or, as one of the most brilliant students ever of American politics, V. O. Key, once put it:

> Triumphant parties that advocate great causes or that come into power at moments of great stress must contrive and enact measures that may be thought, even widely, to be destructive of the principles of the Republic. Yet unless gradual acceptance of such innovation comes about, the cleavage between the parties would grow into a chasm unbridgeable by the compromises of party politics. Or alternations in party control, with the accompanying changes of policy, would jolt the social and economic system beyond the bounds of toleration.[66]

In his 1858 campaign for the Senate, Lincoln argued that "a house divided against itself cannot stand." Lincoln's postulate is especially relevant again today. When the United States is in a perpetual war against invisible terrorists, when so many nations are trying to out-compete the United States in economics, trade, and technological progress, when the dollar is weakening relative to all major currencies, when the United States is suffering unprecedented budget and trade deficits, and when the myth of American military omnipotence has been shattered, is it really viable to argue that a slim majority—and a very small one in the President's popular vote, in seats in the House of Representatives

---

[65] *The Federalist Papers, No. 66* (Hamilton).
[66] V. O. Key, Jr., *Politics, Parties, and Pressure Groups*, 5th ed. (New York: Thomas Crowell and Co., 1964), 223.

and an actual minority in population represented by the Republicans in the Senate—should just write off minority input and objections?[67]*

APPENDIX

ADDRESS OF SENATOR JOHN F. KENNEDY TO
THE GREATER HOUSTON MINISTERIAL ASSOCIATION
Rice Hotel, Houston, Texas
September 12, 1960

Reverend Meza, Reverend Reck, I'm grateful for your generous invitation to speak my views.

While the so-called religious issue is necessarily and properly the chief topic here tonight, I want to emphasize from the outset that we have far more critical issues to face in the 1960 election; the spread of Communist influence, until it now festers 90 miles off the coast of Florida—the humiliating treatment of our President and Vice President by those who no longer respect our power—the hungry children I saw in West Virginia, the old people who cannot pay their doctor bills, the families forced to give up their farms—an America with too many slums, with too few schools, and too late to the moon and outer space.

These are the real issues which should decide this campaign. And they are not religious issues—for war and hunger and ignorance and despair know no religious barriers.

But because I am a Catholic, and no Catholic has ever been elected President, the real issues in this campaign have been obscured—perhaps deliberately, in some quarters less responsible than this. So it is apparently necessary for me to state once again—not what kind of church I believe in, for that should be important only to me—but what kind of America I believe in.

I believe in an America where the separation of church and state is absolute—where no Catholic prelate would tell the President (should he be Catholic) how to act, and no Protestant minister would tell his parishoners for whom to vote—where no church or church school is granted any public funds or political preference—and where no man is denied public office merely because his religion differs from the President who might appoint him or the people who might elect him.

I believe in an America that is officially neither Catholic, Protestant nor Jewish—where no public official either requests or accepts instructions on public policy from the Pope, the National Council of Churches or any other ecclesiastical source—where no religious body seeks to impose its will directly or indirectly upon the general populace or the public acts of its officials—and where religious liberty is so indivisible that an act against one church is treated as an act against all.

For while this year it may be a Catholic against whom the finger of suspicion is pointed, in other years it has been, and may someday be again, a Jew—or a Quaker—or a Unitarian—or a Baptist. It was Virginia's harassment of Baptist preachers, for example, that helped lead to Jefferson's statute of religious freedom. Today I may be the victim—but tomorrow it may be you—until the whole fabric of our harmonious society is ripped at a time of great national peril.

Finally, I believe in an America where religious intolerance will someday end—where all men and all churches are treated as equal—where every man has the same right to attend or not

---

[67] At www.historyplace.com/Lincoln/divided.htm.

*I thank Kathleen Doherty for her excellent research assistance on all aspects of this essay. I also thank Vilma Caraley, James Campbell, Robert Jervis, Walter LaFeber, Andrew Nathan, Ralph Nunez, and Robert Shapiro for reading and making helpful comments on an earlier draft of this essay, although I was not able to incorporate all of their suggestions.

attend the church of his choice—where there is no Catholic vote, no anti-Catholic vote, no bloc voting of any kind—and where Catholics, Protestants and Jews, at both the lay and pastoral level, will refrain from those attitudes of disdain and division which have so often marred their works in the past, and promote instead the American ideal of brotherhood.

That is the kind of America in which I believe. And it represents the kind of Presidency in which I believe—a great office that must neither be humbled by making it the instrument of any one religious group nor tarnished by arbitrarily withholding its occupancy from the members of any one religious group. I believe in a President whose religious views are his own private affair, neither imposed by him upon the nation or imposed by the nation upon him as a condition to holding that office.

I would not look with favor upon a President working to subvert the first amendment's guarantees of religious liberty. Nor would our system of checks and balances permit him to do so— and neither do I look with favor upon those who would work to subvert Article VI of the Constitution by requiring a religious test—even by indirection—for it. If they disagree with that safeguard they should be out openly working to repeal it.

I want a Chief Executive whose public acts are responsible to all groups and obligated to none—who can attend any ceremony, service or dinner his office may appropriately require of him—and whose fulfillment of his Presidential oath is not limited or conditioned by any religious oath, ritual or obligation.

This is the kind of America I believe in—and this is the kind I fought for in the South Pacific, and the kind my brother died for in Europe. No one suggested then that we may have a "divided loyalty," that we did "not believe in liberty," or that we belonged to a disloyal group that threatened the "freedoms for which our forefathers died."

And in fact this is the kind of America for which our forefathers died—when they fled here to escape religious test oaths that denied office to members of less favored churches—when they fought for the Constitution, the Bill of Rights, and the Virginia Statute of Religious Freedom— and when they fought at the shrine I visited today, the Alamo. For side by side with Bowie and Crockett died McCafferty and Bailey and Carey—but no one knows whether they were Catholic or not. For there was no religious test at the Alamo. . . .

But let me stress again that these are my views—for contrary to common newspaper usage, I am not the Catholic candidate for President. I am the Democratic Party's candidate for President who happens also to be a Catholic. I do not speak for my church on public matters—and the church does not speak for me.

Whatever issue may come before me as President—on birth control, divorce, censorship, gambling or any other subject—I will make my decision in accordance with these views, in accordance with what my conscience tells me to be the national interest, and without regard to outside religious pressures or dictates. And no power or threat of punishment could cause me to decide otherwise.

But if the time should ever come—and I do not concede any conflict to be even remotely possible—when my office would require me to either violate my conscience or violate the national interest, then I would resign the office; and I hope any conscientious public servant would do the same.

But I do not intend to apologize for these views to my critics of either Catholic or Protestant faith—nor do I intend to disavow either my views or my church in order to win this election.

If I should lose on the real issues, I shall return to my seat in the Senate, satisfied that I had tried my best and was fairly judged. But if this election is decided on the basis that 40 million Americans lost their chance of being President on the day they were baptized, then it is the whole nation that will be the loser, in the eyes of Catholics and non-Catholics around the world, in the eyes of history, and in the eyes of our own people.

But if, on the other hand, I should win the election, then I shall devote every effort of mind and spirit to fulfilling the oath of the Presidency—practically identical, I might add, to the oath I have taken for 14 years in the Congress. For without reservation, I can "solemnly swear that I will faithfully execute the office of President of the United States, and will to the best of my ability preserve, protect, and defend the Constitution . . . so help me God.